LEGACY

LEGACY

Gangsters, Corruption and The London Olympics

BY MICHAEL GILLARD

BLOOMSBURY READER
LONDON · OXFORD · NEW YORK · NEW DELHI · SYDNEY

BLOOMSBURY READER
Bloomsbury Publishing Plc
50 Bedford Square, London, WC1B 3DP, UK

BLOOMSBURY, BLOOMSBURY READER and the Diana logo are
trademarks of Bloomsbury Publishing Plc

First published in Great Britain 2019
This edition published 2019

A catalogue record for this book is available from the British Library

Library of Congress Cataloguing-in-Publication data has been applied

ISBN: HB: 978-1-4482-1741-0; eBook: 978-1-4482-1742-7

2 4 6 8 10 9 7 5 3 1

Typeset by Deanta Global Publishing Services, Chennai, India
Printed and bound in Great Britain by CPI Group (UK) Ltd, Croydon CR0 4YY

To find out more about our authors and books visit www.bloomsbury.com
and sign up for our newsletters

For fallen colleagues murdered in pursuit of
dirty cops, crooks and the big rich

Who runs things?
The same people who run things everywhere.
The cops, the crooks and the big rich?
Who else.

Hammett (1982)

Contents

Prologue

Going for Gold

The important thing in life is not the triumph, but the fight; the essential thing is not to have won, but to have fought well.

The Olympic Creed

The breaking news sent officials at the Olympic stadium into a panic. London's closing ceremony was just hours away but the heavily choreographed event, themed around the history of British pop music, might have to be cancelled for safety reasons.

Eight miles away, one of the largest waste recycling plants in Europe had caught fire and a menacing cloud of toxic smoke was drifting slowly towards the new stadium. Hundreds of firefighters had been attacking the blaze since the afternoon but couldn't get it under control. The London Fire Brigade told reporters they'd seen nothing like it and feared the heat could trigger an explosion at a nearby oil depot. Scrambled helicopters periodically buzzed above the inferno in Dagenham, filming a spaghetti junction of hoses spraying the burning shell of a one-storey building by the Thames.

The name of the recycling business was of little consequence to short-tempered television types scheduled to broadcast the closing ceremony to an estimated 750 million viewers at 9 p.m. Even if they had looked, the land registry revealed little but an innocuous-sounding company registered offshore in the British Virgin Islands.

In truth, the toxic cloud emanating from the recycling plant represented more than just a threat to the closing ceremony. It was a metaphor for the violent and corrupting influence that its owner, a leading UK crime lord known as 'the Long Fella', exerted over the Olympic borough of Newham and beyond for the last three decades. An alternative battle for gold – one of death threats, broken bones, political chicanery and crooked deals – had recently ended in defeat for a small group of local detectives who were all that stood in his way.

What began as a battle for control of a lucrative strip of land in Newham had become a test of whether London stood for anything more than a cosmopolitan laundry for malodorous men and their money.

In ancient Greece, the Newham crime squad would have been garlanded for putting up a good fight against the odds. But these were risk-averse times of brave hearts led by desk drivers, bean counters and back stabbers; light-touch regulatory times where money had no smell. Still, with one arm tied behind their backs, the detectives had carried on coming forward, determined to expose London's hidden wiring where organised crime, politics and big business met. Until, that is, Scotland Yard decided to throw them under the bus.

Protecting the 'legacy' of the 2012 Games by covering up a scandal of suspicious deaths and corruption was more important to the police and politicians than protecting Londoners from the predatory Long Fella and his friends in suits. For others at Scotland Yard, the crime lord was simply 'too big, too dangerous' to take on which, for all its pre-Olympics bluster, was a sad indictment of the UK's biggest police force.

By five thirty that afternoon on 12 August, Dany Cotton, the director of safety and assurance, was able to announce that her firefighters had contained the blaze and the greatest show on earth could go on. There was just enough time for the ten thousand athletes to take their places in the new stadium alongside Britain's pop aristocracy, politicians and the bloated male relics of the tainted International Olympic Committee.

After several hours of show business, any trace of a toxic cloud over east London had faded away under a dazzling display of fireworks, political hyperbole and The Who belting out 'My Generation'.

This is the story of that smokescreen.

PART ONE

Land of Dope and Gory

I

Children of the Docks

In 2000, the British Olympic Association (BOA) delivered to Prime Minister Tony Blair what they hoped would be the bid that brought the greatest sporting show on earth to London's much-transformed East End.

The BOA was convinced that in the host borough of Newham, a deprived Labour stronghold, London had found the best chance of beating Paris, Madrid, New York and Moscow. The bid document to host the 2012 summer Games was not something the prime minister felt particularly optimistic about. Blair was already working on his own east London legacy to rival predecessor Margaret Thatcher's trailblazing Canary Wharf and Docklands redevelopment. His involved a multibillion-pound project to boost the economy of London, Essex and Kent by reclaiming brownfield land and building new homes along the Thames, right up to its estuary.

The Thames Gateway Development and Olympic projects would eventually dovetail and foreshadow new entertainment hubs, a massive shopping centre, banker penthouses, casinos and pop-ups with deconstructed pie 'n' mash for hipsters. Britons were already binging on a government-sponsored housing and credit boom. The illusion of greater personal wealth hid the toxic truth that debt was unsustainable and financial fraud on the rise, while politicians and regulators turned a blind eye or conspired in the swindle.

According to his autobiography, Blair was sceptical that London could win the Olympic bid against main rivals Paris and Madrid. Nevertheless, forty-eight hours before the vote on 6 July 2005, the prime minister put on that famous rictus grin and lobbied representatives of the International Olympic Committee (IOC) in Singapore. The initial rounds of voting saw Moscow followed by New York and then Madrid knocked out. A little before 1 p.m., IOC president, Jacques Rogge, took to the stage with the rest of the blazerati of largely old, pale, male members to announce the winner.

One of them, however, was missing from the lineup. Ivan Slavkov, the IOC member for Bulgaria, had been secretly filmed offering to sell votes to undercover BBC journalists. He was duped, along with other IOC agents, into believing they were consultants for fictional businesses with an interest in the 2012 Games coming to Newham.[1] The resulting documentary was more powerful because the IOC claimed it had cleaned up its act after a spate of similar scandals, the latest involving Salt Lake City's bid to secure the 2002 Winter Games. The Americans lavished some $15 million on IOC members and their families, and it worked. But no one went to prison when the extent of US largesse was revealed. The bid team said they were simply following an Olympic tradition.

Back in Singapore, some in the UK bid team wondered if the BBC documentary would ruin their chances, despite

[1] *Panorama - Buying the Games* (BBC broadcast: 4 August 2004).

the frantic last-minute schmoozing of IOC members by Blair and his wife.

Standing in front of IOC President Rogge was the nervous figure of Conservative peer Sebastian Coe, a former Olympian and the man in charge of Britain's bid. Next to him was Ken Livingstone, the socialist mayor of London, who was convinced that Paris had won because the media were hovering all over the French bid team. Rogge put paid to the speculation by opening the ornate envelope containing the decision. 'The International Olympic Committee has the honour of announcing that the games of the 30th Olympiad in 2012 are awarded to the city of London,' he declared without dramatic pause.

The ballroom erupted in shrieks and yells as British reserve was abandoned and the bid team, dressed in beige and blue, hugged each other, jumped up and down and punched the air. Losing by just four votes, Paris was praised for a near-flawless bid. The British team kept telling reporters that the IOC had clearly recognised London's ambitious promise of a 'legacy' games, not just for the capital, but also for international youth who it hoped would be inspired to put down their games consoles and get into sport.

'We won't let you down,' Lord Coe told Rogge at the press conference alongside Tessa Jowell, Labour's Olympics minister. She had already pledged £2.37bn to cover the cost of the Games. This, however, was an early fallacy as the experience of past host cities showed the real budget was likely to triple. And it did.

None of the specifics mattered to the hundreds of revellers in Trafalgar Square who also erupted upon hearing the news from Singapore. Moments later they were treated to a fly by from the Royal Air Force's Red Arrows display team, whose jets streamed red, white and blue smoke over Buckingham Palace. In Stratford, where most of the Olympic village would be built alongside a new stadium and the biggest urban shopping centre in Europe, the largely black and Asian crowd greeted the prospect of the Games coming to Newham with equal enthusiasm. For Amber Charles, a fourteen-year-old basketball player, and twenty-nine other school children from the borough who were in Singapore for the ceremony, Newham was finally going to be on the world map for a lot more than extreme poverty, poor health, educational underachievement and gang violence.

Almost 150 years earlier, Charles Dickens, the great chronicler of nineteenth-century poverty, took a trip from central London to the emerging settlement of Canning Town. By that point, in 1857, Canning Town had developed outside the city's boundary and therefore beyond those laws governing standards of sanitation and housing expected in London. Yet the settlement was supposed to house the men and their families building the nearby Royal Docks and working the new factories that helped drive eighteenth-century industrialisation.

Dickens found undignified dwellings backing on to a stagnant, bubbling cesspool where 'ghostly little children' lived and played. Members of the board of health, who lived a few miles north in upmarket Stratford, every so often scattered a ton of 'deodorising' matter over the 'vilest pools' of human and other waste in Canning Town. But it did nothing for the stench. 'Canning Town is the child of the Victoria Docks. Many select such a dwelling place because they are already debased below the point of enmity to filth. The Dock Company is surely, to a very great extent, answerable for the condition of the town they are creating,' Dickens concluded.[2]

The industrialisation of Canning Town started with the Stratford to North Woolwich railway and the Royal Victoria Dock. A law prohibiting harmful trades in London meant polluting factories grew up around Canning Town instead, among them the Tate and Lyle sugar refineries. Working conditions had made the docks a Labour stronghold since the days of Keir Hardie, who founded the party while representing West Ham as an independent MP in the 1890s.

Between the two world wars the government cleared the slum housing and rebuilt more dignified accommodation for the families who kept flocking to Canning Town. But the 1940 Blitz flattened a lot of the docklands and four years later the area was largely rubble. Those who stayed in Canning Town eventually benefitted from the massive rebuilding scheme after the end of the second world war and were rehoused in terraced rows with small front and back gardens. From 1965, Canning Town was no longer 'over the border' from London but formed the southernmost part of a borough called Newham, named after the merging of the East and West Ham districts.

The increased demand for housing led the council to an ill-fated experiment with pre-fabricated high-rise blocks. In 1968, Ronan Point, built by the construction firm Taylor Woodrow, collapsed on one side after a gas explosion in an eighteenth-floor flat. The development had only just opened. Four died and seventeen were injured.

The people of Canning Town were used to looking after their own and the tragedy in such a poor area

[2]Charles Dickens, *Household Words; Vol. XVI* (Bradbury and Evans, 1857).

added to the sense of 'them and us'. Locals distrusted
the police and expected little from the government. That
sense of abandonment was reinforced when a strategic
plan to rescue the dying docks in the 1980s (a result
of containerisation and increased trade with Europe)
excluded Canning Town, despite its lack of facilities and
green space. Almost all past central government funds
had gone into the elevated, criss-crossing road and rail
system above their heads that carried the more fortunate
from London to the Essex countryside.

The Thatcher government envisaged the old docks as
a new financial centre. London City Airport and Canary
Wharf were early developments. The Docklands Light
Railway from Tower Bridge and plans to extend the Jubilee
line certainly had deferred benefits for Canning Town but
the immediate impression was still one of abandonment
by the state. A young, wiry Scotsman with a chemistry
degree wanted to change all that. Robin Wales was first
elected a Labour councillor in 1982 while still in his late
twenties.

Wales came from the right wing of the Labour
movement and was made leader of Newham council
shortly after Tony Blair took over a rebranded New
Labour party in 1994.

Both men shared a vision for the Docklands that
attracted not just new business but a new type of resident,
drawn from the ranks of young professionals already
gentrifying deprived, multi-cultural boroughs such as
Hackney and Lambeth in search of affordable private
housing and expensive coffee.

Since its creation, the London borough of Newham
was largely white, working class and overwhelmingly tied
to social housing. The seventies had seen the far-right

National Front party achieve its biggest vote in Canning Town. 'The area had the highest unemployment and the worst elements of racial harassment. For a long time black and Asian families didn't want to be housed there,' recalls former deputy leader Conor McAuley. But by the nineties whites were in flight to Essex and Kent as the borough rapidly became more ethnically diverse with large Indian, Pakistani, Bangladeshi and African immigrant communities moving in and eventually buying their own homes. By 2000, when Blair had Wales knighted, Newham was over 60 per cent Asian and Black. Two years later, Wales became the UK's first directly elected mayor, and politically benefitted from a £3.7 billion regeneration package for Canning Town, the ward he once represented, claiming the central government funds would raise residents out of poor health, low education and poverty through work opportunities.

There was certainly much work to be done. 'Deprivation is high with much of the area falling within the 2 per cent most deprived areas within England and Wales,' a planning document revealed. 'In recent surveys, 17 per cent of the local working-age population have a limiting long-term illness, 17.5 per cent claim income support and 49.7 per cent of 16-74 year olds were identified as having no formal qualifications,' it continued, without the pathos of Dickens. The original regeneration plans were modified in 2005 after London won the right to host the Olympics, most of which was going to take place in Newham. Canning Town alone would host the boxing, wrestling, weightlifting, fencing, judo, taekwondo and table tennis at the recently built ExCel centre.

'There has been an exceptional level of developer interest in the clear opportunities the area has to offer,' the council cheerily announced. 'Canning Town and Custom House will become a destination for those who wish to enjoy the modernism and vibrancy of London's East End. The place will be as welcoming to newcomers, as it is to those who already reside in the area.'

Overlooked in all this Olympic euphoria was what to do about the grip of fear and corruption that violent and organised crime had on the area.

2

2

The Silvertown Strip

The Royal Docks historically had attracted a certain type of domestic villainy that went beyond the theft of the odd barrel of whisky or some meat for the family table.

Organised gangs with distribution networks were expert at looting a ship's cargo while it was unloading dockside. Some of the spoils found their way on to stalls at Rathbone Street market, alongside Moody's Sarsaparilla stand and Olley's pie and mash restaurant, or they were hawked around the many pubs which served as community centres where dockers, criminals and union men did business and met their future wives.

By the seventies, the volume of goods coming off the Royal Docks had spawned a bold and lucrative crime, excelled at by some of Canning Town's most violent sons. These 'jump up' specialists hijacked lorries by ejecting or forcing drivers at gunpoint to divert their load to 'a slaughter' – the location from where it could be dispersed away from prying eyes. Until recently, the UK hotspot for finding slaughtered lorries was under a flyover at Canning Town. The proximity to the docks was the initial reason for this odd distinction, but when they closed down in

the eighties the spaghetti junction of roads left behind
was ideal.

Silvertown Way was the first flyover built in Britain.
Caxton Street and Peto Street, the slip roads on either
side of it, descend towards menacing, dark arches under
the flyover where frightened lorry drivers watched their
hijacked load being scattered to the black markets of
London and beyond. The Silvertown strip, or simply the
strip, are the slivers of land on either side of the elevated
section of the flyover where this story violently unfolds.
For decades, extended crime families involved in armed
robbery, fraud and drug trafficking controlled the area.

The infamous strip evokes mixed memories of excite-
ment and fear for the organised crime detectives who
secretly policed it. One of them, Michael Carroll, spent a
lot of time conducting surveillance there during the 1980s.
'It was a city of thieves where anything nicked in the UK
would end up,' he recalled. Another former detective,
who didn't want to be named, said the local police had a
derogatory but Dickensian term for families that lived in
the terraced social housing off the strip in the seventies.
'Canning Town feet', he explained, was a description of
the kids who ran around barefoot outside houses that were
immaculate inside and full of stolen goods, some still in
the boxes fresh from slaughtered lorries.

'That den of iniquity,' said Carroll, 'was such that at
any one time you could have five squads all on different
wavelengths and not talking to each other.' The level and
variety of criminal activity was so high that at times more
detectives were secreted around the strip than villains
under surveillance. The strip remained the epicentre of
villainy in the decade running up to the 2012 Olympics,
only now the local organised crime families were sitting

on real estate whose value had rocketed. The Bowers, the Matthews, the Allens and the Sabines all had colourful histories and in some cases intense rivalries. But if they and other crime families could agree on ownership and put aside past feuds, there was a golden opportunity to make millions.

Newham is united by a love of West Ham United Football Club but divided by districts, each with a claim to producing the most feared men. Canning Town, that child of the docks, was an undisputed incubator of no-nonsense women, canny criminals and fighting men. Among its many claims to fame, the area has a long and glorious boxing history, which made it seem right that British fighters hoping for Olympic glory would be battling it out at the nearby ExCel centre.

Canning Town has produced great professional boxers and world-class trainers such as Jimmy Tibbs, who came from a respected crime family involved in the scrap metal trade. The Tibbs' also owned a cafe on the Silvertown strip doubling as a *spieler* – an illegal gambling den. Jimmy's own promising career in the ring was cut short when a rival family 'took liberties' and cut his brother's throat. Blood was thicker than boxing glory, and the Tibbs family went to war with the Nicols and their associates in the late sixties and early seventies.

Tit-for-tat shootings, stabbings and beatings ended in murder and bombing until Commander Bert Wickstead, one of the last high-profile Scotland Yard detectives, got hold of the case. The 'Old Grey Fox' came from Newham and once dreamt of a career playing for West Ham, but his forte was gangsters and bent detectives. Wickstead ensured the Tibbs family went away for a long time, hoping to send

a message to other local crime families that gang warfare in
the East End was not a wise choice for those who valued
their liberty, whatever the liberty taken.[1]

In 1973, while many of the Tibbs family were in prison,
two teenage brothers also from Canning Town came
up with the idea of starting their own boxing gym in a
council-owned building. In their telling of the story, Tony
and Martin Bowers persuaded the local Labour councillor
that this would be good for the community. As the venture
grew in popularity, the Bowers moved the gym above the
Peacock pub, from where it took its name – the Peacock
Gym. In 1993, they relocated once more to an old canvas-
making factory on Caxton Street on the Silvertown strip,
where it remains to this day.

The Charity Commission's decision to grant the gym full
charitable status that year certainly raised eyebrows back at
Scotland Yard. The Peacock was not just, as local folklore
would have it, an international boxing institution where
world champions came to train and the youth avoided drugs
and gang violence. It was also the headquarters of a criminal
gang of brothers who, through violence and corruption
mixed with charm and charitable acts, infiltrated all aspects
of Newham life. A police intelligence report commented
that the Bowers had developed a high profile in the borough
through associating with celebrities who loved the frisson
of being around hard men, in and out of the boxing ring.
More disturbing was the report's suggestion that the Bowers

---

[1]Jimmy Tibbs emerged from prison in the early eighties to train boxers with
Terry Lawless until they eventually opened a gym above the Royal Oak pub in
Newham. Tibbs also found God and went on to be Britain's greatest trainer and
corner man for world champions, among them Barry McGuigan, Frank Bruno
and Nigel Benn.

rubbed shoulders with 'police officers and local politicians', some of whom were vulnerable to compromise.

The police report named an insider at the gym as someone who could bridge the gap between Canning Town and other London crime families, in particular the Adamses and Rileys in Islington and the Arifs and Brindles across the water in Bermondsey. The insider was 'frequently called upon to act as go-between in negotiations,' it was claimed.[2] In 1999, Scotland Yard's Specialist Intelligence Section targeted the brothers at the Peacock Gym in a covert operation codenamed Deenside. Tony, Martin and Paul Bowers were suspected of being involved in money laundering, lorry hijacking, tobacco and alcohol smuggling, and drug trafficking using European and Chinese contacts – some from the world of boxing.

Operation Deenside detectives wanted to bug the boardroom above the gym and tried the ruse of asking to use it as a secret observation post to tackle the high level of car crime. But on the advice of a friendly retired detective and patron of the gym, the Bowers politely declined the request. It took longer, but the Yard's covert entry team eventually bypassed the alarms and bugged the boardroom anyway.

The Bowers family also owned a pub on the Victoria Dock Road side of the Silvertown strip that was renamed The Peacock. Local politicians drank there and associates of the brothers played late night card sessions in a shed next to the pub. This too was bugged. According to the police intelligence report, the Bowers co-owned the pub with Stephen Clark whose father, a scrap metal dealer, was a key player in the iconic Brink's-Mat robbery in November

[2]Operation Tiberius Strategic Intelligence Report 2002.

1983, a watershed in British crime that ended badly for all involved. The group of mainly southeast London robbers stole £26 million of gold bullion from Heathrow Airport with the help of an inside man. The size of the score was unexpected and a network of enablers, from smelters, fences, lawyers, bankers and accountants, were required to launder the money. Much of it was cleaned through investing in the first phase of Docklands development, which is where Clark's father came in.

Patrick 'bolt eyes' Clark was jailed for conspiring to launder the proceeds of the Brink's-Mat robbery. His son, Stephen, described in court as a restaurateur, was acquitted and briefly teamed up with the Bowers as co-director of Abbeycastle Properties, the company through which they owned the renamed Peacock pub.[3] In 2001, detectives received intelligence that the Bowers were seeking to cash in on the second phase of Docklands regeneration in Canning Town. Tony Bowers was 'considering a £6 million investment in a business venture involving the construction of a hotel and casino complex,' a police report noted. The Bowers' timing was impeccable, as the Blair government was already relaxing gambling laws to offer new licences for supercasinos. The brothers lobbied local Labour politicians and were invited to the House of Commons. To raise finance for their development project, the Bowers didn't go the route of normal businessmen and ask the bank for a loan. They robbed one instead.

[3]Company House records show that Stephen Clark was a director from November 1995, when Abbeycastle Properties was incorporated, to June 1996. In 2001, Mr Gisa Troy from New York was the majority shareholder in Abbeycastle Properties followed by John Sharp from Canning Town. Tony and Martin Bowers were minority shareholders.

The bank job was referred to as 'the big one'. There were similarities with the 1983 Brink's-Mat heist in that the Bowers also posed as guards from the security company in order to steal cash from HSBC bank's depot at an airport, this time it was Gatwick. Detectives, however, were listening to the whole criminal conspiracy unfold via the bug in the boardroom. In March 2003, they arrested the gang as they were leaving the cargo terminal with a £1 million score. The Bowers brothers eventually pleaded guilty. In mitigation they claimed the heist was conceived to keep the Peacock gym open after their landlord had quadrupled the rent. The implication was that they were already doing community service by preserving an essential space for deprived youngsters.

Unimpressed, the judge doled out big sentences with Tony getting the largest, twelve years. The brothers would later complain that the judge had reneged on a secret deal to give them lesser sentences for their guilty pleas.[4] Nevertheless, with good behaviour the Peacock gang, as the press now dubbed them, were guaranteed to be home with their wives and children in time for the opening ceremony of the 2012 Olympic Games.[5]

[4]See *Private Eye* 'Peacock and Bull' No 1158, 12 May-25 May 2006.
[5]Nine others were convicted, significantly John 'square' Turner, a top Bowers lieutenant who grew up with the brothers and was part of a group of violent football hooligans that supported West Ham. The Inter City Firm or ICF enjoyed organised fights with rival supporters, especially Millwall and Tottenham. But some of its leaders were also middle tier criminal muscle providing security to clubs and raves, which went hand in hand with the supply of cocaine and ecstasy. Turner had already gone to prison in 2000 for drug trafficking courtesy of operation Deenside detectives. Soon after his release he was jailed again over the Gatwick robbery.

Prison is rarely a deterrent for family-based organised crime gangs. It is looked on more as a right of passage – an occupational hazard, an informal tax even – and when it happens, control invariably passes to another family member or close associate. That was certainly true of the Matthews crime family, who have as colourful a history on the Silvertown strip as their neighbours, and allies, the Bowers.

Charles 'Chic' Matthews, the head of the family, was born in 1934. After fifteen years at school he apprenticed at a local turf accountants before two years of national service. On his discharge in the mid-fifties, Matthews entered the scrap metal game. The post-war years had made it a tough but lucrative business that attracted villainous types willing to receive and steal metals from other yards. British Rail and construction companies were good targets.

Matthews earned early convictions for such larceny and the odd bit of violence. By the time he hit his mid-thirties he'd also moved into the vehicle trade, a natural ally of criminally-minded scrap metal dealers. If you can judge a man by the company he keeps, Matthews was by now knocking around with the up-and-coming faces of Newham. Among them Frankie Sims, Patsy 'bolt eyes' Clark and members of the Hunt and Ferrier families. However, it wasn't until 1972 that 'Chic', as he was known, made the national news whilst on the run, following the hijacking of a lorry carrying £400,000 worth of silver bullion.

The robbers' escape plan was foiled by an Essex milkman who refused to allow their getaway car to pass, forcing them to take slower roads and eventually abandon the car to run across fields with as much of the stolen silver they could carry. Matthews eventually handed himself in along with the others. Some claimed the reason they had been on the run was nothing to do with the robbery, but to avoid being drawn into the Tibbs family's Canning Town war. The jury didn't buy it, and all but Matthews, who wisely didn't give evidence in his defence, were convicted. Chic Matthews raised his arm in a victory salute and told the press outside the Old Bailey that he wished the others 'good luck.' The same two words were later sent in an anonymous New Year's card to Scotland Yard's drug squad, who, in 1986, were attempting to locate a massive amphetamine sulphate or 'speed' factory in Canning Town. After receiving a tip-off that the police were on to them, the factory was hastily relocated from arches under the Silvertown flyover to a warehouse in Tidal Basin Street and the cheeky good luck card was sent.

The regional crime squad based in Barkingside were brought in to follow Matthews, who unwittingly led them from his scrap business, Vitoria Metals, to the relocated factory down the road. Both places were now under observation from land owned by a police informant who would become Chic Matthews' archenemy, and another important figure in this story – Canning Town businessman, Billy Allen.

By February 1987, the regional crime squad was forced to raid the speed factory earlier than they planned because local police had apprehended one of their targets on suspicion of robbery; an example of different police teams not communicating with each other, and therefore hindering operations on the strip. Matthews was arrested at his business premises and £250,000 worth of wrapped speed was seized from the nearby drug factory. At the trial the following year the jury were given round the clock protection to prevent any intimidation or bribes from the millions of pounds the police estimated that the defendants had salted away.

Matthews was eventually convicted of conspiracy to supply. As he left the dock, the 50-year-old shouted defiantly at the detectives present, 'You didn't get my money.' Though he may well have been rolling in drug cash, Matthews was also looking at the thick end of a ten-year sentence before he could spend any of it. However, just two years later, in 1990, the real possibility emerged of overturning his conviction as a miscarriage of justice, not because he was innocent, but because the police were corrupt.

It all started with an incredible exchange of letters that Matthews initiated with a Barkingside regional crime squad detective, who was now serving a seventeen-year prison sentence for an audacious blackmail plot. Rodney Whitchelo had tried in 1988 to extort almost £4 million from food giants Heinz and Pedigree after spiking their products with caustic acid and broken up razor blades. The blackmail plot had been forming in Whitchelo's mind while he was part of the police surveillance operation on Matthews and the drug factory.

In his opening prison letter to the disgraced former detective, who was serving his hefty sentence in another prison, Matthews initially struck a threatening tone:

I wouldn't want to be in your shoes for love nor money. Well in court you said you was fitted up, that's what I said, but you know and I know you was part of the team who fitted me up, you ain't only a liar, your (sic) a pervert as well, fuck me a policeman pervert and nonce you've got some chance you have, perhaps you can start helping yourself by telling the truth for once.

Whitchelo wrote back wryly thanking Matthews for his letter then told him, 'we both know you were bang to rights, don't we?' It led Matthews to mellow somewhat and assure Whitchelo in his next letter that he wouldn't 'punch his teeth down his throat' if their paths ever crossed in prison.

...but you know I'm not the sort of bloke to start kidding you to ask favours ... You know I'm not a drugs man, I'm one of the old school, fuck the drugs. I've always got a good living without any of that ... so watch yourself, I mean I ain't made up my mind what to think of you, anyway be lucky.

Whitchelo's response was dynamite and set a course of events that would rock Scotland Yard:

No way will you ever convince me you weren't involved ... Having said that, I do think you were hard done by. Not only a bloody long sentence with little prospect of parole but yes, you were given a 'leg up'. You all were. But not by me ... I knew that the officers were committing perjury at your trial and I considered what could be done about it. I decided to do nothing because in my heart I knew you were all guilty of conspiring to manufacture and supply. If I was going to go out on a limb it would be for someone that was innocent ... What I can do is to explain to your solicitor how he can prove that logs which were kept on [the drug factory] were not written contemporaneously.[6]

This so-called 'noble cause corruption' – the fabricating of evidence to ensure the conviction of those the police believe are guilty – was a significant problem across the forces. In the course of their correspondence, Whitchelo also confirmed to Matthews that Billy Allen was the informant on Operation Trooper, the codename for the drug factory surveillance. Whitchelo said he met Allen during the operation and had used his Brunel Street land to covertly photograph Matthews at Vitoria Metals. The land Allen owned on Tidal Basin Road was also used to spy on the amphetamine factory.

Whitchelo, who by now hated the police, more so when they took away his pension, repeated his claims to the Yard's anti-corruption squad in 1993. He added that a kilo of drugs had been planted to shore up the evidence against Kevin Hole, Matthews' son-in-law. Based on Whitchelo's revelations, Matthews and his accomplices appealed their 1988 convictions and, in November 1996, three appeal court judges found that the police had indeed fabricated evidence. The surveillance logs could not be relied on, they said, and therefore the convictions of Matthews, Hole and Joey Pykett were unsafe.

Matthews had already completed his sentence but the appeal court ruling meant that he was now in line for a significant compensation payment from the state. The money did little to assuage his anger, which was not so

[6]See Court of Appeal judgment in the case of Charles Matthews, Joseph Pykett and Thomas Hole. 27 November 1996.

much directed against the police – none of whom were ever prosecuted – as against the informant who had allowed the regional crime squad to use his land on the Silvertown strip for surveillance: Billy Allen

Matthew's resentment toward Allen, mixed with old fashioned criminal greed, was about to fuel an all-out war for control of the strip in the run up to the Olympics.

3

Billy Liar

There was a sombre and anxious mood on the streets of central London. It was 8 July 2005 and the capital was gingerly returning to its frantic pace just twenty-four hours after home-grown jihadists exploded a series of bombs on the transport network, killing themselves and fifty-two others.

Only two afternoons earlier, Londoners were celebrating being named the 2012 Olympics hosts. Now they were wondering if they would even make it to and from the office alive each day. Billy Allen, though, had reason to be cheerful. Land on the Silvertown strip that had been in his family for twenty years was now worth a lot more thanks to the International Olympic Committee's decision. He was stuck in traffic in Whitehall whilst on the way to meet his lawyers on the eve of a court hearing to determine ownership of the land that had been squatted. If the case went his way, which he expected it to, Allen told his legal team he was going to put together a consortium of developers that would hopefully meet the approval of Canning Town and Olympic planners.

As the traffic shuddered forward towards the Cenotaph memorial, the driver of an oncoming car caught Allen's eye.

It was someone he recognised from the strip and whose presence instantly jolted Allen into considering whether he should abandon his car and flee on foot. But he quickly reasoned that with armed police and soldiers everywhere no one would try anything, especially outside the prime minister's official residence. Time would shortly tell as by now the driver was almost level with his window down.

'So, you *are* going to court tomorrow?' the man asked calmly holding Allen's stare. And as their cars passed he made a slow throat slitting gesture. There was no mistake, Allen informed the police. It was a message on behalf of Chic Matthews.

The Allens had roots in Canning Town going back to the early 1900s and the Royal Docks. Jimmy Allen and his son, Billy, were natural entrepreneurs and an inseparable presence on the Silvertown strip where they ran a successful business selling commercial vehicles.

Their individual reputations among Canning Town criminals, especially with the Matthews family, however, were in stark contrast. Jimmy Allen had been in prison in the 1950s for handling stolen goods from a safe deposit robbery, but he was respected among straightgoers as a loyal friend, while maintaining friendships with some of east London's heavy villains of his generation.

Conversely, Billy Allen was despised, hated even, for being a police informant. He was also feared, though not as a local hard man, but as an only child rumoured to possess the necessary evil to kill his own parents.

'I was born in 1959. My parents never wanted me to go to school in the East End because my father found the people of Canning Town distasteful,' Billy Allen explained during one of many meetings, usually in the grand

surroundings of the Wallace Collection dining room or
Fortnum & Masons. This partly explained why the Allen
family moved from Canning Town to Ilford in Essex in the
early 1960s. 'I had a happy childhood ... I was the blue-
eyed boy. My first car was a Mercedes Sports at sixteen. Me
and my dad was like brothers. We did everything together.'

Billy Allen speaks quickly, as if second-guessing what
you are thinking and trying to head it off before the
question is asked. 'The thing that annoys me the most is
my dad was my best mate,' he volunteered, knowing the
elephant in the tea room was the view held in some police
and criminal circles that he had got away with killing his
father, and possibly his mother too.

Jimmy Allen started renting land on the Silvertown strip
in 1982, for his second-hand vehicle business, from local
legend Charles 'Wag' Bennett. Wag ran a famous body
builders' gym in Newham and is credited by Arnold
Schwarzenegger with mentoring him for the Mr Universe
competition. Arnie would run laps around the strip –
down Peto Street, under the flyover into Caxton Street
North to Chic Matthews' scrap metal business, onto
Brunel Street, past Jimmy Allen's vehicle yard before
coming to rest at the Tibbs' cafe.

By 1984, JW Allen Commercials was doing well enough
that they bought the land from Wag for £106,000. They
also invested in land on the other side of the Silvertown
flyover on Tidal Basin Road.

'I ran a really good business with my dad and we
earned a fortune – legitimately,' Allen said, keen to draw a
distinction with the criminal element on the strip. 'Dad's
motto was to stay away from all them people in Canning
Town because he thought they were scumbags.'

The claim is at odds with Jimmy Allen's criminal record and his business arrangements with his neighbours. For example, he allowed Chic Matthews to store scrap on his Brunel Street land as overspill from Vitoria Metals. It was an arrangement that continued under Billy's management when his father stepped back from business to take his beloved wife on world cruises for months on end.

'As far as I was concerned I had hit utopia. Life couldn't have been better if I tried. I wanted it all. I wanted to buy everything and be the biggest property owner,' said Billy.

At the time, the Docklands was going through its first phase of development and the opportunity was there for locals with knowledge of the financial system and raising loans. Billy Allen's ambition was also his undoing as he got into bed with some dodgy Canning Town 'faces' involving overseas land deals in Ireland and the US.[1] He also started trading on his own in Saudi Arabia, buying second-hand Volvo lorry tractor units and fraudulently selling them in the UK to construction giant Taylor Woodrow as brand new.

The good times began to go bad in April 1986 when Billy lost his mother. The effect on his father was immediate, he said. '[Dad] refused to return to the family home after the funeral. He stopped caring about his appearance, no longer wearing a suit and tie.'

Unable to adjust to life without his wife, Jimmy was saved by an invitation to visit friends who were having an extended one-way vacation on Spain's Costa del Sol. Freddie Foreman, John Mason and Ron Everett were part of the team that robbed a Security Express van in Shoreditch

[1]VAT fraudster Peter Pomfrett was in on the Dublin land deal with Allen, who says he also bought a cat litter mine in Denver, Colorado, and a mill in Accrington, Lancashire.

in April 1983, making off with £6 million – the largest cash robbery at the time. Along with Ronnie Knight, the former husband of *Carry On* and *Eastenders* star, Barbara Windsor, they bolted for Spain, which was yet to formalise its extradition treaty with the UK after a recent transition from fascist dictatorship to left-leaning democracy. Terry Perkins, the other robber, chose to remain in the UK and, as a result, was serving a 22-year sentence for the robbery while his associates drank sangria in the sun.

Jimmy Allen had known the fugitives since the 1950s, when he too was involved in the armed robbery game. After his wife's death, he accepted Foreman's invitation to stay with him in Puerto Banus, that gaudy playground in Marbella for the super-rich and blue-collar criminals. As the months rolled by, he even considered relocating there permanently and buying a yacht with his £500,000 savings. But in December 1986, the widower was brutally murdered during a trip to London.

According to Billy Allen, his father was already suffering from peritonitis of the gall bladder when he went to Spain in the spring of 1986. Months later, in November, Foreman called to say that Jimmy had fallen badly. Billy told the police he immediately flew to Spain and returned to the UK the next day with his father. For reasons unknown, Jimmy wanted to stay in a motel in Epping where, days later on the night of 3 December, he was attacked by an intruder who tried to suffocate him before running off. Nothing was stolen.

The incident was reported to the police and Billy arranged for his father to receive some medical treatment. When Jimmy was well enough, he opted to stay in a flat owned by a friend in Romford who needed a sympathetic ear after the death of his own wife. However, on the night of 17 December, Billy said he got a call to come to the flat because his father was unwell, only to discover he had been murdered. The police told him there had been a break in and his father was fatally struck with an iron bar while in bed. From the outset, Billy felt the police were more interested in using him to get Foreman and the other Security Express robbers back to the UK than solving his father's murder. Nevertheless, he agreed to talk because he believed Foreman was behind his father's death. Furthermore, when murder detectives examined the Allen family business they discovered Billy's fraudulent activity, and he claims they used this to pressure him into making a statement against Foreman and the other fugitive robbers.

Billy had already given two pieces of intelligence about the gang gleaned from his father and from his own visits to Spain, but he had no desire to put his name to a witness statement and stand up in court.

The first nugget he passed to the police was the alleged location of the Security Express van slaughter. Billy told them that the silver bullion had been divided up at Henlow Health Farm near Bedford. The second piece of intelligence was the name of the bank that allegedly laundered some of the proceeds of the crime. Billy named a manager of the Allied Irish Bank who he said had dined with Foreman, Mason and Everett at Silks Restaurant in Puerto Banus after the robbery. Billy insisted to the police that the three robbers were responsible for his father's murder and claimed the invitation to Spain was part of a 'softening up' because they wanted Jimmy to bring passport photos of them and money. The plan to return to the UK on false identities somehow went wrong, he claimed, and the robbers had his father killed but blamed him for it.

The murder squad was not initially suspicious of Billy Allen. His constant and 'close contact', especially with lead investigator detective superintendent Ronald Chapman, was viewed with considerable empathy at first. In a summary report, Chapman described how he started off feeling that Billy was trying to 'fill the void' of his father's death because witnesses had spoken of their 'utter devotion' to one another. Gradually, however, Chapman and his squad came to believe that calls made to his father before his death were to check on his whereabouts so a hit man could strike, and that the intense and voluntary engagement with the murder squad was a ruse to get an inside track on their investigation.[2]

A 'further complication', Chapman noted, was that Billy Allen was a police informant. He was registered in Scotland Yard files on 21 October 1986, seven weeks before his father's murder, and had contacted his handler on the day of the first failed attack in the motel and on the morning and evening of the murder two weeks later.[3] This fitted the emerging police theory that Billy was 'using his informant status to disguise his involvement' in a crime

[2]Report by Detective Superintendent Ronald Chapman, January 1989. Allen made 74 of 76 calls to the police, had two meetings and ten informal interviews before he was arrested.

[3]Detective sergeant Peter Avery was named Billy Allen's handler in the Chapman report. Allen admits knowing Avery and allowing his land on the Silvertown strip to be used for Operation Trooper against Charles Matthews, but denied being a registered informant. In the way of these things, it's possible Allen was unaware of how the informant system worked and didn't know he was formally registered. But in east London police circles he was known as 'Peter's man.' Relationships with the police appeared to run in the family. Allen admits his father was friendly with Commander Bert Wickstead, but denied that Jimmy Allen was the Old Grey Fox's informant. He claimed the pair probably met when they were on a cruise with their respective wives.

that had 'all the hallmarks of a deliberate murder made to look like a routine burglary.' Chapman's team believed Billy was trying to mislead them with 'false information' about the robbers in Spain, so they pumped him for everything he knew before Billy figured out that *he* was their main suspect.

It was when detectives followed Billy to a meeting with a business consultant that they started to uncover the multiple frauds, using the land he owned on the Silvertown strip as a lure. A theory was emerging that Billy had got into financial problems through these frauds and contracted a hit man to kill his father as the sole beneficiary of the will.

In a bizarre twist, this led police to suspect that Billy might also have killed his mother, the original beneficiary of her husband's estate. They exhumed Louise Allen's body when it became clear that the family GP had signed the death certificate without ever seeing her body.[4] Given the developing complexity of the case, Chapman split his team. One group of detectives investigated what he described in his summary as 'the tangled web of fraud throughout England, Jersey, Isle of Man and Eire.' This freed up Chapman to investigate the murder.

The first step was to go to Spain in May 1988 to bottom out Billy's suggestion that the fugitive robbers were behind the murder. 'There is a deal of fact in what Allen says but this is far outweighed by the multitude of lies,' Chapman wrote. Billy, he continued, had 'used every opportunity to exploit his father's associate[ion] with various fugitives residing in the Costa del Sol.'

By far the most significant was Freddie Foreman or 'Brown Bread Fred' as some knew him on account of

---

[4]Billy Allen told the author his mother died of a blood clot.

the work he did for the Krays in the Sixties. Foreman
had been jailed with the twins for luring two criminals
to their death, dismembering the bodies and disposing of
the remains in Newham.

The murder of Jimmy Allen, however, apparently
disturbed Foreman so much that he agreed to meet
Chapman, only not in a Spanish police station. The
fugitive was wary of ongoing efforts by Scotland Yard
to have him extradited or deported so he chose the
Andalucia Plaza Hotel in Puerto Banus where on 23 May
he immediately denied phoning Billy Allen to alert him
to his father's fall. Foreman said he wasn't even aware his
friend of thirty years had left Spain or been killed until he
saw it on the news. He immediately suspected Billy Allen
was behind the murder.

Superintendent Chapman believed Foreman was
genuinely upset and shared his view about who was
responsible. The detective left Spain believing that Billy
had misled him about the health and future intentions of
his father and furthermore had obstructed inquiries into
the family business to prevent discovery of the fraud. Allen
was in financial difficulties after some bad investments and
needed his father's £500,000 savings. This, the detectives
now believed, was the real motive for the murder.

Chapman returned from Spain in late May 1988 and
arrested Billy for murdering his father and for a £1 million
fraud.

Also arrested was east London hit man, Kenneth Kenny,
aka Kenny Beagle. Chapman's team was initially convinced
that Kenny was the killer, particularly when his wife, who
was unhappy in the marriage, grassed him up. According
to Chapman's report, Mrs Kenny revealed that on the night
of Jimmy Allen's murder, her husband returned home in

'a state' and 'splattered' with blood. He burned his clothes and gave her a watch to bury in the garden. However, searches didn't corroborate these claims and she declined to make a witness statement against Kenny, who had to be released. A public appeal nevertheless linked Kenny to Billy Allen through a hired car, but the man arrested for allegedly destroying the getaway vehicle also would not make a statement, the report noted.[5]

Ultimately, the evidence against Billy Allen was deemed by prosecutors to be insufficient to charge him with murder. But in November 1988 he did stand trial for incitement to murder his father and for fraud. By unravelling Billy Allen's complex financial transactions and land deals, detectives got to Anthony Smith, a business associate, who confessed his role in the fraud. Smith, more importantly, also claimed that in November 1986 Billy Allen had asked him to kill Jimmy because he was dying of cancer. Smith said he went along with the murder plot to get the money Billy owed him from the frauds, but in the end he couldn't go through with it.

Following a two-week trial, on 8 December 1988, Billy Allen was found not guilty of inciting Smith to kill his father. The evidence against him for the £1 million pound fraud, however, was more concrete so he pleaded guilty and was jailed for seven years.[6] The east London underworld was delighted to see him behind bars. Not

---

[5]Kenneth Kenny was shot dead in a Romford car park on 1 November 2000. See Michael Gillard and Laurie Flynn, *Untouchables: Dirty Cops, Bent Justice and Racism in Scotland Yard* (Cutting Edge, 2004).

[6]Billy Allen had used 1-7 Brunel Street on the Silvertown strip as collateral to fraudulently raise £500,000 from Barclays bank. He then used the same land as collateral to borrow money from others.

just for thinking he was too good for Canning Town, but because word was out that he had grassed up Foreman and the other fugitive robbers. Allen believed the police had leaked this out of spite. Either way, from then on he was known as 'Billy Liar.'

Chic Matthews was already serving his ten-year sentence for the drug factory in Canning Town when news reached him that Billy Allen, the man he blamed for his downfall, was now in prison too.

By the time Matthews was released in 1992, he returned to the Silvertown strip harbouring some very bad feelings towards his duplicitous neighbour. Allen was also released that year but sensibly stayed away from the strip. He had been made bankrupt and his interest in the plot of land at 1-7 Brunel Street was by now assigned to his trustees. However, the recession made it hard to sell and pay off his creditors. A plan by London Underground to compulsory purchase the land as part of the Jubilee Line extension had also come to nothing. In any case, Allen's freedom was short-lived as by 1996 he was back in prison serving a six-year sentence, this time for a vicious assault. The rumour mill on the Silvertown strip had it that he almost bludgeoned his stepdaughter to death with an ashtray. When the victim, Allen said, was her black boyfriend.

It wasn't long before Matthews had his revenge. Before emigrating to Spain in 1992 and handing over the day-to-day running of his scrap metal business to his sons, Matthews squatted Allen's land anticipating the major regeneration of Canning Town. His plan was to eventually seek adverse possession under a law that granted title if a tenant could show a continuous presence of twelve years.

Matthews' eldest son, Charles junior, was fresh from prison for VAT fraud when he took over the scrap metal business now called London City Metals and situated in one of the units under the arches of the Silvertown Way flyover opposite Allen's land at 1-7 Brunel Street. Junior formed a second company, London City Self Storage, and began renting out large shipping containers, which were stacked up on Allen's land without his knowledge. Inside prison Allen befriended fellow prisoner Michael Relton, a corrupt solicitor who had helped the Brink's-Mat robbers launder the stolen gold bullion through the first phase of the Docklands development. It was clear this second phase was going to be even bigger and Allen planned to put together a consortium of developers on his release.[7]

That day came in 2000. Allen was now forty years old and ready to make his mark in the property game. During a stock take of his assets he visited the land at Brunel Street only to discover the Matthews family had been squatting it since 1992 with no intention of leaving. However, the assets were under the control of Allen's trustees in bankruptcy who were sceptical about spending money on lawyers to evict the Matthews family from Brunel Street.

[7]In 1999, the Canning Town Partnership, a consortium, wanted to buy the whole Silvertown strip and build a mixed residential and commercial development with a hotel. The plan chimed with the regeneration vision of Newham council, who also owned some land on the strip, which it rented to various businesses and contractors. Lawyers for the consortium made inquiries about Allen's land and discovered the recent history of murder, drug dealing, fraud and violence. Their clients eventually backed out after realising it was too complex to secure an unencumbered freehold from so many colourful private owners and tenants.

For the next four years Allen reinvented himself and worked on developing new business opportunities. Being a discharged bankrupt and convicted fraudster didn't make that task any easier but Allen had powerful friends in the property game who were unconcerned about his past and others who didn't know about it. In 2004, when it was clear that billions of pounds would be flooding into Canning Town for regeneration, Allen told his trustees that he had found a private funder willing to pay the legal costs of removing the Matthews family from Brunel Street. This would make the land sellable to developers. Alternatively, Allen said he would try and raise private finance to develop it through a consortium of investors. Either way, his creditors would get paid and he would make money on the deal.

Chic Matthews was served with a writ ordering him off the land but he immediately countersued for adverse possession claiming a presence since 1987. Luckily, Allen had a spy in the Matthews camp in the form of his cousin, Terry Sabine. His family had rented a corner of the Brunel Street land from the Allens to run a car valeting business since the late eighties. While Billy Allen was in prison, the Sabines remained on the land and co-existed with the Matthews even when they moved all the shipping containers onto it for their London City Self Storage business. But after the legal action started in 2004, Terry Sabine sided with Billy Allen, who promised to cut him into any future development deal.

It wasn't long before Allen started receiving threatening anonymous phone calls and texts. A typical message read:

YOU LITTLE CUNT BACK OUT NOW IF YOU KNOW WHAT'S
GOOD FOR YOU. YOU ARE GETTING OUT OF YOUR DEPTH.

Usually the threats arrived just before a court hearing. Allen logged most of it with his legal team but, in July 2005, when London won the Olympic bid, matters escalated. A wreath was sent to his home in Hampshire where he had moved with his second wife, Lorraine, a former prison nurse, and their profoundly disabled young son. On other occasions, letters with London postmarks dropped through the door. One had newspaper lettering of two words, 'Shooting' and 'Bill' stuck to a piece of paper.

Another said:

DON'T EVEN CONTEMPLATE TURNING UP IN COURT. YOU WONT SEE IT COMING.

All this was racing through Billy Allen's mind that day on 8 July 2005 in Whitehall when an associate of Matthews made a throat slashing gesture as he drove past. The incident convinced him to finally report the history of threats to Hampshire police. He also decided to invest in some personal protection.

Newham gangster Danny Woollard was happy to take the well-paid job. He knew both sides in the battle and was familiar with the land being fought over.

In the nineties, the police suspected Woollard of murder and had bugged his yard near Stratford, as well as Sabine's car valeting business on Allen's land. The intelligence gleaned from these bugs helped put Woollard away in 1996 for his involvement with the robbery of a cash-in-transit security van and for gun running. Allen needed someone of Woollard's standing to get him safely to and from court, and the 61-year-old overweight thug obliged. Matthews certainly took notice when, at the next court hearing in October 2005, Allen turned up with six minders, one of them a champion bare-knuckle fighter.

The case was adjourned until February 2006, when a two-day trial would finally determine ownership of the Brunel Street plot of land. Allen was expecting victory. Woollard and his five gorillas were expecting another easy payday.

Neither of them could have been more wrong.

4

The Aladdin's Den

Billy Allen's iPhone didn't stop ringing during the car journey to London on 6 February, 2006. As usual he answered with a broad East End accent that he'd done nothing to soften in forty-six years.

It was immediately apparent that his next caller wasn't from the new world he now inhabited as a property developer; a world of offshore companies, multi-millionaire suits sealing deals in Michelin-starred restaurants to expand London's skyline. This caller was most definitely from an East End past that Allen was trying hard to leave behind.

'You fucking cunt,' said the male voice. 'We've just watched your wife put the rubbish out. We'll kill you and your family if you go to court.'

'It's another threat,' Allen informed his solicitor who was sitting next to him. 'I've got to call my Lorraine and James to see if they're alright.'

Allen's wife confirmed that she had put out the rubbish at 8 a.m. Lorraine didn't spook easily, but Allen assured her he would insist Hampshire police sent someone to the house while he faced down Chic Matthews over the two-day hearing.

Land disputes are rarely that interesting for barristers on either side. Technical issues and adverse possession law are usually as unremarkable as the clients and as dry as the land being fought over. But the run-down strip under the Silvertown Way flyover was now highly sought after real estate. The £3.7 billion regeneration fund had turned Canning Town into a building site more reminiscent of the Blitz. With the Olympic Games just six years away, local crime families were already trying to cash in.

The Bowers' early effort to raise money for luxury flats and a rooftop casino on the Silvertown strip had resulted in long prison sentences after their failed robbery of the HSBC depot at Gatwick Airport. Money tends to have no smell when the Olympics come to town and HSBC bank were now talking with Allen, a convicted fraudster, about building a rival citadel of greed and algorithmic thuggery to Canary Wharf across the river.

Just before 10 a.m., Allen's car pulled up in a London crescent near Regent's Park outside a Regency building that looked more like the entrance to an embassy or government ministry than a court of law. Woollard and the other minders emerged from a support vehicle and surrounded Allen on the short distance to the entrance of the Central London County Court. He immediately relayed the latest phone threat to his barrister, Jane Giret QC, who in turn brought it to the attention of the senior judge hearing the case within the hour.

'My client informs me that he has recently been subject to death threats,' Giret told Recorder Stuart Bridge in his rooms.

'Have you any further details?' he inquired.

The threats were anonymous but definitely related to the case, she replied, adding that the police had been alerted and were now investigating. There was little the judge could do except start the trial. On entering the small courtroom, he couldn't help but notice a row of 'physically imposing' men at the back dressed in dark overcoats. As the hearing progressed it became clear they were not witnesses but Allen's bodyguards. The protection team included Woollard's son, Danny junior, bare-knuckle fighter Matty Attrell, Nicky Cook and Shane Stanton, who used to bodyguard Robbie Williams. They struggled to stay awake as the mind-numbing nuances of property law were argued in front of the judge over the long morning session.

While that played out, a tall man in an expensive grey suit contoured around a muscular physique quietly entered the court building and made his way to the canteen looking for Woollard, Allen's chief minder, who was nursing a cup of tea. Woollard greeted the greying 45-year-old visitor with respect. There weren't many real criminals, especially from Newham, who didn't know of the Long Fella.

He usually operated in the shadows at arm's length, but by turning up at court he was making a point beyond showing his support for Allen's rival. The Matthews were family friends who the Long Fella knew from growing up in Canning Town.

'This land ain't worth nothing like the £110 million odd that Billy Allen is telling you,' he calmly explained to Woollard. 'Maybe it's one and a half mil tops, but if you think it's more you're being mugged off, Danny,' he continued.

After explaining his interest in the case, next came the threat to Allen. 'Hand him over and walk away or tell him to walk away for his own good,' the Long Fella warned Woollard.

'If I'd known you was involved I'd never have taken the job. I don't go against pals,' Woollard replied. 'But I'm committed now. Maybe we can all have touch. I'll speak to him. You know what Billy's like.'

'He's a fucking grass!'

Woollard was left to finish his tea and wonder whether the next drink would be through a straw. That afternoon, Allen emerged from court in a buoyant mood. He was not for backing down when the case was going so well.

The Long Fella, however, was not a man many said no to. At 9.23 a.m. the following morning he was the first to arrive at court, this time dressed like a football thug with a long-sleeved white fleece, purple tracksuit bottoms and trainers. Seconds later his older brother entered in similar attire followed by two extremely heavy-set men. They milled about in the court lobby with their hands in their pockets, keeping an occasional eye on the entrance. After ten minutes, other familiar faces arrived. One by one the ten men respectfully emptied their pockets of phones and keys for the two skinny security guards manning the door-framed scanner at the court entrance.

The intimidating mob – black and white, young and old, some so wide they went through the scanner sideways – paced the lobby for the next twenty minutes.

Chic Matthews, then aged seventy-one, and Billy Ambrose, an equally elderly former Canning Town boxer, were outside enjoying a cigarette when at just after 10 a.m. Allen arrived with his minders. Allen immediately noticed the welcome committee waiting in the lobby area and stopped short of the scanner. He chatted nervously to his solicitor while Woollard and three other minders emptied their pockets for the security guards. As he collected his belongings, the CCTV caught a grimace on Woollard's face when the Long Fella approached and whispered something in his ear.

Moments later the lobby exploded with violence. Allen's protection team were bundled into a corridor where there were no cameras to record the bloodletting that followed. As soon as the violence started Allen bolted for his car. Inside the building, stunned court staff and legal professionals froze against the walls. They had never seen anything like it and never wanted to again. A rain of clenched fists the size of hams and boots like anvils stomped all over Allen's protection team, who only managed to get a few of their own blows in before collapsing in a foetal position on the court floor.

The violence stopped as quickly as it started and the victorious mob casually strolled out of the court in single file, leaving the walls and flooring splattered with the blood of others. One by one Woollard and his men struggled to their feet, humiliated but too dazed to leave the court before the police arrived.

By now, Allen was driving the wrong way down one-way streets to get as far away as he could. Constantly checking his rear view mirror, he calculated on getting to his nearby Grosvenor Square office to dump the car and make good the rest of his escape on foot. In the end, he hit a clear patch of road and headed for his family in Hampshire.

Back at the court, the senior clerk caught Judge Bridge just before he left his rooms to start the second day's hearing.

'Sir, there's been a disturbance in the court to do with the case. About fifteen men carried out an assault on three men then left before the police arrived. The ambulance has been called.'

Judge Bridge called both legal teams into his rooms where Giret explained that her client had fled the scene and the police were advising he stay away. The judge adjourned the trial until further notice, but not before calling both legal teams back to the courtroom to formally put his concerns on record.

'It seems apparent that attempts are being made one way or another to intimidate those who are involved in this case,' he began. Matthews sat still and without expression.

'It is impossible to say which party is implicated or indeed whether both parties are implicated. All I can say is it seems to me to be an appalling situation that has arisen.'[1]

Two weeks later, on 21 February 2006, Billy Allen received another unwelcome letter. This one wasn't anonymous but the content was as alarming as all the others that had come to his home.

'Information has come to my attention, the existence of which I believe you should be made aware,' wrote a detective from Hampshire police in strangulated terms. 'The information relates to your personal safety and indeed concerns a potential threat to your life.'

The letter was an official warning that the police had credible intelligence that Allen's life was in danger. Such notifications, known as an Osman warning after a European court ruling, are usually the result of an informant tip-off, phone taps or bugs and legally require that the police offer protection to the intended target.

---

[1]Details of the attack at the court on 7 February 2006 are taken from witness statements, the court hearing, the police investigation and interviews by the author.

The Hampshire detective urged Allen to make contact but said he would not be able to reveal the source of the threat. The Osman warning left Allen feeling like a sitting duck and, after talking to his wife, they started to pack. Overnight, he moved his family and changed his phone.

The next day another letter arrived at Billy Allen's solicitors. This one was from lawyers representing Chic Matthews who claimed their client had nothing to do with the violence in court and no connection to the Long Fella.

Danny Woollard, who told detectives he was 'pissing blood for days' after the attack, scoffed at the suggestion and gave them his understanding of the Long Fella's true involvement in the land dispute. Matthews, he said, owed £600,000 to the top gangster and had done a deal over the land as payment. The story according to Woollard was that the north London Adams crime family were originally involved with the Long Fella in a plan to develop the land, but pulled out because the legal case with Allen was making it all too messy.[2]

Despite this circling of gangsters and the recent attack on his minders, Allen told potential investors that he

---

[2]Certainly the Adams family was sniffing around the Silvertown strip in recent months. The local crime squad in Newham had stopped Steve Bryant, a trusted senior lieutenant, in Caxton Street in late 2005. Bryant explained that he was simply scouting for local pubs to buy. And in the summer of 2006 a detective on Operation Trinity – a major National Crime Squad investigation that led to the break up of the Adams crime family – told DCI Dave McKelvey, the head of the Newham crime squad, that paperwork concerning the Silvertown land was discovered during a raid on a suspected money launderer in Gants Hill, Essex. Detectives believed that Tommy Adams, who at the time was on bail for money laundering, had an interest in Canning Town.

was still determined to evict Matthews from 1-7 Brunel
Street and buy up enough of the Silvertown strip to
develop a world trade centre to rival Canary Wharf.
However, as a discharged bankrupt with significant
creditors he needed a proxy, or front man, to operate
through. Allen cast around and through his relatives
in Canning Town alighted on a local young Asian
businessman with good contacts in Newham council's
planning department.

Biju Ramakrishnan's property and finance company
offered Allen's trustees in bankruptcy £8 million for
the freehold of the Brunel Street land, subject to vacant
possession and 25 per cent more if there was planning
permission. Another £1.5 million was on the table as a
full and final settlement to Allen's creditors.[3] While the
trustees considered this offer, in late February the Long
Fella approached Allen through an intermediary with an
offer to resolve the Brunel Street land dispute and avoid
a costly retrial, now scheduled for June 2006. Allen had
no intention of being bought out but wanted to end
hostilities. Ramakrishnan agreed to represent him at the

[3] Documents show that in August 2004 Allen's trustees received a valuation on the
1-7 Brunel Street plots of £1.75 million. In August 2005, Biju Ramakrishnan's
recently incorporated company Samsen Limited offered £8m. On 15 March
2006, Ramakrishnan's new company, Raymont Limited (now Opulen Asset
Management), made a 100% offer to pay off Allen's creditors and trustees' fees.
The trustees had only anticipated a 19.25% return for creditors. The trustees
asked for proof that Raymont Limited had £1.5m and on 30 March 2006, the
Royal Bank of Scotland in the Isle of Man obliged with a letter that said a
company called Governside Limited was a 'highly respectable and trustworthy
company' it had known for over 10 years. Governside was one of the investor
companies Ramakrishnan called on to provide proof of funds when structuring
property deals. He ended up falling out with Allen and claimed he had lost
£100,000 by getting involved.

sit down with the Long Fella and see what was on the table. Allen was willing to offer up to £1 million for the gangsters to walk away and leave him alone.

However, the meeting set for 1 March 2006 at the Custom House Hotel never took place because that morning, to everyone's surprise, the police raided the land on 1-7 Brunel Street. Detectives from the Newham crime squad had received a tip-off that there was a load of stolen copper at the Matthews' scrap metal yard in Caxton Street. And in the course of the search they also discovered that another of their family businesses, London City Self Storage, was on the nearby disputed land at Brunel Street and searched that too.

Allen knew nothing about the raid and the Newham crime squad knew even less about the violent gangland war over the very land that its detectives were now searching with gusto. But to others on the strip it looked like Billy Liar was up to his old tricks. Later that night, Allen claimed the Long Fella called and accused him of being the grass behind the raid.

'Liberty taking cunt,' a voice growled down the line. 'You'll get a bullet through your head.'[4]

The Newham crime squad had come to the Silvertown strip looking for stolen copper. It wasn't supposed to be a massive operation, just another cleanup strike in line with local policing and mayoral priorities for the Olympic borough.

Instead, the detectives discovered an Aladdin's den of over £1 million of luxury goods that had been stolen during a series of lorry hijacks and warehouse robberies.

[4]Operation Houdini Crime Report entries on 19 September 2006.

The swag was stored in forty-one freight containers stacked on top of each other in 1-7 Brunel Street. The containers were rented to customers, many who turned out to be as false as their business addresses in the files of London City Self Storage. Among the stolen goods were cases upon cases of fine wine and designer clothes, shoes and handbags destined for Harvey Nichols, Liberty and other London department stores.

After six days, on 6 March 2006, all the items were traced. Most were the result of lorry hijacks and warehouse robberies going back three years that had taken place in Essex to the east and Hampshire to the southwest. Among the other stolen items were cloned vehicle registration plates, a bug detecting device and £800,000 worth of safes complete with blank keys and lock-picking equipment. In one safe, detectives found jewellery from a £350,000 heist in Hatton Garden, the heart of London's diamond trade.[5]

Chicky Matthews junior was arrested and later charged with conspiracy to steal and handling stolen goods. He denied it but distanced himself from the stroage side of the business. Similarly, he claimed not to know that the jewellery, which he claimed to have bought 'off a Chinaman', was stolen.[6]

A financial search revealed the Matthews family had withdrawn £1.6 million from their Lloyds business

[5]Giggy's on the corner of Greville Street and Hatton Garden was robbed over a weekend in November 2004. The robbers bypassed a sophisticated ADT alarm and picked the lock of the fully-stocked safe. Giggy Kyriacou told the author (interview 17 February 2009) that until some of the jewellery was discovered in Charles Matthews' possession some suspected that he was behind the robbery in order to make a false insurance claim.
[6]Defence case statement of Charles Frederick Matthews 14 August 2007.

account over thirty-two months, drove Bentleys and had a boat, *Options*, moored at the nearby Galleons Reach Marina and properties in London and Spain. Not bad for scrap metal dealers. However, the Newham crime squad only learned about the link to the Long Fella when Allen approached them weeks later on 1 May 2006 and explained his battle over the land and the recent fight at court.

Detective chief inspector David 'Mac' McKelvey was instantly wary of Allen and pulled his massive file from Scotland Yard's registry. Although the property developer insisted that he had nothing to do with his father's murder, Mac was concerned about some of the evidence and warned his crime squad to be careful about taking 'Billy Liar' at his word. That said, Allen clearly was a victim of violent crime and needed police protection in the run-up to the next court hearing in a month's time.

But equally, Mac didn't have to take over the case from Hampshire police. The truth was that at forty-three, a time when most detectives with twenty-four years on the force are thinking of seeing out their service behind a desk, Mac couldn't resist an opportunity to take a crack at the biggest gangster on the block. The Untouchable. The Long Fella.

Unlike most of his colleagues, Mac can remember the exact moment he decided to join the police. It was 1981, he was nineteen years old, and out with friends at the Green Gate nightclub in Barkingside, Essex.

'There was a massive fight and two blokes destroyed this poor sod for no reason. I wanted to do something but couldn't. It was the standing there helpless, not being able to do nothing. That was always something that followed me through my service – being able to do something when someone is not doing anything; catching the bad guys, people who was violent for no reason.'

The McKelveys came from Irish stock and moved to Newham with a proud tradition of public service behind them. Mac's great grandfather helped build the trams in Ilford, Essex. His grandfather was shot in France during the first world war and returned home to champion council residents.

Mac did well at school and opted for a career in banking during the first Thatcher government, whose politics he admired. He was being groomed for the trading floor while the Iron Lady deregulated the financial sector and pushed Docklands as a new bankers' casino. However, in February 1982, the lure of cops and robbers following the nightclub incident drove him towards the Metropolitan Police. It's an illustration of the detective he would become that Mac can still recount details of his first arrest, a prostitute, in the way another man might remember losing his virginity.

His first posting was Stoke Newington in Hackney, later one of the five Olympic boroughs, where large West Indian and African communities were already on the receiving end of racist, violent and corrupt policing. Mac shared the siege mentality of most police officers working tough inner city boroughs where crimes from drug dealing to armed robbery crossed ethnic lines and much of the community referred to you as *the Filth*.

'I nicked someone every day for five years. There wasn't someone I didn't nick for something. It was all overtime,' he recalled. Mac was drunk on being a police officer, a condition known internally as *job pissed*.

'All I wanted was to be a detective. I've got paperwork saying, "He's [job] pissed about being a detective."'

That wasn't the only paperwork he treasured. From the first day of his police service to his last, Mac kept old-fashioned scrapbooks of the cut-and-paste kind where every notable arrest, commendation and mention in the media was preserved in chronological order. There was one scrapbook entry in 1983 that marked his first experience of the Long Fella. Three drunk associates were threatening a Newham landlord while Mac sat alone, off duty, nursing a pint. He tried to intervene but the thugs had no fear of assaulting a policeman and one of them slashed Mac across the backside before help arrived and arrests were made.

At court, detectives from a covert operation approached Mac to educate the impressive young constable about who he was going up against. They took him to their secret base where a wall chart depicted the scale of organised crime in Newham. It was the first time Mac had heard of the Long Fella, who, like him, was only in his early twenties and ran a crew of lorry hijackers, the detectives explained.

'The trial led to the conviction of two of them and a third bloke was tried separately and jailed for attempting to intimidate the jury,' Mac recalled. 'After seeing the [intelligence] material and having my windows put in I got myself a gun. I was part of a shooting club. I also moved house and got a Rottweiler.'[7]

---

[7] David McKelvey recalled that Frankie Thompson junior was convicted of threatening the jury in the case of Tony Martin and Anthony Payne, the pair convicted of the assault on the pub landlord.

In 1987, Mac was finally transferred to detective training school shortly before Stoke Newington police station imploded in a massive corruption scandal. He remembers the ten-week training course as the best days of his life.

'It created a bond among us the like of which doesn't exist anywhere else. Complete strangers become brothers. You'd form bonds that went on forever. Being a detective was everything. Once you got that Detective in front of your name, you'd made it. It wasn't about getting promoted it was getting the best job off. All I wanted to do was arrest people. The reason for being a detective was I wanted to nick bigger and better villains. I wanted to put it right.'

It seemed logical but not planned that Mac would fall in love with a girl whose father was also a dedicated policeman. She'll understand my obsession with nicking gangsters, he reasoned, wrongly as it turned out.

'The first time I saw her I thought she is the most stunning woman I've ever met, and I was her first real love.' The couple married in 1992 but Mac didn't wear his uniform for the wedding ceremony. He'd done everything to get into plain clothes and wasn't going back now.

Children followed, three of them in the nineties, created between the long hours of surveillance and tearing about east London with a gun. Mac tested his wife's love every day with acts that showed where his real priorities lay. On learning about a drug importation through the Channel Tunnel, for example, he picked up his son from school then drove to Dover. Mac's mother had to collect her grandson, who had been left in the car while daddy pursued the baddies onto the train.

'In reality there was home life but my life was in the police. The term *job pissed* sums it up adequately,' he said.

Inevitably, a vocational copper is going to end up on a specialist squad. The regional crime squad was Mac's first but he found the Brentwood office to be a hiding place for the lazy and unmotivated. So with other like-minded detectives they went to work on taking out the untouched local criminals.

'There was freedom to develop long and short-term bits of work against top villains. And during this period in the late nineties, including a spell on the National Crime Squad, I came to realise just how sophisticated British organised crime in east London had become in the era of drugs and money laundering.'

In 1996, for example, Mac arrested Canning Town criminal Terry Sabine, who ran the car valeting business on Billy Allen's plot of land on the Silvertown strip. Sabine worked from a Portacabin, which the police had bugged. They had also tapped his phone and discovered he was moving large quantities of ecstasy to feed the expanding tribe of British ravers. As luck would have it, the Portacabin also doubled as a drop-in centre for criminal associates to slag off rivals and brag about capers past and present. Sabine was not just a friend of Allen, but also of the Long Fella and Danny Woollard, who all popped in for a natter.

Detectives listening in were delighted to get real time notice of the latest criminal plans as they were hatched. It made a change from relying on informant tip-offs or weeks on end following villains around the strip. 'It was great,' said retired detective chief superintendent Albert Patrick. 'We had something almost every day of the week.' And for some light relief, there was also a chance

to catch up on Sabine's latest call to an exotic sex chat
line. Sabine and Lenny Naylor were eventually arrested
with over 5000 ecstasy tablets. However, the surveillance
logs for the operation, codenamed Fairway, went missing
in the run up to their trial. 'Albert Patrick put the word
out that he wanted them returned or someone would be
killed,' Mac recalled. 'A word was had in a suspect officer's
ear and the logs reappeared.'[8]

For him the war on drugs was all about 'nicking villains'.
For other officers it was all about nicking. 'You knew who
they were, what they were doing. You stayed away from
them. You never ever believed they had crossed the line
and were working for the baddies. There were people in
the office you would and would not work with. People
got complaints for stealing and you didn't want to go out
with them and get in the shit. Usually, they weren't the
best police. You knew who the vocational police officers
were. It was the kudos of pitting your wits against the
baddies.'

The bugging of Sabine's Portacabin had some unintended
consequences for Scotland Yard. As well as intelligence on
Canning Town criminals, those listening in also picked up
the names of detectives said to be in their pockets. Some of
this chatter could be written off as bravado among crooks
trying to outdo each other by claiming to have a copper
'squared up'. But the volume of intelligence so alarmed senior
management back at Scotland Yard that they launched a

[8]Sabine and Naylor were both jailed but Naylor was executed shortly after his
release in 2001. The grapevine had it that the murder was revenge for his attack
with a machete on criminals who'd disrespected him in a Canning Town pub.
Terrence Barry was jailed for 18 years in October 2017 for conspiring to murder
Naylor following a cold case review by Kent and Essex police. Robert Blackwell
and David Carvell were found not guilty.

Ghost Squad (Operation Othona) to secretly scope the force's exposure to corruption. The highly politicised anti-corruption probe would run until 2002 with very mixed results.[9]

The intelligence from bugs secreted in various Canning Town premises developed in two separate silos: There was the Ghost Squad looking at bent officers while other detectives targeted organised crime in east London, when, arguably, it would have been more effective to examine the problem of police corruption and organised crime together.[10]

Analysts looking at the latter sifted the intelligence to create 'packages' for operational detectives like Mac to work into arrests. A 1998 intelligence package gave Mac his first insight into the crossover between gangsterism and the financial world. A key target of an operation codenamed Beregon was suspected money launderer Iraj Parvizi, whose family ran a kebab house. A tap on Parvizi's phones revealed his association with the north London Adams crime family and, more importantly, an unlikely romance with the wife of a Bank of England insider.

Parvizi, who played the financial markets and was a prolific gambler, allegedly pumped the woman for priceless inside information on whether interest rates were going up or down. So sensitive was the leak that

---

[9]Operations Crocus, Fairway, Frantic and Fantasy. See *Untouchables*.
[10]The organised crime intelligence cell was initially based at the old cadet centre in Wanstead, then moved to Woodford police station and finally to Old Ilford police station, where we pick up its activities in Chapter 8. In a bizarre coincidence, one of the intelligence officers who ran the cell was the son-in-law of the best friend of Jimmy Allen whose flat he lived in when murdered in 1986.

MI5 took over from Mac and his team.[11] Meanwhile, a police bug inserted into an east London warehouse visited by Parvizi had captured an incredible conversation, which suggested that the major organised crime families in the UK met regularly and worked together like a cartel. Mac took the recording to his boss who refused to accept the notion, much to his undisguised annoyance.

UK organised crime was certainly not structured or interconnected like the Mafia in the United States. British criminals, outside of the family-based organised crime networks, tended to be lone wolves or specialists who came together for one job and were then in the wind. That's not to say major UK organised crime networks wouldn't invest in the same large shipment of drugs, but the enormous profits made what alliances there were very precarious and prone to violence. Greed, treachery and drug-induced paranoia were frequent problems in organisations that lacked a Mafia-style or military sense of discipline found among some international rivals, such as those coming from the former Soviet Union.

In 1999, Mac was moved from the National Crime Squad (NCS) to a more routine policing role in Enfield, a lively north London borough. The transfer was a punishment for inadvertently and indirectly assisting a former Stoke Newington detective, Martin Morgan, who was the secret target of a major anti-corruption investigation.[12] Mac felt

[11]See Michael Gillard, 'Sex, Lies and Interest Rates' *Buzzfeed*, 30 July 2015. Iraj Parvizi could not be identified at the time of the article as he was facing a separate trial for insider trading. He was acquitted in 2016. For more on the trial See Private Eye Numbers 1411, 1414-16 and 1419, February to June 2016.
[12]DC Martin Morgan was the main target of Operation Greyhound. He was initially suspected of corruption during his time at Stoke Newington police station and those suspicions continued through his career until he was sacked and jailed. See Chapter 8 and *Untouchables*.

this was unfair – he didn't even like Morgan – and maybe it was. A senior police source, who reviewed the file, said the sudden transfer was more down to Mac's personality than his integrity. His sometimes abrasive and arrogant style had, it seemed, angered key managers at the NCS who seized on the incident to transfer him.

After almost four years at Enfield, during which time he had been promoted to detective inspector, Mac was itching to return to a specialist unit. His application in 2003 to join the east London office of the Flying Squad, which deals with armed robbery, was approved then suddenly blocked following the intervention of a senior officer who had seen his file or heard whispers and decided there was a whiff about the candidate. Unfortunately for detective chief superintendent Sharon Kerr, she mistakenly called Mac and relayed her concerns before he was able to interrupt and identify himself as the very officer whose transfer she was blocking. Now aware what was being said about him, Mac appealed Kerr's decision and, remarkably, she was ordered to apologise.[13]

'DI McKelvey is clearly an able detective and he has achieved impressive results throughout his career. He delivers results and gets things done. I note he has amassed a wealth of commendations. His involvement at the cutting edge of crime fighting, particularly in east London and Essex, has meant that his name has been linked to both corrupt officers and corruptors of the same. In my experience this should not be seen as unusual and should not necessarily attract adverse comment. I have seen no direct evidence to suggest

[13]DCS Kerr told the anti-corruption squad it was always her intention to speak to McKelvey and there was no inadvertent disclosure of information to him.

that this officer is corrupt and to label him so cannot be justified on the material reviewed,' wrote deputy assistant commissioner John Yates, who had made his name in the anti-corruption squad of so-called 'Untouchables'. Nevertheless, Mac was told he had shown poor judgement and must remain on borough policing for another 18 months before applying again to join a specialist squad.

The experience got him thinking that there were some senior managers at the Yard who had it in for him. Only a fool ignored how jealousy, personality clashes and patronage in a 33,000-strong rank-based organisation could undo a promising career and make an unremarkable one.

In March 2003, Mac transferred from Enfield to Newham borough, which was awaiting the decision of the International Olympic Committee on whether London would host the 2012 Games. As a detective with an encyclopaedic knowledge of East End villainy, he was put in charge of the borough's proactive crime, drugs, robbery and motor vehicle squads based at police headquarters in Stratford. Mac had around fifty detectives and uniformed officers of varying levels of experience under him. He therefore made it his mission to create, through mentoring, an effective pool of proactive officers led from the front. Drawing on his own drive to make detective, he trained junior ranks in-house and rotated them on different squads to get a rounded experience. Mac gave them loyalty and demanded it in return. This style of leadership was going out of fashion in the new 'dog eat dog' London force where many senior officers drove desks and were loyal only to their own promotion prospects.

At the time, Stratford was undergoing major redevelopment. Westfield, the commercial developers, had a £1.5bn plan for a retail complex erected around Stratford's soon to be upgraded transport hubs linking the Docklands Light Railway to Canning Town and to the High Speed line and eventually Crossrail. Stratford was also the proposed gateway to the London 2012 athletes' village intended to be a residential and commercial space called Stratford City after the Games. The International Olympic Committee considered public security a key factor when deciding between candidate cities. This meant the London bid team and Sir Robin Wales, the newly-elected Newham major, had to get on top of their significant street crime problem.

Wales was 'breathing down the borough commander's neck' to sort it out, a senior police source said. The New Labour mayor already had his own controversial street enforcement team of civilians, made to look like police but without their powers, to patrol the borough's few green spaces and many run-down streets.

Mac was pulled into the borough commander's office and given a speech rarely heard these days. 'Money's no object, just reduce street crime and burglary because it's out of control,' he was told. Mac interpreted the order as carte blanche to combat crime in all its forms. Maybe borough policing wasn't that boring after all, he convinced himself.

Early success came in an operation against Vietnamese gangs running skunk farms. The hydroponically grown, high-strength cannabis was popular with the youth and, as well as being the graveyard of ambition, when over-indulged caused psychosis in some users, with all the attendant effects on the social fabric of the Olympic

borough in-waiting. Mac was given two weeks to make a
dent on the problem. He took four months and crushed
it. The ringleaders rented residential homes and modified
them, using their own plumbers and electricians, to serve
as a round-the-clock nursery that yielded a crop worth
£40,000 every six to eight weeks.

After one raid, where the *Evening Standard* was
authorised to tag along, a senior officer at Scotland Yard
rebuked Mac for describing the skunk farms as 'organised
crime' in Newham. It was the first sign that he might not
be on the same political wavelength as his bosses.

'There's only a small number of cannabis farms in the
borough,' the deputy assistant commissioner insisted by
phone.

'We've raided over 100 farms, Ma'am, deported many
people and convicted seven ringleaders,' Mac replied,
saving his best for last. 'One farm was next door to Forest
Gate police station!'

While Scotland Yard and the mayor of Newham
continued to present a distorted reality of crime, Mac
converted seized assets from the Vietnamese and other
drugs raids into resources for further proactive operations.
But when Scotland Yard needed his help, the Newham
crime squad was ready to heed the call and show they
could punch above their weight. In this instance, the
haulage and cargo industry around Heathrow Airport
was particularly concerned about the volume of lorry
hijackings. Many of the lorries were being slaughtered
on the Silvertown strip, in Caxton Street to be precise,
where the Matthews and Bowers crime families operated.
In some cases, the hijackers were using police identities to
dupe haulage companies and warehouses into diverting
their lorries to the strip.

Feeling the Yard's oversight was more 'talking shop' than action, Mac came up with his own proactive operation: A bugged lorry baited with a high-value load and an undercover officer posing as the driver.

The Newham crime squad targeted the strip and developed informants among the business and criminal communities who worked there. It was one of these informants who provided the tip-off about the stolen copper at the Matthews' yard, which in turn led to the discovery of the Aladdin's den of hijacked goods in containers stored at 1-7 Brunel Street. By the time Billy Allen met the Newham crime squad in early May 2006, back at Scotland Yard Mac was seen as something of a loose cannon. His can-do attitude and enthusiasm for policing made some of his superiors feel uneasy, cowardly even, and therefore prone to believing the worst of him.

The line between personal and commercial violence becomes blurred in the world of 'illegal capitalism', Newham-born criminologist, Professor Dick Hobbs, observed in his book *Lush Life*. In general, criminals are good capitalists and know that violence is bad for business because it attracts the wrong kind of attention.

After Allen's visit In May 2006, Mac viewed the CCTV footage of the court fight that had taken place three months earlier in February. The disregard for the law and cocky recklessness intrigued the detective.

Mac had risen through the ranks listening to war stories told in hushed tones about how the Long Fella was unlike other gangsters: His psychopathic nature, his cunning, his ability to avoid prosecution and his 'friends' in the police and maybe even the intelligence services. Mac requested everything that the registry held on his new adversary. Nothing, it turned out, was in one place but spread among the filing cabinets of different squads and the fractured memories of detectives who had gone up against the enigmatic gangster since the early 1980s. Mac avidly digested what he could find. The reports were full of violent incidents and implicit warnings about cops whose careers had been destroyed after taking on the Long Fella.

There was certainly enough to make any other detective think twice, particularly one heading for a life of risk-free desk driving and a retirement pension as a superintendent. But the idea of an untouchable criminal offended Mac and went to the heart of his reasons for joining the police – to put things right. It also appealed to the righteous and possibly cocky reckless side of his own nature.

Mac scoured the files for a weak link. Every villain has one. Drugs, booze, a perversion maybe, or someone they care for who's on the pipe or the pole. Something that made them act in a way likely to make them vulnerable.

The Long Fella's Achilles heel was staring Mac in the face in the most recent reports about the fight at court. What sort of criminal thinks they are beyond the law in today's surveillance society?

The files revealed a pattern of behaviour that a psychologist might call a personality disorder and a dramatist might portray as a fatal flaw. Narcissism was the Long Fella's weakness, an obsession with being respected or, put another way, not being disrespected. The flaw was his belief that any slight, however minor, if left uncorrected would undermine his power and leave him exposed. This survival of the fittest mentality, combined with a willingness to use extreme violence, rendered him vulnerable to any detective game enough to go after him, especially one with the backing of his own force.

The police files revealed how almost a decade earlier in 1997 Scotland Yard had come the closest ever to putting the Long Fella away after an explosion of violence that saw a man have his throat cut following a minor matter of disrespect.

Mac learned that the detectives investigating this serious assault were greatly assisted by a criminal associate and former friend of the Long Fella called Jimmy Holmes. Their spectacular falling-out was the stuff of underworld legend and Mac discovered from reading the files that Holmes was still alive, still active and still very angry. But it was still the case that after two decades of throwing everything Scotland Yard had at him, with six years to go before the Games, the Long Fella was more powerful than ever; a crime lord of the Olympic borough and beyond.

Mac gathered his squad together for a briefing. His instructions were simple:

One: Tell no one outside the team what you're up to.

Two: Expect criminals and bent cops to make violent or corrupt approaches.

And Three: Find Jimmy Holmes.

PART TWO

The Long Fella

5

Snipers

Jimmy Holmes is no run-of-the-mill villain. The self-described 'avant-garde' gangster honed his jazz-meets-Miami mobster dress code and eclectic musical taste while acting as an enforcer for his mentor, Bernie Silver: Soho's Godfather.

Silver, an East End Jew, had risen to the top through an alliance with gangsters of Maltese origin in the 1950s. Their outfit, known as the 'Syndicate', ran *spielers*, cinemas, clubs, clip joints and brothels in that patch of central London demarcated by Oxford Street and Regent Street, Shaftsbury Avenue and Charing Cross Road.

No one opened a rival business in Soho without the approval of Silver and his high-level corrupt police contacts. The second world war veteran was even said to have helped British intelligence set up brothels in Northern Ireland to honey-trap republicans into turning against the IRA.[1] But when his police protection waned after a series of newspaper investigations into corruption and vice, Silver was eventually jailed in 1974 for living off immoral earnings, and then for murder a year later.

[1]'British set up bugged brothels to trap IRA killers', *Daily Mail* (7 February 1976).

Opportunistic criminals with animal cunning can sense weakness in their prey and Silver's operation needed extra muscle when rivals started running prostitutes from properties without paying rent to the fallen godfather. In 1978, Silver's murder conviction was overturned and he was freed on parole. He returned to his Soho throne, but the once dapper, Rolls Royce-driving vice king cut a different figure. He now walked around Silver City, as it was known, looking down at heel and much beyond his fifty-six years.

Holmes was part of a group of thugs put together to remove the squatters and scare off their pimps.[2] Although he never said it, from the way Holmes talks about his criminal past, Silver was clearly something of a father figure to him. Holmes recalled with genuine sorrow how, on his release from prison, Silver took to buying multiple pairs of the same brown moccasins, cords and tops from Marks & Spencer, which he wore until threadbare. 'He would also fix the television sets of a select group of Soho residents.'

Between these eccentricities, Silver made time to teach Holmes the tricks of the porn trade: how to use front men, rent collectors, false nominee directors and offshore companies to hide ownership of leases and freeholds from the taxman, honest coppers and journalists. Holmes didn't trust easily but he enjoyed the company of Silver, who could talk with authority about any subject, especially antiques.

The pair often met at the Victoria Sporting Club for a morning catch-up on the night's events. Holmes also

---

[2]Jimmy Holmes says the French family, a criminal gang in south London he ran with in his early twenties as an apprentice armed robber and enforcer, approached him to work for Silver.

enjoyed gambling trips to Monte Carlo. Silver would get him to drive his Volvo stuffed with cash from London to Monaco, where the Soho Godfather laundered money and gambled heavily at the casino tables. However, behind this extravagance was a shrewd and slippery mind. Silver reminded Holmes that the secret to holding on to criminal wealth lay in the hidden arm's length offshore ownership of property. He had earned and kept millions of pounds from the taxman and was a sharp observer of trends in London's property market.

During one of their chats in 1984, he suggested that now his 25-year-old mentee was earning good money as the leaseholder of various clip joints, porn shops and brothels, he might also want to invest in the East End.

'It's a shit hole now, but mark my words Jimmy, it won't be for long,' Silver counselled.

The Thatcher government was already lubricating public and private partnerships to invest in a new business airport and a railway system connecting the City to a new financial district – Canary Wharf. These infrastructure projects were some years off completion, but there were any number of old pubs, clubs and shop fronts that could be picked up cheaply to launder criminal activity and service the sexual urges of, initially, traditional East Enders, the growing immigrant community from the Asian sub-continent, and later, young professionals.

Opportunity knocked when Holmes was asked if he wanted in on an investment in Newham. Days later at a *spieler* over a second-hand furniture shop, veteran south London villain, Ronnie Olliffe, laid out the proposition. Holmes knew Olliffe through the porn game and supplied him with dirty magazines and videos. At the meeting, Holmes was told that 'a young up and coming

face called Davey Hunt from Canning Town' had a gym
that wasn't making money. The building on the Barking
Road was ripe for converting into a dodgy sauna cum
massage parlour.

Hunt had a reputation for uncompromising hardness
that was now extending beyond Canning Town. Holmes –
bored of Soho and looking for misadventure – thought he
would take a look at this similarly-aged criminal upstart.
He might have thought differently had he known just
how much heat was on Hunt at the time – the Long Fella
was already the police's public enemy number one in east
London.

On 18 September 1984, a detective chief inspector at
Plaistow police station, which covers Canning Town,
sent an illuminating dispatch to his superiors requesting
immediate help.

'This report,' he wrote, 'concerns a group of people
operating in the East End of London, particularly in the
area of Plaistow and Canning Town, whose influence
on crime in London and the Home counties has grown
steadily over a period of eight to ten years. In proportion
to this growth has been the development of fear that they
engender in the local population until a point has now
been reached where the indigenous population would
rather tolerate the outrageous behaviour of these people
than become involved as a witness.'

The 'evil group of people' terrorising the area had
emerged from a local football team attached to the
Mayflower Youth Club. They gave themselves a name that
reeked of adolescent self-regard and the gang's founders,
by then aged between twenty-five and thirty-five, were
regarded locally as 'untouchable', the report continued.

The so-called Snipers were about fifty-strong with a feeder pool of young recruits. These 'Mini Snipers' were selected from Canning Town's white youth, some as young as eleven, who had shown an appetite for violence, cunning and respect for the underworld hierarchy.

A strong racist current flowed through the Snipers who, as well as dedicating themselves to crime and supporting West Ham Football Club, were attracted to the British Movement and National Front, who happily stoked local resentment of the Asian influx into Canning Town. However, it was armed robbery and protection rackets that most concerned the police. Menacing local businesses to pay a protection fee or risk violence and financial ruin was a staple of criminal gangs the world over. The police calculated that the Snipers operated protection rackets from the edge of the City of London seventy miles east to the Essex coast. They provided security to pubs and clubs and then abused the business as their personal VIP lounge.

The Snipers showed no fear of the local police. In fact, three weeks before the report was written, a group of them had thrown nitric acid in the face of an officer attending an incident at the Tropicana Wine Bar, and then driven a car at him. One of the perpetrators was now in custody but it was the same story – no witnesses would come forward to identify the others. Attached to the detective chief inspector's report was a list of twenty-three 'original Snipers'. One family, the Hunts, dominated the list. Six of them, all with criminal records, were named.[3]

Davey Hunt and his brother, Stevie, were among eight Snipers in custody or awaiting trial, but this did not

[3]Joseph, Kevin, Paul, John, Stephen and David Hunt.

diminish the gang's influence, the report noted. 'Witnesses go missing, are "got at" or just forget their evidence,' it said. By 1984 Hunt, then aged twenty-four, had not only dominated his twelve siblings, but the Canning Town kid was top dog in the Snipers.

The detective chief inspector signed off his report with a call to action by others as he was weeks away from retiring. 'The Snipers,' he wrote, 'represent the single most serious crime threat in the Division, their sphere of influence is growing and their territory widening. The type of crime they undertake is becoming ever more serious.' Nothing short of a 'concerted attack' by the police was needed to restore public confidence among a local population who now believe the gang is 'invincible', he concluded.

The warning did not go unheeded. Within three weeks a recently formed covert police intelligence unit was staking out Hunt and his Snipers in Canning Town. The Intelligence and Surveillance Unit (ISU) operated from a secret office miles away on the Caledonian Road. The team of detectives had the latest surveillance equipment, trackers, cameras and covert cars necessary to build an intelligence picture about the Snipers without being spotted. Their targets always went out under the cover of darkness, usually in BMWs, scouting for commercial warehouses, parked lorries and containers to rob.

One Sniper car would shadow a van that had been hired on a stolen driving license or recently bought for cash at auction. Its purpose was to transport the stolen material back to Canning Town. If the police happened to make a random stop then the Sniper in the BMW was prepared to act as a decoy, including smashing into the police vehicle, so the van could escape.

The ISU followed the gang for weeks, on one occasion as far as Falmouth in Cornwall. But it sometimes felt that the Snipers were too good at anti-surveillance or had inside information that they were being followed. To overcome the problem, the ISU 'lumped up' the Sniper cars with magnetic tracking devices placed under the chassis and followed from a distance.

There was no shortage of cannon fodder in Canning Town willing to help the gang. The Snipers recruited from a snooker hall on the Barking Road, which led the ISU to give its surveillance operation the codename Soldier 3. 'The snooker recruits represented soldier ants and number 3 was the Met police division of east London,' an ISU veteran explained. Unusually, the operation had its own dramatic logo of a silhouetted paramilitary figure with a gun. Faxes with the logo went to every police force listing the make, model, number plate and registered owner of all the vehicles the ISU had observed. Forces from Nottingham to Devon and Cornwall were warned that the men behind the wheels were violent and details of all stops should be passed back to their unit. The response was enormous, and one detective had the sole task of collating all this incoming intelligence on a massive spider chart on the wall of their secret office in north London.

At first it was not apparent who occupied the centre of the web. The Snipers would return to Canning Town at around 6 a.m. and park in the dimly lit arches underneath the Silvertown Way flyover. Buyers were waiting to collect the stolen goods for onwards sale across London. From these dark arches, the Snipers were followed a short distance along Victoria Dock Road to a corner pub. The Prince of Wales was 'one of those dens of iniquity where they could smell old bill in their cars,' said Michael

Carroll, one of the ISU detectives on the job. So he hung
back. It wasn't just out of fear of acid in the eyes but also
new, disturbing intelligence that the Snipers were turning
the tables and had the police under surveillance.

'To date a number of police officers have been physically
attacked. A woman police officer has received continuous
threatening phone calls, whilst a police officer's house
and other police property has been damaged. On one
occasion a police officer giving evidence at court had his
house broken into before he could get home after his
home address was given out in evidence. Members of
this organisation have also been known to disrupt court
proceedings and generally jeer and jostle witnesses. More
recently they have threatened officers in the street and
have taken vehicle registration numbers of cars parked
outside police officers' home addresses,' an internal ISU
report warned at the time.

The Snipers, it turned out, were stopping at the
Prince of Wales for a 'debrief' with their boss. The ISU
quickly identified him as Davey Hunt. Detectives were
told the Long Fella had taken control of the pub by
forcing protection on the licensee, who refused to make
a complaint. It took three months for Operation Soldier
3 to establish a complete intelligence picture – Hunt was
the young general masterminding the distribution of the
Sniper's hijacked goods. It was these ISU detectives who'd
taken Mac into their confidence after two Snipers slashed
the young constable's backside during the attack on a pub
landlord.

As the criminal money flowed, the ISU observed Hunt's
gang enjoying nights out with their wives. A 'steak and
two bottles of Moët' was the usual shout at the Apollo, a
famous steakhouse in Stratford, and also at Venus, another

steakhouse and bar popular with West Ham footballers
and Page 3 girls.

It was not the ISU's job to make arrests but to build
an accurate intelligence picture. In that, it had been
successful. However, a progress report in January 1985
said that, in the meantime, the Snipers' influence had
'widened' because local detectives lacked the resources to
stem the tide.

'[The Snipers'] growing influence on the supply of drugs
is particularly worrying,' the report noted, and revealed
that a drug factory was now operating in Canning Town
but had not yet been located. This would turn out to be
the amphetamine factory connected to Chic Matthews,
which Billy Allen helped identify. The proposed solution
to the wider Sniper problem was for a special squad of
detectives to start making arrests based on the ISU's
intelligence. A senior officer agreed and, at the beginning
of 1985, authorised the setting up of a seventeen-strong
squad of detectives who were tasked with putting right
the past 'failure to tackle this aspect of organised crime' in
Newham borough.

Weeks later, Holmes met Hunt for the first time to
discuss investing in his Canning Town gym. It went well,
and the two men impressed each other with their swagger
and criminal arrogance. They agreed to partner with
Ronnie Olliffe, who had introduced them, buy the lease
and convert the building into a massage parlour on the
first floor and a hardcore cinema named the Swedish Club
above. The existing gym, Abigale's, would be kept open
for criminal friends to meet and for Hunt and Holmes
to peacock over their obsession with banging weights
and hitting the heavy bag. Hunt stood out beyond the
premature greying of his thick black hair and a gold

left front tooth, all of which gave him the look of an edgy Vogue model, Holmes observed. His new business partner also didn't booze or use recreational drugs. Sport and fitness were the Long Fella's highs.

'He was bright as a button,' recalled one former detective, 'with a memory for the faces of police officers who had nicked him in the past, like me. There was something about him, but you'd never have known he'd go on to be what he was.'

Hunt had left the local Woodside Secondary School in 1977, aged sixteen, for a promising career with Millwall Football Club that was cut short due to injury. Luckily, his real talent was in amateur boxing. Hunt retired from the ring an undefeated light heavyweight with a terrific right hand, which he continued to throw while working as a bouncer for various rowdy local pubs in his late teens and early twenties.

Though the shorter of the two by a considerable way, Holmes had a solid upper body that served him well as a kick boxer. 'I once fought behind the Iron Curtain,' he bragged to Hunt.

The pair shared an inner rage that would explode in bursts of expert violence. Holmes, for example, by far the more outgoing of the two, spoke of his love for beating up 'nonces' in Soho's neon backlit street who'd come looking for child porn or an underage prostitute. By his own admission, Holmes had 'declared war on the world' long before he met Hunt and was a veteran of many acts of violence, not just against child abusers. Privately he knew his way of being was ultimately 'a declaration of war on himself'; a misplaced anger about being sexually abused as a young child in Bermondsey, a once tough southeast London borough, where he was born in July 1959.

Living off adult prostitution – or *poncing* as it was
informally known – didn't trouble Holmes, but he firmly
drew the line when it came to *noncing*. He knew from
personal experience its everlasting damage, which he hid
through kickboxing, street violence, alcohol and drug
binges.

'Once you've been fucked up the arse, you stay fucked
up the arse,' he liked to say when explaining how as a
boy he had drifted from sex for pay with men in toilets
to being a rent boy hanging around the 'meat rack'. This
was the notorious stretch of Piccadilly Circus, opposite
Wimpey's flagship restaurant, where male prostitutes of
varying ages, strays and strung-out runaways would drape
themselves over the railings that separated the pavement
from Shaftesbury Avenue, waiting like low-hanging,
bruised fruit to be picked by passersby.

It would be a while yet before Holmes opened up
to Hunt about his abusive past and sexuality. Coming
out would be a tricky matter as his business partner,
like wider society, held typically homophobic views
where the difference between 'poofs' and 'nonces' went
unrecognised. Also, on a practical level, Holmes could
see in Hunt a predator's eye for weakness. Happily, they
bonded over another of Hunt's great passions: racing
pigeons. As a boy he was shown how to care for, train
and race pigeons over long distances. Hunt longed to be
a champion pigeon fancier. It therefore helped cement
their friendship when Holmes told him the 'best flyer
out of east London', a man Hunt thought highly of, was
his uncle. It was this, plus his propensity for violence and
business acumen (Holmes was introduced as someone
with a 'Midas touch') that guaranteed him a place on
Hunt's firm.

However, their first joint venture was not going to plan. Olliffe was slow to invest in the new massage parlour and cinema business. The two violent upstarts didn't want to upset the south London villain because he offered introductions to other criminal enterprise and underworld contacts, but decided to run the new business without him. In the end, Olliffe was not put out because his real motive for getting close to the youthful pair was not business but personal security. It turned out Olliffe needed fresh blood to protect him when Freddie Foreman, his business partner and friend, went on the run to Spain after the 1983 Security Express robbery.[4]

Meanwhile, the new seventeen-strong squad of detectives were all over Hunt who, a 1985 police report observed, 'is very quickly moving up the ladder of importance. He has now, in the main, progressed from the actual physical involvement in crime, to the organisation of criminal activity and the placing of the stolen property

---

[4]According to Holmes, Ronnie Olliffe was feeling vulnerable to reprisals following the recent murder of Peter Hennessey at a boxing charity event. Freddie Foreman later wrote that the fatal stabbing split south London and sparked a war. Paddy Onions and Jimmy Coleman were acquitted of the murder. Michael Hennessey, Peter's brother, was shot before he could exact revenge on the pair, but survived.

Separately, Holmes claims that Olliffe was also plotting to rip off one of the armed robbers behind the £26 million Brink's-Mat gold bullion heist in 1983. Gold bars that hadn't been smelted were secreted around London. According to Holmes, Olliffe was trying to enlist criminals to help steal the share of gold belonging to 'mad' Micky McAvoy – by then serving a twenty-five year sentence for the robbery. His share was apparently hidden in the chimney of Patrick 'bolt eyes' Clark's house in Chislehurst, Kent. Olliffe even mentioned it to Holmes, who lived in Chislehurst at the time and was minded to case the house but said he thought better of ripping off such a heavy and well-connected criminal.

obtained. His involvement in crime includes robbery, theft of loads and drugs etc.'

On 15 April 1986 at 4.30 p.m. the Long Fella was sitting with his brother, Christopher, and two others in the office hut of a new scaffold business in Back Lane, Stratford, when detectives burst in. The premises had been under police surveillance for some time as part of Operation Trooper, which also was targeting Chic Matthews over the amphetamine drug factory. Detectives uncovered £5000 of stolen men's clothing and, significantly, a sawn-off 410 shotgun. Both barrels and the butt had been shortened.

'As your honour is well aware, this type of weapon is widely used in the commission of robberies and I can think of no legal use for [it],' an officer wryly told the judge in a bid to deny the Hunt brothers bail.

To make good his point, he explained how his witnesses were afraid and recounted a conversation overheard by a court officer in the cells. The Hunt brothers were talking to one of their co-accused, who was about to be released.

'Get the wreckers to go round tonight,' he was ordered. The judge then heard how that night a pub in Canning Town was broken into and 'GRASS' daubed in red paint on the walls of every room, some of which were set alight. Hunt eventually pleaded guilty to handling stolen goods. He received nine months but the sentence was suspended meaning he never had to go to jail.[5]

His brother was not so lucky. He pleaded guilty to possessing the sawn off shotgun without a permit. It left

[5]David Charles Hunt CRO 209288/80H was sentenced at Southwark Crown Court on 13 July 1987.

detectives suspecting that Christopher had agreed to take the rap for his younger brother.

Despite all this police attention on his partner, Holmes wanted to get the firm further into the drugs game. One day, while Hunt was racing pigeons, Holmes headed for Blackpool to look at a potential peep show investment. The contacts he made there led to a deal to buy two hundred bars of Moroccan cannabis resin. The drugs were meant for Olliffe, but Holmes explained to the northerners that he was on the run from Flying Squad detectives still doggedly investigating the laundering of Brink's-Mat gold. Holmes stepped in and shadowed the van carrying the drugs to the Prince of Wales pub in Canning Town where it was distributed to local dealers and, he calculated, brought in £160,000 for the firm.

Meanwhile, Operation Trooper continued its surveillance on Hunt and saw him meeting with Chic Matthews shortly before his arrest over the drug factory. Cash was certainly flowing into Canning Town's criminal fraternity from protection rackets, robberies and drugs, but there was a lack of sophistication about how to spend it. Many did up their modest terraced houses, bought flash cars and treated the family and mistress. Any detective following the money had little difficulty working out what had gone on.

Holmes decided it was time to teach Hunt some new tricks, just as Silver had schooled him. He was already quite alarmed at his partner's lack of financial smarts. Until then, Hunt invested his money in property and home improvement. He had a mortgage just like any civilian, but was 'clueless', thought Holmes, who in times like these missed the sophistication of the Soho vice kings. Hunt's outlook was also very parochial. His financial empire existed within a ladder of streets between Freemasons Road and Prince Regent Lane. On the ladder was the terraced house in Garvary Road, where he grew up with a dozen siblings, and in Varley Road was the first house Hunt bought in 1983 for £22,000 with an Abbey National mortgage.

Soho could be a heavy criminal environment at times, but it had nothing on the casual violence and villainy Holmes was now experiencing in the East End. More importantly, Hunt, the man at the top of that group of criminals, was not someone to make feel stupid, so Holmes had to tread carefully. An opportunity arose to broach the subject of financial management following the 1986 murder of Peter Morris, owner of a club in Canning Town called Galleons Reach.

Morris had been a well-known face whose club, almost opposite the Prince of Wales pub, acted as a watering hole for an older generation of criminals not the arrivistes. The takeover of Galleons Reach followed a familiar pattern. Billy 'Jango' Williams, a man described by the police as 'Hunt's Monster', was sent in to terrorise the place until the manager saw the sense of having new protection.

Galleons Reach was a money-spinner and Holmes eventually suggested they buy the freehold through his offshore company, Winton Investments, which was incorporated in September 1987 in the Isle of Man. Hunt agreed and the firm now had its own club renamed The Bancroft. Every proper firm should have a club and Hunt wanted to be like London's other top crime families with a recognised venue for entertaining.

For his part, Holmes was now feeling he belonged to 'a tight unit', whose key players were Davey Hunt and his brother Stevie, with the Snipers as their wrecking crew. Stevie was still very much his own man who did his own thing, usually involving cars. But when you crossed Davey Hunt you also had his fearsome older brother on your case. People called them 'Doom and Gloom', though not to their faces. To Holmes it very much looked like the two Hunt brothers were modelling themselves on those other gangster siblings, the Krays, who terrorised the East End in the sixties until hubris, mental illness and the law finally caught up with them.

Ronnie Kray had sent word that Hunt should visit him at Broadmoor, the secure psychiatric unit in Berkshire. Holmes agreed to come along for the craic, noticing his business partner's pride in being considered heavy enough to parlay with one of the Krays. The meeting, however, was a high camp affair with the two rising criminals kicking each other under the visiting room table like schoolboys when Ronnie, in his monogramed jacket, cufflinks and slippers, made lascivious suggestions about Hunt's model good looks.

The business at hand was a film about the twins. Roger Daltrey, frontman of The Who, had bought the rights to John Pearson's *The Profession of Violence*, the best book on the twins' rise and fall. The singer, who co-produced and starred in the 1980 film *McVicar* about the eponymous London armed robber and prison escapee, had also done a deal with the twins for their support. Ronnie Kray, however, was livid when he learned Daltrey had sold the project to another company. The madder of the two Krays had an inflated sense of his influence in the real world and wanted Hunt to bring the singer to Broadmoor so he could 'cut him'.

Reggie Kray was not happy with Ronnie's approach, and when Hunt and Holmes visited him in Gartree prison a better plan to win over Daltrey was hatched. It involved using Reggie's former prison boyfriend, a wannabe singer, as an intermediary.[6] Nothing came of that intervention and Holmes and Hunt eventually walked away from the project. However, a year or so later a film was made with the Kemp brothers of new romantic band Spandau Ballet playing the twins.

In a strange homage to the East End legends, Hunt later insisted on naming a new club in Soho after the Krays' mother, Violet. The venue used to be a clip joint controlled by Holmes, but after a fire it was converted into an upmarket celebrity hangout in partnership with Soho landlord, Frank Spiteri.[7] At its peak in the late 1980s, Violet's attracted a trendy crowd of celebrities, among them singers Sade and Neneh Cherry, Levis' model, Nick Kamen, and the usual assortment of terminally hip Soho night dwellers. The club had a 'nice vibe' and Holmes was very comfortable there. For starters, he loved outlandish clothes and had befriended Mark Powell, a rising bespoke Soho tailor who mixed Edwardian and Mod cuts with gangster-style and a Saville Row ethic.

A strong believer in 'the power of dress' – a working class pride in looking sharp on a weekend – Powell had rented his first shop from Holmes in nearby Archer Street. There he met Hunt and through him got involved in the ill-fated Kray film project. Powell agreed to be the immaculately dressed front of house host for Violet's. Holmes flitted seamlessly between the club and other

[6]Peter Gillett.
[7]52 Rupert Street.

Soho haunts, including the Wag, Gossips and Ronnie
Scott's, where he queued as 'a civilian' until his personality
and spending power got him noticed and through the red
rope quicker. In general, the dandy gangster preferred to
night trawl without Hunt. It wasn't just that his partner's
abstinence was a downer for the self-described 'party
animal' who loved alcohol, drugs and music. Hunt also
had an unnerving habit of scanning a venue for someone
to fight.

'Do you think he can have a tear up?' he would ask
Holmes, who tried his best to steer his business partner
away from violence on their night off. Sometimes, though,
it was inevitable. One night Gary Stretch, a good-looking
British super welterweight boxer, attended the same event
at an East End pub. Hunt felt Stretch was belittling one
of the staff and confronted the boxer. Stretch gave Hunt
short shrift. Hunt gave Stretch a lesson in boxing. The
vanquished champ, said one observer, was then made to
repeat Hunt's name until the Lancastrian could pronounce
it like a Londoner, while Holmes and the rest of the firm
finished off his friends.

'That's his pre-eminence in life, that he can have a tear
up. And fuck me he can have a tear up,' Holmes reflected.
'He judges everyone by that manner. Then money. He's
never been beaten in a tear up.'

Back at Violet's, Hunt's Canning Town gorillas were
running amok with a volatile mix of gun-toting lairiness
and being star-struck. Holmes felt their presence was
lowering the tone and would eventually ruin the club
vibe that he and Mark Powell were building. Matters
escalated when Hunt suggested that rather than split the
profits with Spiteri they should take it all for themselves.
It was this type of short-termism that made Holmes

sometimes regret his association with the Canning Town gangster.

It didn't make financial sense to pick a fight when the firm was laundering good money through the club and making a profit. There was enough to go around and more opportunities on offer in Soho. Having over Spiteri would only send word out that they were no good. Holmes, after all, had a reputation to preserve and was always planning to return to his beloved Soho.

The area, however, was changing in the late eighties and Bernie Silver continued to move with the times. The Soho Godfather could not resist the pink pound behind a gay community intent on creating an alternative scene in the heart of London. Silver wanted to sell up and offered some of his leases to Holmes, but they were too expensive and he couldn't compete with Paul Raymond, the well-established Soho landlord and pornographer. At the time, Holmes said the firm was leasing a property belonging to David Sullivan, another of the newer vice kings who had cornered the market in mail-order dirty magazines. Unlike Hunt, Sullivan revelled in publicity. No opportunity was missed to promote his magazines and shops through interviews he often granted at his Essex mansion.

The Long Fella, meanwhile, was attracting renewed attention of a different kind – from the police. Only this time, the detectives on his case were prepared to take the fight to Hunt's door and, if necessary, slug it out toe-to-toe in Canning Town.

But first, they had an enemy within to confront.

David Easy was posted to Plaistow Division in 1988 as a newly-made detective chief inspector in his early thirties. His brief from on high was to 'clean it up'. This meant rooting out the suspected corrupt links between detectives and Davey Hunt's crime group, whose control over the area had created no-go zones for the police. This too had to stop, Easy was told.

He soon identified problem officers and gently eased them out 'in a nice way', he recalled. However, one veteran detective, Taffy Howells, he found very unwilling to go. Easy didn't get the measure of Howells until he was shown around Canning Town and introduced to local publicans, often the source of good intelligence and the gatekeepers to an after-hours drink. By the third pub it dawned on Easy that he was being 'set up' for a reverse ID parade. Howells was showing him off to all the criminals so they would recognise the new man in charge.

Undeterred, Easy formed a small unit of experienced detectives to take out Hunt. The operation was codenamed Tiger, as befitting a top gangster in the concrete jungle. Among the new team was detective sergeant John Redgrave, a ginger giant who'd just come off the Flying Squad's ongoing Brink's-Mat investigation. Easy was certain the new recruit, who he referred to in one appraisal as 'hard as woodpecker lips', would soon be making his physical presence felt. The pair shared an intolerance of no-go areas and bullying gangsters, which was always going to put the ginger giant and the Long Fella on a collision course.

Such was the concern that criminals had penetrated Plaistow police station, Easy moved his team to a small, secure office in north Woolwich near to the newly-opened City Airport. Howells was sometimes seen in a timber yard behind Plaistow police station that was connected to Hunt. It was a standing joke among the Operation Tiger team that the suspect detective must have 'the biggest fence in the world'. Easy warned Howells that if he ever tried to gain access to the new office he would be done for.[8]

Meanwhile, the Operation Tiger team quickly immersed themselves in all the past intelligence reports on Hunt's network. It was clear that local witnesses were too vulnerable to intimidation. The new strategy was simple: take out the 'soldiers' and try to get them to roll over against Hunt in return for a lighter sentence and maybe a change in scenery. In an early show of strength, Easy and Redgrave went with another detective to Hunt's club, The Bancroft, for a drink. It was a bold move never done before. Regulars bristled as 'the filth' entered until one snapped and threw a soft drink at them. The ginger giant threw a hard right. After a standoff, three scotches were sent over to the detectives as a peace offering. They declined, poured the drinks on the floor and left. No one had disrespected Hunt's club like that.

Intelligence had meanwhile come in that the crime boss was carrying a silver-plated handgun. It didn't stop the detectives from drinking wherever they chose, which some publicans welcomed. During one 'big drink' at the Red House on Barking Road, Hunt entered the pub with two others 'on their rounds' for protection money. The locals parted and Hunt stared out Easy and his detectives at the bar then turned and left without saying anything. It was the only time he came face to face with Hunt.

---

[8]Sources say that several years after Operation Tiger, DCI Easy was asked by a senior officer to review a photograph and recording of Hunt meeting Howells and another detective at a sauna in Plaistow. The matter was never referred to the Met's anti-corruption squad and the photographic evidence apparently destroyed.

Operation Tiger had one key advantage over the other police attempts to take on the Long Fella. Their intelligence cell had nurtured quality informants at the heart of his crime group, including one who said Hunt had been carrying the handgun during the Red House showdown and another who revealed details about the prison visit to the Krays and meetings with the twins' accountant. On the wall of their office detectives updated the spider chart showing three types of criminality – 'Protection' at pubs, 'Prostitution' in Soho and 'Drug premises'. All lines flowed back to Hunt, the principal target. Holmes was named as the first of the Long Fella's six close associates[9] and Violet's and The Bancroft were identified as two of five clubs linked to 28-year-old Hunt.[10]

Operation Tiger had initial success in taking out five of his top soldiers. None, however, rolled over against him. Billy 'Jango' Williams, the loyal former boxer with a screw loose who was sent in to 'slice up' non-compliant publicans, was an early scalp. Then there was Lenny Price. He was arrested for possessing a shotgun under his bed. On his release, the criminal grapevine had it that Redgrave had murdered Price. It wasn't true, but the Operation Tiger team did nothing to put the record straight. The intelligence front of the war in Canning Town meant both sides played psychological games, or what the police now call 'disruption'.

Hunt was both a beneficiary and victim of his own reputation for ruthlessness, and the police were sometimes wrongly tipped off about crimes he had nothing to do with. It is an occupational hazard in the underworld that

[9]Paul Edmonds, William Jacobs, Bobby Reading, Frank Spiteri.
[10]Others included the Phoenix and Roxannes.

lesser criminals falsely drop the name of top criminals
to further their own crooked enterprise. But this was
definitely not the case when it came to a group of violent
West Ham supporters who had moved into the emerging
Acid House rave scene. Their association with Hunt was
very real and the Bowers brothers from Canning Town's
Peacock Gym were leading members.

'In the late eighties we teamed up with other criminals
to supply ecstasy to the rave scene,' said Holmes. 'The
two big raves we were involved with were Raindance and
Sunrise. We also became involved in a large one hosted
by Gerry O'Dowd, the brother of Boy George. During
the rave, the Inter City Firm (ICF), a notorious gang of
football hooligans, muscled in on the event and stole the
takings. Using [Hunt's] criminal reputation we made a
meeting with Danny Harrison and Andy Swallow, known
as leading figures in the ICF, and were able to get the
money back from them. We kept it ourselves.'

Detectives on Operation Tiger also believed that ICF
leaders had formed alliances with Tony Bowers and Terry
Sabine, Billy Allen's cousin, and were 'a syndicate' that
controlled the door and therefore the supply of drugs to
raves in the East End and Essex. As with any overt link to
prostitution, Hunt hated the idea of being thought of as a
drug dealer. Holmes said he often ranted that such people
weren't 'proper men'. At this stage in their friendship,
the hypocrisy didn't trouble Holmes, who happily sold
drugs and said it was 'good grace' to get high on your own
supply. As in all successful partnerships one side has to
put up with the other's bullshit, until they can't, and that
day was still a long way off.

By now, Holmes was in and out of his business partner's
family home at 143 Varley Road, where Hunt lived with

his wife, Tina, and their two young children. Holmes even babysat when the couple stepped out and was godfather to their first-born son. But the two gangsters couldn't ignore the inroads that Operation Tiger was making. The game changer for Hunt was in 1988, when detectives paid him an unannounced home visit.

One of the two detectives chosen for the job was John Redgrave. Hunt immediately jumped up and went eye-to-eye with the ginger giant when the detectives entered the sitting room. Redgrave offered a provocative smile that dared Hunt to throw a punch. The ginger giant also boxed as a heavyweight for the police and was willing to put his warrant card in his back pocket if Hunt wanted a straight up fight on the cobbles. But the gangster knew better than to raise his fists and stepped back.

'What are you doing here?' he asked.

'You gotta go,' Redgrave replied.

'Go where?'

'I don't give a fuck, just pack up and leave Canning Town.' With that, the two detectives headed back to the office.

The ultimatum was not strictly speaking lawful. But in the war on crime, with its invisible front lines, fuzzy rules of engagement and a confused vision of what victory looked like, telling Hunt to leave town made sense to Operation Tiger and felt good. Back then, the police had control of the streets and were willing to physically confront violent youth gangs and seasoned older villains who thought otherwise. Realistically, though, displacing Hunt did not mean his criminal reach in Canning Town would diminish. The police visit was more a piece of macho theatre, a modern scene from an old western.

Hunt had a difficult choice ahead of him. He could defy the police and stay where he had grown up and forged his reputation, but this meant constant harassment and disruption of his family life and criminal empire. Alternatively, leaving was the equivalent of being run out of Dodge, which directly undermined his reputation for not backing down. There can be no knowing for sure what affect it had on Hunt. Certainly, some officers doubted the ultimatum would work. But months later in October 1988, he left Canning Town for good, moving his family to a big, detached house near Epping Forest in Essex, obtained with a fraudulent mortgage.[11]

The following year, Operation Tiger was wound down when the money ran out. Easy understood the need to fund other local policing priorities, but he had a furious and ultimately unsuccessful row trying to get Scotland Yard's specialist organised crime units to take over. Hunt, he was told, was not yet on their radar. However, that changed when several of Easy's team were transferred to the regional crime squad office in Barkingside, Essex. Hunt soon got to hear that he was at the top of their list and realised it was only a matter of time before the detectives came for him at his new Epping home.

A forward-thinking criminal knows when to be proactive in his own defence and one day it surprised detective sergeant Michael Ellis to take a call from Hunt, who wanted to discuss a proposition with his boss, detective

---

[11]Hunt bought 20 Rahn Road in Epping in October 1988 for £169,995 with an 85% mortgage from Abbey National. Holmes had introduced Hunt to his mortgage broker, Ben Stronge, In the mortgage application Hunt claimed he had no criminal record and didn't own 147 Varley Road but rented it from tailor Mark Powell.

inspector Peter Avery. He had handled Billy Allen as an
informant during the investigation of his father's murder
and the arrest of Chic Matthews for the drug factory in
1987. Avery thought Hunt wanted a similar arrangement.
The Long Fella insisted they met alone in a remote location
on the Essex and Suffolk border. Avery was willing but
brought Ellis along to watch his back from a distance. As
soon as he entered the house, Avery was asked to strip to his
underpants. He complied, assuming Hunt was concerned
about being secretly recorded while offering to be a grass.

'I'm going places. You're going places,' the gangster
began. 'Maybe we can go places together, help each other
out,' he suggested to the now near-naked detective.

It wasn't the proposition Avery was expecting. Instead
of offering to become his informant, Hunt wanted the
up and coming detective to continue rising through the
ranks and be *his* inside man. Avery declined while getting
dressed.

'What did he want?' Ellis inquired, when his boss
returned to the car.

'He was looking for someone to help him because of
the someone he has become,' Avery replied enigmatically.

The corrupt approach was not reported. In those days
it wasn't the way things were done. There was little sense
of the need to cover your own back in these early days
of the war on drugs. But Avery did confide in colleagues
who, like him, wondered just how many other front line
detectives young Hunt had tried to compromise and,
more importantly, how many times it had worked.

The intense surveillance on Hunt's gang between 1984
and 1990 revealed more than how he ran his wreckers.
Detectives also discovered Shani Whincup, a long-term

mistress, whose home in Plaistow doubled as a safe house
for the firm.

Holmes dropped by in the afternoons, sometimes
finding Hunt lying on the sofa staring into a blank
television screen. He imagined his friend was plotting
who to have over next while Shani prepared tea and cakes
using her ornate china. Hunt didn't allow a landline in his
mistress's house. Instead, the phone number of her elderly
neighbour was given out and she would knock if Hunt
had a call. Only a select group of villains in business with
the firm had the number, said Holmes. Among them were
the Adams brothers from Islington in north London, the
capital's leading organised crime group.

Terry, Patrick and Tommy Adams hailed from a large
Irish Catholic family on the Barnsbury estate and served
their apprenticeship as thieves, enforcers and armed
robbers. They also cut their teeth helping launder some
of the Brink's-Mat gold in 1983. By the early nineties,
the Adams brothers were bringing in large quantities of
cannabis, ecstasy and cocaine with the cash laundered
through clubs and pubs across London. Hunt and
Holmes were relative newcomers to the drugs game when
notorious brothers Albert and Bobby Reading from
Canning Town and Jimmy Coleman, a south London
associate of Ronnie Olliffe, introduced them to the older,
more established Adams family.

Holmes said the firm bought into major drug
importations with the Adams brothers by ripping off
low-level drug dealers who believed they had bought
protection from such a possibility. To Holmes' great
relief, Hunt never tried to rip off the Islington mob. Terry
Adams, the head of the family, was not someone Hunt
feared but he knew the brothers were no strangers to real

violence. It was said that if you cut an Adams 'they all bleed.' The same was not said of the Hunts.

Terry and his brothers usually held court on Thursdays at their RaRa bar on Islington High Street where thirsty Arsenal footballers rubbed shoulders with villains who were invited to share a line of coke with a flute of champagne before getting down to business. Holmes thought Hunt secretly envied the ease with which the Adams brothers moved in limos and nice suits between the Islington of Tony Blair's New Labour project and the cool of Soho. They knew how to party loudly and talk quietly – only their mullets let them down. By contrast, Hunt's firm was brash and its leader always intent on baring his teeth. It privately embarrassed Holmes when the Adams and other quality villains visited The Bancroft. There was no cream of West Ham Football Club among the clientele and, on Sundays, the club was even somewhere you could buy a goat.

Despite this snobbery, Holmes enormously respected Hunt as a fearless gangster and among his most cherished goofy photos was a sepia-tinted snap of them as Butch Cassidy and the Sundance Kid – a memento of a day out at the seaside. They were certainly outlaws, but the police didn't view them as the likeable rogues of the silver screen. In fact, intelligence at the time suggested the double act was a lot more sinister than previously thought and that Hunt and Holmes had allegedly developed a side-line as contract killers.

Hunt has always denied any involvement in murder but Holmes is less emphatic. 'We moved into serious armed robbery, drug smuggling, pub protection rackets, porn, prostitution and other more serious stuff, which I can't mention specifically because loads of it is still on old Bill's open files,' he said. One cold but still open case involves 39-year-old Terrence Gooderham and his girlfriend Maxine Arnold whose bodies were found in the boot of their Mercedes on Saturday 23 December 1989. The couple had been shot twice in the head at close range with a 12-bore shotgun the evening before. Gooderham was a self-employed stock taker for over 300 pubs in east and north London, Essex and Hertfordshire. Arnold was in the proverbial wrong place when the couple were kidnapped at home and taken by gunpoint to their execution in Epping Forest. Homicide detectives tossed around several theories about who did the killing and why. The most constant hypothesis was that Gooderham had fallen foul of criminals in the licensing trade, who put out a contract to have him killed.

Six months after the murder, detectives were linking the deaths to 'prolific organised crime operating primarily in east and north London.' Intelligence came in that the Adams family put out the contract on Gooderham for having his hand in the till and Holmes and Hunt had picked it up.[12] A May 1990 report summed up the police dilemma this way: 'It is not known what the present relationship is between Hunt and the Adams family but up to two years ago Hunt was arranging the distribution of the Adams' drugs. Both Hunt and Holmes are equipped with bearcats, which can monitor any police

[12]Holmes, like Hunt, continues to deny any involvement in the Gooderham and Arnold murders. However, Holmes does suggest that the pair carried out contract shootings, but not killings. 'I can ride a motorbike,' he enigmatically told the author. 'So sometimes I rode a bike for him.' When pressed if Hunt had any involvement with the murder, Holmes said: 'Some things I just can't go anywhere near and I wouldn't like to speculate. I've been put in the frame for that. There are certain things I can say and I can't say.' Author's interview with Jimmy Holmes in 2010.

radio transmissions, and are very surveillance conscious, as are the Adams' … It is said by sources that very little of what occurs in Plaistow police station remains secret from this criminal fraternity and they even target this police station with long range listening devices.'

Police corruption was a serious problem for the murder investigation. But a bigger obstacle was the reign of terror that both crime families exercised over the pub and club trade. Detectives believed that trade sources could not be approached without putting them at risk of being killed. One extraordinary feature of the report was that just weeks after the Gooderham and Arnold murders detectives received fresh intelligence that Hunt had 'accepted' and 'sub-contracted' out a new contract to kill someone else.

Holmes, Hunt and a member of the Adams family remained under suspicion for involvement in the Epping Forest double murder, but intelligence is not evidence and none of them were ever charged with the crime. That didn't stop *Daily Mirror* crime reporter Peter Wilson approaching Hunt for comment at his home in Rahn Road, just a short car journey from the murder scene. The journalist fled Epping with an experience that has never left him.

The police had briefed Wilson in March 1992 that Hunt was a dangerous suspect, but the crime reporter had no real idea whose bell he was ringing. Hunt's wife told him her husband was out but invited Wilson inside where he explained the purpose of his visit. Sitting in the kitchen over a cup of tea, the reporter suspected that Hunt was lurking somewhere in the house listening to his every word. He left his card promising to call back in a little while.

When he returned to the cul-de-sac, Wilson told his photographer, who was driving, to keep the engine running in case they needed to make a quick escape and to try and snatch a shot of Hunt on his doorstep. Wilson rang the bell again and waited. Presently, he heard the sound of the side gate opening. Hunt was walking towards him like a man on the warpath. Instinctively, Wilson knew to retreat. He walked backwards towards the car keeping his eyes on Hunt and hoping the photographer was doing the same. But the gangster was soon on him and grabbed the terrified journalist by the lapels, shaking him, Wilson later described, 'like a rag doll' in the jaws of an attack dog. The journalist was head-butted with such force it smashed his right eye socket.

'You fucking cunt! I'll up you, talking to my wife about fucking murder,' he shouted, then dropped Wilson to the ground and walked off.

Concussed and bleeding, the reporter returned to the car, which was already rolling out of the cul-de-sac. 'Did you get it?'

'No,' the terrified photographer replied.

Sitting in front of an Essex constable hours later, Wilson recounted details of the assault.

'Are you willing to go to court?' the officer asked.

'Yes,' the reporter replied emphatically.

The policeman paused.

'You do know who you're talking about?'

Days later, Wilson bumped into Jeff Edwards, the chief crime reporter for a sister newspaper. Edwards had earned his spurs on the *Newham Recorder* in the seventies and maintained one of the best contact books. When he learned that Wilson was intending to doorstep Hunt he had advised against it and now, looking at the bruised and broken face of his colleague, he felt he was about to make another mistake. Wilson was already having second thoughts about going through with the complaint and told Edwards that he no longer left work through the front entrance in case he was followed home and threatened. He dropped the case after hearing Edwards' advice.

'Peter,' the more senior reporter counselled. 'You don't want to be looking over your shoulder for the rest of your life.'[13]

---

[13] The assault on Peter Wilson took place on 19 March 1992. Hunt was arrested the same day and charged with actual bodily harm but the case was discontinued.

6

Poofed Off

Jimmy Holmes's life of violence was getting to him like never before. At the age of thirty-two he feared being 'ironed out' by a rival gangster, his drug use was spiralling out of control and the thought of going to Canning Town now filled him with dread.

Lately, Holmes was thinking a lot about his relationship with Hunt. It was the early nineties, and after more than five years together he wondered whether they were still equals. A creeping suspicion gnawed at him that his partner was secretly taking the lion's share of the spoils, secure that no one would challenge him. The signs were there from the beginning, Holmes told himself. A security van driver who used the same gym had offered to be his inside man in return for a share of the loot. The robbery went well, but the driver was shot in the leg to disguise his role. Holmes raised an eyebrow when Hunt held on to the takings until the heat died down. The driver claimed the van was carrying £240,000. Hunt told the firm it was £150,000 and refused to pay the inside man, said Holmes.

The driver wasn't the problem; he couldn't exactly hobble over to the police. The real issue vexing Holmes was why he never confronted Hunt about the size of the score. He knew the answer, but couldn't yet admit it to himself. The truth was that Holmes no longer fancied he could take Hunt in a fight. He'd seen him vanquish too many hard men 'on the cobbles'. So, he stayed silent and let his suspicion and creeping emasculation get the better of him.

While his business partner grew in confidence, Holmes headed in the opposite direction. Hunt, for example, appeared to show no fear for the consequences of ripping off freelancers in the fractured drug trade that attracted fly by night operators and first timers looking to get rich with one deal. The firm, said Holmes, used these easy scores to buy into the bigger consignments of cannabis. These came across the water in lorries often organised by a consortium of higher echelon criminal investors from the UK, Spain and Holland, and also the IRA. Ripping off these men was inviting a world of pain.[1]

Holmes felt more exposed than Hunt, who tended to stay 'on the plot' in Canning Town where he was top dog and had a network of spies to spot a hitman coming. By contrast, Holmes saw himself as a pan-London, avant-garde gangster and felt more vulnerable to being kidnapped or killed in Soho or on the way to his new, swanky Docklands apartment near Tower Bridge. Ironically, it was the police who got to him first. Detectives arrested Holmes for robbery and possession of a gun but also interviewed him about a number of other serious crimes,

[1] The seizure of drugs at a port is usually down to a tip-off not a random stop because the volume of moving cargo is simply too great. Drug traffickers understand that losing the occasional load is the cost of doing business, but expect proof of loss. The haulage company will eventually receive official notification of the stop and seizure. It is this document that proves no one is being ripped off.

including the 1989 murder of Gooderham and Arnold in Epping Forest.

Days before the arrest, Holmes had received a £150,000 share of a drug deal. He was planning to deposit the cash into the bank account of his offshore company, Winton Investments Limited. However, detectives raided his solicitor's office before he had a chance to make the drop. They identified the offshore company from seized documents and spoke to the nominee directors in the Isle of Man, who immediately resigned. Holmes didn't care too much; he simply used one of his aliases to replace them. Offshore banking secrecy laws did the rest, putting the company's assets beyond the reach of the law.

However, detectives finally caught a break from other seized paperwork. It turned out that Holmes was engaged in a complex mortgage fraud using false identities named after characters from *One Flew Over the Cuckoo's Nest* to hide control of premises used for the harder end of the porn game.

'The porn was heavy, never child porn, but anal, you got five years for that back then, and bestiality. No kids' stuff. I'd never have entertained that,' Holmes explained.

Ultimately, the robbery and weapons offences were not pursued but instead used to keep him on remand in a holding prison until he was charged with the mortgage fraud, where the evidence was strong.

Strong enough that soon after his trial started, Holmes put his hands up. 'I changed my plea to guilty because I didn't want any of our business associates to be dragged through the courts,' he said. 'The judge allowed me a month to sort out my business affairs before he passed sentence.'

What happened next changed his relationship with Hunt and put the two villains on a collision course that would ultimately provide detectives with their best opportunity to break up the Canning Town firm.

Holmes didn't sweat when the judge handed down a 30-month sentence. Soon he was in an open prison where the low security conditions suited his chancer nature.[2] Confinement aside, he was grateful for the 'lay down'. It was time away from his overbearing criminal life, the drug use and, he had to admit it, Davey Hunt. Lying in his cell at HMP Ford he started to consider going it alone when he got out.

All that was stopping him from leaving Hunt was a large amount of cash invested with the firm before he went inside. 'We had a couple of knockbacks before I went in and we did genuinely lose some loads [of cannabis],' he said.[3]

As a result, the firm had to dip into their own profits to finance new drug runs. Holmes said he invested £250,000 in the belief that his stake would be doubled when he got out of prison. However, it was only a matter of time before doubts emerged. One day an inmate

---

[2]Holmes claims he took advantage of the prison governor's good nature and with other criminals used a charity front to leave HMP Ford and conduct various drug deals in Holland and the UK. He would then return to prison with the authorities none-the-wiser.

[3]Holmes said that shortly before his arrest the firm had lost money in cannabis deals with Bobby Reading and Jimmy Tarrant from Canning Town and Clifford Norris from Chislehurst, Kent. Norris was on the run at the time and an associate of the Frenchs, who Holmes had worked for as a younger criminal. Clifford was the father of David Norris, later jailed for the murder of Stephen Lawrence.

from east London took him aside with some hard to swallow news.

'You heard? The Long Fella's bought my mate's massive house in the countryside.'

Holmes was shocked. But he couldn't show it and lose face for not knowing about his business partner's move up the property ladder. And what a move it was – from a detached house in Epping to a 1920s, eight-bedroom mansion set in twenty acres of walled grounds with lake, tennis court, outdoor and indoor swimming pools, gym and separate lodge house.

The Morleys mansion is reached via a long gravel drive from crested wrought iron gates on the main road running through the Essex village of Great Hallingbury, a quaint but unremarkable place on the border of Hertfordshire and Bishop's Stortford. On paper it was an amazing success story. In ten years, 32-year-old Hunt had taken his family from a terraced house in Canning Town worth just over £20,000 to a mansion worth £600,000.

Sitting in his cell that summer of 1993, Holmes suspected some of his £250,000 had gone towards the asking price. He also thought that Hunt was taking a risk with such an upwardly mobile move without the legitimate income to explain his conspicuous consumption. Certainly, the Morleys mansion purchase had not gone unnoticed by the police or the taxman. A few months later, when Holmes was allowed out of prison on day release, Hunt explained that he'd bought Morleys from Alan Sewell, an Essex scrap metal dealer who also had the distinction of being Rod Stewart's best friend. The deal Sewell struck with Hunt on 27 August 1993 was complex. It involved

Hunt swapping his Epping home as part payment for the mansion.[4]

Part of the balance was raised by a fraudulent mortgage that Hunt took out with Portman building society in May that year. He had applied for a £250,000 loan by falsely claiming a self-employed annual income of £140,000 and ticking the box that said no criminal record. To complete the deception of the bank, Hunt valued his Epping home at £400,000, more than double what he bought it for five years earlier. Less than a year later, Sewell sold the Epping property for £235,000.

A police financial report concluded that the house swap was structured for a specific purpose. 'Copies of the Land Registry documents suggest this was done to avoid Stamp Duty and the Sewells received £250,000 from the Hunts when they exchanged their properties.'[5]

By the end of 1993, the Long Fella had bought a £600,000 mansion and fully paid off his £144,000 Abbey National mortgage on the old Epping place. The taxman, however, had yet to see a penny on any of his supposed six-figure income as a self-employed scaffolder and part-time bouncer.[6]

The mansion swap was suspicious enough until Holmes learned that a new drug run in Holland had gone sour

[4]According to a Scotland Yard financial report, in June 1993 Portman Building Society valued Morleys at £600,000. Sewell had bought it five years earlier for £850,000, made high-quality improvements and declined an offer of £875,000 before selling the mansion to Hunt.
[5]Police financial profile of David Hunt 11 November 1998.
[6]The monthly £2,555 mortgage payment to Portman Building Society was paid from Tina Hunt's Barclay's Bank account. The mortgage for Morleys was in her and David Hunt's name.

and his £250,000 investment was apparently lost. 'Hunt went on to say that he couldn't go to Amsterdam himself because the police were watching him very closely. Despite being on home leave from prison and therefore not allowed to leave the country, I volunteered to go in order to protect my interests.

'Having flown to Amsterdam on a fake passport, I met with Tattoo and Ronnie in a hotel in the centre of the city. Ronnie told me the people we were doing business with had a small chain of restaurants called Happy Families. He then said that the man who took the five hundred thousand pounds was nicknamed Rico, and that he had phoned him on his mobile, and said he was taking the money because he didn't believe Ronnie when he said that a previous load of cannabis he had supplied him had been confiscated by Customs at the port of Dover.

'After intense discussions we agreed the best thing to do was kidnap Rico's father and hold him hostage to get the money back. Ronnie phoned two Dutch brothers who brought a small handgun to the hotel. Myself and Ronnie discussed the plan to carry out the kidnapping, but he began to get very nervous and said he didn't think he could go through with it, so the mission was aborted. It was then that I began to get suspicious that something was amiss.

'That night I made a phone call to David Hunt. I spoke to him for a while and during the conversation he mentioned to me he thought that it was possible that Tattoo and Ronnie could be double agents working with Rico. He said that if this was the case he would have them both killed. He then went on to say that the lorry that the drugs were due to be loaded onto would be passing through the outskirts of Amsterdam the next day, and we had to get a load on board to make up the total of what another gang was also putting on board, or else all of us, and especially him, would lose credibility with the other gang. He also told me he had organised a safe house for us to stay in Amsterdam to give us a better place to sort things out.

'Hunt then provided me with the directions to a small log cabin in the back garden of a very run-down hotel near Amsterdam's red light district. When we got there I checked out the layout of the premises and became very nervous. I pointed out to Ronnie and Tattoo that it would be very easy for a hit man to plot us up and kill us there because of how secluded the place was. In the event I was not happy with the location and so we moved to another hotel. Much later that night I managed to track down a friend of mine, German John, who was also involved in large-scale cannabis smuggling. He agreed to provide me with two hundred kilos of cannabis on loan, with the agreement that his money would be repaid as soon as the drugs were sold in the UK.

'With the deal done I met up with the other gang from Canning Town, representatives of the Sabine family, who were also due to put their own cannabis load on the same lorry. Once the deal had been concluded I returned to the UK without having tracked down the missing five hundred thousand pounds, and headed straight back to Ford prison, where over the next few weeks I maintained regular phone contact with Hunt. During those phone conversations he told me that everything was fine regarding the cannabis load I had organised, and that my friend, German John, had been paid back in full.'[7]

[7]Law enforcement intelligence files corroborate some of Holmes' account. In particular, a report from detective inspector John Redgrave to his superiors dated September 1992 seeking permission for an informant known by the pseudonym

Holmes was released from Ford prison in late 1993 determined to find out what happened to his money but wary of how his questions would be received. He had expected Hunt to pick him up, but instead made his own way to Plaistow where his business partner was waiting at the safe house.

'We left east London and drove to his new house. As we drove up the gravel drive I was astounded that he could afford it, knowing he had not long spent a large amount of cash on redeveloping his bungalow in Epping. He informed me he had not yet paid the owner and was to due pay him in cash instalments over the coming year.'

'George Wimpey' to travel abroad. Apparently, the informant had been asked to help David Hunt with problems some of the Wright family had with a drug gang operating in Holland and Spain. According to the report, brothers Eddie and Jason Wright owed 'in excess of £1 million for drugs already supplied.' The drug gang had apparently seized the Wrights' property in Spain and they enlisted Hunt to help resolve the situation.

Holmes identified to the author Jason Wright as the man he called Tattoo. Efforts to contact Jason Wright through his former lawyer, Chris Williams, and brother, Mark, were unsuccessful. Similarly, Eddie Wright didn't respond to a request for an interview through his brother, Mark.

George Wimpey's real name was Brynmor Lindop. He ran a haulage yard in Canning Town and was an armourer for organised crime. His murder in January 2002 remains unsolved.

Further corroboration came from another informant codenamed 'Richard Harris', who was close to Hunt and according to reports acted as a money mover for a range of London and northern Irish criminals. He sometimes moved as much as £750,000 packed into a Suzuki that he drove to Holland. His handler recorded in an informant's log that Hunt has lost £250,000 in a drug deal in Holland and had an ex-British army sniper as his Netherlands representative looking for it.

The Serious Organised Crime Agency also held intelligence that in the 1990s Hunt was working with Ronnie Johnson bringing in between 1.5 and 2 tons of cannabis per week from Spain in lorries.

Morleys had marble floors and, like all guests, Holmes was made to take off his shoes. He laughed inwardly during a tour of the mansion as he slid through the columns, past the massive bust of a Greek or Roman figure and steadied himself against the suede wallpaper.

'The next morning I broached Hunt about the whereabouts of my money and he became extremely aggressive towards me, asking if I was accusing him of stealing it. Having witnessed, and taken part in many violent criminal acts with Hunt, I became very nervous and declined to say that I did believe he had stolen my money, but I was sure he was not being straight with me. He went on to say that he was working on things and that I would get my money in due course.'[8]

Alsatian dogs patrolled the 20-acre grounds and CCTV cameras were dotted around the mansion. The firm had invested in a building company that Hunt was using to renovate the lodge house for his elderly, widowed father. Like Holmes, the builders were generally frightened of Hunt. An inoffensive aside cost one of them dearly on the drive home one afternoon.

'Davey, I've gotta say, since you moved down here you've really mellowed,' the builder innocently remarked.

'Yeah? What do you mean?' Hunt asked.

Holmes, driving, cringed. He knew the signs.

'You know, before you were het up, but now, since you moved here...'

Hunt suddenly told Holmes to pull over, got the builder out of the car then 'smashed the granny out of him. And left him at the side of the road.'

[8]Jimmy Holmes' statement to the author in 2010.

Driving off, Holmes could only imagine what he would do if pushed further over the missing money. 'He'd cut me up into a million and one little pieces.' Nevertheless, he still vowed to leave the firm – and not without his cash.

In December 1993, Hunt's father died. The funeral was a typical East End affair. The churchyard in Canning Town was full of mourners and local faces in Crombie overcoats and dark glasses there to pay respect to the local crime boss. Not all were welcome.

'D'you see who's over there?' Hunt asked Holmes as they alighted from the car outside the church.

They had both clocked the south London villain who had first introduced them back in 1984. Ronnie Olliffe was with two minders, Jimmy Coleman and 'Mad' Micky Behara.

'Keep an eye on it,' Hunt told Holmes as he headed towards the church. Before long, Behara approached Holmes and, after pleasantries, came to the point.

'Ronnie's still waiting on that bit of dough.'

Holmes knew Mad Micky was referring to the Blackpool drug deal when Olliffe was laying low after the Brink's-Mat robbery.

'At a funeral? It's a bit out of order Mick.' he replied under Hunt's distant gaze.

'Well, Ronnie's over there and he wants to know what happened to his money,' the minder continued.

'It's a bit of liberty,' Holmes repeated before walking into the church to find Hunt.

'What did that cunt want?' he asked.

'You ain't gonna believe it, but he wants that money from the puff deal.

'That's a fucking liberty. Why didn't you do him?'

'How could I? It's your dad's funeral.'

'You got to do it,' Hunt told him.

When the service was over and the coffin started its final journey in a carriage slowly drawn by two black horses, Holmes calmly walked over to Behara and suddenly smashed the butt of his gun into his face. Other members of the firm joined in and stomped all over Mad Micky as Olliffe and Coleman watched nervously.

'He didn't get killed but he might as well have been,' recalled Holmes. An eyewitness saw Behara 'make a run for it before the police and ambulance arrived.' Olliffe also scarpered knowing he was now at war with the Hunts.

The fear of being 'ironed out' only worsened for Holmes when he became involved in the kidnapping of another serious criminal. The victim this time was said to be a major cannabis trafficker based in Spain who regularly came to the UK to collect drug money stashed in a car. 'The Bug' apparently made six runs a year and each time would pick up a Citroën parked in a secret London location, which he then drove back to Spain. Holmes claims the Bug was kidnapped on a visit to London and tortured to within an inch of his life before revealing the location of £500,000 secreted in the car. Hunt, he said, was particularly vicious. '[He] went mad on [the Bug] and smashed him so bad. He was nearly dead … The beating he took I don't think he was ever going to be the same man again. He was begging to be killed.'

A bad feeling grew inside Holmes as he minded the barely breathing body for a few hours on his own. A line had been crossed and reprisals, he felt, were sure to follow. Of course, Holmes' drug use throughout 1994 didn't exactly reduce his fear of being killed. It was yet another reason for hating Hunt. 'He was getting me so much above my head I was going mad. I was taking so many fucking drugs because it was non-stop ... All the enemies he was making, I was making. Every time he went out he'd do something and I'm part of that ... Fearing for my life I purchased a brand new .22 Beretta semi-automatic gun with a silencer. I also purchased a shoulder holster and began to carry the gun with me at all times. I was now resigned to the fact that I would not see my money again.'

Holmes owned a number of properties on the south coast through a complex offshore corporate veil involving Winton Investments.[9] He relocated to a luxury seafront apartment in Sussex Square, Brighton. With its long history hosting the UK gay scene, Brighton was somewhere Holmes could live away from the predatory violence of Canning Town. By now he'd come out to Hunt. To his face, at least, Hunt was not uncomfortable that his business partner was gay. But Holmes suspected that behind his back and for appearances he was being 'poofed off' to other less enlightened members of the underworld.

Brighton was not just a sanctuary for Holmes, but also an opportunity to make money from the pink pound. He had his eye on a gay bar on the seafront.

'As the project took shape I realised I was around seventy-five thousand pounds short for my share, and so I once again approached [Hunt] and enquired about my missing funds. He responded once more by screaming

[9]Holmes said he and Hunt controlled the lease for 32 Preston Road in Brighton, which was used as a hardcore cinema with video rental on ground floor. Winton Investments held the lease to Preston Road, he said. Hunt admits having joint interests with Holmes in Brighton.

and shouting at me, saying he was still working on sorting things out. A few weeks later he informed me he had found an investor who was interested in putting in the seventy-five thousand pounds to help me out of my current situation. The investor, whom I also knew, was a drug dealer called Colin. Needing to secure the money I met Colin and showed him the bar, and he agreed to buy in.

'I subsequently met [Hunt] and he handed me a carrier bag full of money which Colin had given him. Hunt told me that he had taken out twenty-five thousand pounds, which he needed to put to work to help me get my outstanding money back from the people he said had stolen it. I protested as it left me short of money for the bar, but he just basically told me to lump it or leave it. A month or so later I then found out that he had also just purchased a new safe house in Buckhurst Hill, Essex, and was at the time having a swimming pool installed at the property. Despite the shortage of money, I eventually opened the bar.'[10]

On 15 January 1994, Hunt took a table at a gala dinner for UK pigeon fanciers. His wife, Tina, and her friend accompanied the Long Fella to the ball. Well-known racers, trainers and journalists mingled at the upmarket affair in the Chingford assembly rooms, swapping gossip and tips before sitting down for the meal and speeches.

Hunt was now an accomplished pigeon fancier. But his success had ruffled the feathers of some rivals who whispered that his reputation was underserved or at least

[10]Jimmy Holmes' statement to the author in 2010.

should be shared with his trainer, the real talent behind the success of Hunt's birds. A pigeon fancier and contributor to *The Racing Pigeon* magazine who had picked up on these rumblings was also at the gala dinner. Hunt approached 60-year-old Jean Andrews and discussed her coverage. He was unhappy with the ranking she had given him. The journalist robustly defended herself with no idea that she was jousting with an ascendant local crime boss. Hunt, she thought, was just a businessman with a bit of money.

After the exchange of words, Andrews sat down with her daughter, Tilly, who had brought her mild-mannered boyfriend, Stuart Everitt, to the dinner. As the drink flowed, an altercation broke out in the Ladies toilets. Tina Hunt and her friend were clashing with Andrews and her 27-year-old daughter. Sipping water and scanning the room, Hunt saw Everitt get up and walk towards the ruckus. He followed a few paces behind. This time the two men clashed and Everitt came off worse with twelve fractured teeth and a haemorrhage to his right eye. Hunt then intervened in the fight between Tilly and his wife. The journalist's daughter claimed he hit her too. Stuart Everitt and Tilly Andrews complained to the police and Hunt was charged with grievous bodily harm and causing actual bodily harm.

The trial, however, was not due to take place until the following year. The complainants had no idea that the UK's biggest police force by this stage considered Hunt an 'untouchable' who evaded justice through witness intimidation and jury nobbling. They soon found out when Derek Everitt, Stuart's father, was approached at his local pub with an offer he was told it would be unwise to refuse.

Levi Smith, a heavy set 54-year-old builder of Gyspy stock, offered to pay an out of court settlement if the case against Hunt was dropped. The offer was declined, but Smith was not deterred and on 27 June 1994 he left a note at Derek Everitt's home with a telephone number to get in touch. Everitt did call back but on a police phone that was recording the conversation. His repeated refusal to accept the offer drew an incriminating response from Smith. 'I don't give a fuck, Derek. Listen, it's up to you. Do you want your throat cut? It's up to you. You go by the law too much.'

Two days later, Smith was arrested for perverting the course of justice, but never admitted acting for Hunt.

In April 1995, the Long Fella stood trial separately for the assault. The police had made no application to protect the jury. Nor were they told about Smith so as not to prejudice the trial. Hunt denied hitting Tilly Andrews and claimed self-defence against her boyfriend. The pair was stunned when the jury acquitted him after just one hour's deliberation. A court reporter noticed Hunt smiling broadly and then thanking the jury before embracing his wife. Outside the court he said: 'I am very relieved. This has been fifteen months of hell. I want to get on with my life.'

Levi Smith was less fortunate. Passing a nine-month sentence, Judge Aglionby told him: 'Although [Hunt] was acquitted, that has little to do with the gravity of your actions. What you did was to indicate that violence would or may be used on Derek Everitt and this is not a suggestion that you would have committed that violence. You were a conduit for the threat you were passing on. It cannot be emphasised that any action of this kind, threats or bribery, goes to the heart of the criminal justice system in this country.'[11]

Holmes couldn't avoid it any more. The not knowing what happened to his missing money was tearing him up. And he'd recently learned that the friend who helped rescue the Amsterdam deal by putting up 200 kilos of cannabis on spec had also not been repaid.

'I asked [Davey] about the fact that my friend German John had not been paid for the cannabis deal I organised, and he told me that the load had been discovered and confiscated by Customs at the port of Dover. I said I would need proof of the arrest to show German John, as I had personally vouched for the load and was financially responsible for it. Once again, Hunt screamed and shouted at me, saying that as I was his partner I should take him at his word and not ask for paperwork.

'I returned to Brighton convinced [he] had taken not only the money I had left with him before I started my prison sentence, but that he had also stolen the drugs advanced to me by my friend.' On the drive home, Holmes cursed Hunt for showing him so little respect, but he cursed himself more for allowing it.

---

[11] *The Court News UK*, 2 November 1995. David Hunt said at his 2013 libel trial against *The Sunday Times*: 'These were Gypsies, Sir, and I believe this is the way they deal with things amongst their community, but I knew nothing about this. What had happened was at that trial Mr Everett – he was very intoxicated that evening with drink and he said he would like to have a straight fight with me, Sir, and this was arranged through the Gypsy community and this is how I knew they were Gypsies, Sir.'

Hunt, meanwhile, was making a bold move into the world of waste management and scrap metal. In May 1994, he struck a deal for some industrial land on the Thames gateway in Essex and made it the headquarters of his emerging business empire.

Chequers Lane off the A13 leads to a bleak plot of land where the waste management business was soon to be incorporated as a limited company called Hunt's Iron and Steel. The 99-year lease was bought for £90,000 from a businessman who generously allowed Hunt to operate before the deal was formally completed. The businessman held the lease in an offshore company set up by a crooked Jersey-based accountant who he advised Hunt to look up.[12] It was an offer Hunt would take up shortly. But first Holmes had come to him with a new opportunity in Soho to expand their porn interests. However burnt out he felt, however much he hated his business partner, Holmes was always looking for ways to recoup his losses and leave the firm. When things were going well between them, Holmes had taken over a lease on a Soho brothel linked to Bernie Silver. Now the chance had arisen to buy the freehold.

2 Green's Court is on one of the three short passageways off Brewer Street that are notorious for purveyors of fine porn and 'walk ups' – those anonymous doorways with handwritten signs advertising 'models' and the promise of an unencumbered ejaculation. The building served many desires. In the basement was a clip joint – a dive bar where suited saps are rinsed of cash for the privilege of buying watered-down alcohol and indifferent women. On the ground floor was a sex shop offering hardcore

[12]Joseph Chamberlain owned 75-77 Chequers Lane through an offshore company. His scrap business was called Chequers Iron & Steel.

porn. Prostitutes occupied flats on the first and second floors and the attic was rented to a regular tenant.

The building's owners were now looking to sell the freehold due to financial problems with their bank. 'I informed Hunt that the freehold could be obtained for somewhere in the region of two hundred thousand pounds. Hunt told me he could raise his half of the money, while I in turn told him I did not have the cash for my share at that time. But I also told him that it would be a good idea to have his share of the money ready, and that I would approach my own contacts in Soho to raise my share, so that when the time came I would be ready.'

This was the beginning of the sting Holmes had been waiting to execute on Hunt. And, as luck would have it, another opportunity arose to leave the firm with even more money. 'Skinny Gary', a former armed robber turned drug trafficker, had apparently approached Hunt wanting to launder several hundred thousand pounds through the firm's business interests. In return, Gary offered to partner up on some cannabis and ecstasy deals.

'Although I was unhappy with Hunt, now knowing he had stolen my money I agreed to go along with doing business with Skinny Gary because I was hoping to garner in some new finances. I took Skinny Gary under my wing and began to show him a good time in the West End, as well as taking him around to see [our] Soho and east London operations.'

Holmes discovered that Hunt was lining up Skinny Gary to be ripped off on the next drug deal so he decided he would get there first and also have Hunt's money for the Soho brothel. It was a bold and dirty plan but before he could implement it Holmes suffered a severe 'nervous breakdown' and locked himself inside his Brighton flat for a two-week bender. Every time he regained something resembling sobriety he'd do another fat line of cocaine. The only people who came to the door were his dealer and the pizza deliveryman. The deep pan couldn't be posted through the letterbox, so Holmes reluctantly opened his front door wearing dark glasses and a dressing gown. With the inevitable come down came periods of depression. Holmes found himself reaching for his shotgun, putting it in his mouth and deliberating whether or not to pull the trigger.

Hunt got word that his business partner was losing the plot, the thought of which only fed Holmes' paranoia. He imagined that Hunt was on his way to Brighton to kill him for being a weak link. For days, he waited with a shotgun in one hand and a rolled up twenty-pound note in the other for his appointment with death or freedom. As soon as he heard the door knock and Hunt's gravelly East End tones pretending to be concerned, he planned to shove the shotgun through the letterbox and blast away the Long Fella's crown jewels. But there was no knock. Just the rattle of Holmes' drug addled brain, which finally came to rest, allowing him to re-join the firm in Canning Town.

He wasn't fixed, not by far. Worse still, his deep-seated fear of Hunt was crystallising into the idea that as well as taking the money and running, he had to kill or be killed.

Holmes was still coked off his head from the night before and the day before that. Dressed like a Soho jazz cat, he slouched in the back seat of a red Mercedes, the Hunt brothers up front oblivious to his rage and paranoia. Stevie was driving with Davey in the passenger seat boasting about the recent waste recycling site deal.[13]

This riled Holmes further. 'Yeah, that's right. You're a proper man and everyone's a cunt who isn't from Canning Town and doesn't think you're the dog's bollocks,' Holmes rapped silently to himself. 'You're a psychopath. You enjoy hurting people. You get a kick out of it. I know how you are when you are going to do someone – the quiet, then that ghostly-white face of yours when it's done. You couldn't wait to poof me off to the others. Always going on about fags. Why do you hate them so much? Maybe there is something in there that makes you hate yourself so much,' he continued.

Holmes was experiencing the same emasculation and self-loathing felt by the many others who believed the Long Fella cheated them but were too afraid to do anything about it. Only, the residual cocaine needling his brain gave him the necessary bump to think he could be the one who finally stood up. It was then that Holmes reached into his jacket and pulled out the Beretta from its shoulder holster.

'I just had enough. He was going on and on. I knew he had fucked me up. But I couldn't prove it ... I just wanted to get out of it. I was fucked, really mentally fucked. I nearly topped myself a couple of times. I'd gone through all that and then I'm sitting there listening to all his bollocks about what a proper man he is and I know he's fucked me for a lot of money. When we went to Amsterdam someone got killed when I was out there. I knew that had happened. I fancy he'd set it up. And I thought, what am I doing with this cunt?'

---

[13]Hunt said he divested from Quick Skips and put the £90,000 into buying the waste management site in Dagenham, which became Hunt's Iron & Steel.

Holmes stuck the gun into the back of the front seat. It felt good to have Hunt's life in his trembling hand.

'It was the nearest I've come. But it was just strange. I thought the bullets would bounce off him. He had convinced me over the period we were together that he was invincible. It's very hard. It's like if you look at Adolf Hitler. Any one of the Nazi storm troopers could have turned round and fucking beaten him up. He was a little insignificant man. But once someone has beaten you psychologically, they've fucked you. No one was safe. Hunt could have easily been overthrown. But there's an aura around him that people invested in. That was the problem. That's what got me and I've seen him do some wicked things. And I thought if I fire and he don't die, he's going to do me.'

Seconds passed but still he couldn't pull the trigger. In those moments of vacillation Jimmy Holmes, avant-garde gangster and Soho dandy, finally accepted what he had long suspected: Hunt had defeated him psychologically. Like a boxer beaten before entering the ring, Holmes imagined the car stopping, being dragged out screaming and made to suffer until he begged to die.

'Get your head right first Jimmy,' he told himself while re-holstering the Beretta.

Holmes was not even a shadow of the man Hunt had met ten years ago. Mentally and physically he was done. All that was left was to run and repair with as much cash as he could cram into a suitcase.

The drug deal with Skinny Gary came good and Holmes said he picked up £400,000 cash in two suitcases from a southeast London gym, where he was friendly with the owner.

'I phoned Hunt to say that all was well and that I was going to lay the money low for a few days and get it counted out to make sure it was all kosher. I took the money straight to a [unit I'd hired in a] storage warehouse on the outskirts of Brighton, and [then] went back to my Brighton flat. I then hired a removal company to take [my] furniture and clothes to the same storage unit where the drugs money was stored.'

Next, Holmes went to Hunt's to get his £100,000 share for the Soho brothel in Green's Court. The unsuspecting Long Fella handed him five cheques, each for £20,000. It was the last time the two men would see each other. Holmes needed this moment. All the times Hunt had made him believe they were equal partners, all the times he was told to trust him. Now it was his turn to do the same. Holmes knew that when word got out the humiliation would eat away at Hunt, not least because on the day of reckoning he had looked him in the eye with all the sincerity possible, shook his hand and fucked him with aplomb.

Back in Brighton, Holmes opened up the bar and stood in the middle of it. 'The cunt's not having this,' he told himself before smashing the place up.

Several days after the handshake, Holmes got word that Hunt was wondering about his whereabouts so he left Brighton and booked into the Cavendish Hotel in Soho and waited for the five cheques to clear. Holmes had enough time before fleeing the UK to brief his mentor, Bernie Silver, and take Gary Oxley, the man who managed his Soho assets, into his confidence. Oxley not only collected rents but was the eyes and ears of Holmes' porn empire and supposedly beyond Hunt's reach. To ensure it stayed that way, Holmes offered him half of the weekly takings.

'I explained to [Gary] that I had learnt that Hunt had stolen a large sum of money from me, and that as far as I was concerned he had forfeited our partnership. I asked Gary if he would be interested in coming in on a partnership deal, and went on to explain that I was going to lay low in America for a while and come back when things had calmed down, as I had taken back money I was owed from Hunt. I told Gary that all he had to do was keep my paperwork safe, and carry on picking up the rents from the various Soho properties under my control. He said he wanted in, and so I handed him over all my company papers, freehold title documents and solicitors letters, which he told me he would put somewhere where he could access them, as and when I needed them.'

On the next plane to San Francisco, Holmes felt a surge of release as he took off. 'Psychologically he had me fucked. I was so fucked I was a shell. Gone.'

Away from London he felt he could change. 'Hunt will never change but I can,' he told himself. He needed to. He didn't want to be violent, to be angry, to carry a gun anymore. Between the brothel and drug deal, Holmes had left the UK with half a million pounds at his disposal. 'I took £200,000, which I considered mine [but] which Hunt considered his. He was trying to fuck me and I got the money, which I knew was mine. It was small but it weren't fuck all. I had other things, which he didn't know about.'

Holmes settled in a small coastal town in southern California and began negotiations to start up a small business certain that back home Hunt was putting the blame on him for all the firm's rip offs.

Reflecting on that period in his life, Holmes said of his former business partner and best friend: 'He fucked my life up in a way. I'm not blaming him. I blame myself for letting him do it to me. But at the end of the day I had the bollocks these so-called villains didn't. I took the money and looked him in the eye.'

7

Cut

Paul Cavanagh regularly tells God that he would never have pursued the life of a career criminal had his father just offered him the chance to be a sports reporter.

His father, a well-liked and connected tally clerk logging what came on and off the ships at the West India Docks, just didn't trust his first born to hold down a job without scamming it. Cavanagh is gregarious and can spin a witty yarn but, unlike his father, he had sticky fingers from an early age. 'I started thieving at eight and getting caught on my own. Then I had a paper round and would fiddle it. I'd nick all the papers. Then, when I was fourteen, it was all about gambling. A mate of mine's dad was taking me to Hackney dog track. I loved it. I couldn't wait to get back. It was the people, the characters, the *spielers*.'

The young teenager found a part-time cash-in-hand job with a contract cleaner. But with the cash came demands for hand jobs from his paedophile boss who sexually abused him over two years, he said.

Cavanagh's hardworking parents were unaware and despaired at their son's developing waywardness. At sixteen he'd already earned two burglary convictions and spent three months in juvenile detention.

The sports reporter opening on an East End newspaper came up in 1973, by which time 21-year-old Cavanagh was earning reasonable money from crime. He felt perfect for the job having spent so much time at the racetrack and in betting shops where he studied the odds and the progress of Bobby Moore's West Ham United. But his father put forward his other son for the job.

'That should have been me. I fell out with my dad over this. I wouldn't have been sitting here with you now if I'd got that job. He never got me in the docks either because he thought I'd have half of it away in a fortnight. My uncle George said he'd take me. He had a haulage firm. But my dad stopped that for the same reasons.'

An acerbic put-down from his father, who had agreed to advance his rent one day, has stayed with Cavanagh forever. When the bank teller remarked that the rent cheque was unsigned, senior pointed at his apprentice fraudster son and said, 'Give it to Joe Cunt, he'll sign anything.' Snubbed by a father he loved, Cavanagh teamed up with a group of young men he'd met at the snooker hall and started on a spree of armed robberies and lorry hijacks. 'There was never any question of getting caught. We kept it right tight. The secret to it is doing your homework. They never had DNA then. And the only thing we'd do if we had it off was put a suit on and go to the Room At The Top in Ilford. There were bottles of champagne. We knew the bouncers. They probably knew. Look at these lot they've had it off again.'

The crime spree went on for four years. 'Then I packed it in. We all did. We'd had about one hundred and fifty grand with no one having a clue.'

Cavanagh put down his gun forever and picked up a pen as the weapon of his new criminal direction – fraud. A bent postman passed him blank chequebooks. He also learnt to forge banker's drafts with signatures lifted off the back of credit cards. The frauds earned him his first spell in grown up prison in 1978. It was only three months but he emerged keen to hone the skills of a new fiddle – insurance.

By 1983, aged thirty-one, Cavanagh was an accomplished fraudster who had fallen in love and married Sheron Morris, the daughter of Canning Town 'face', Peter Morris. His new father-in-law owned the Galleon's Reach club across the road from the Prince of Wales pub where a young Davey Hunt and his Snipers were making quite a name for themselves.

It was over a game of pool at the Prince in 1984 that Cavanagh first met the man who would almost kill him thirteen years later.

'[Davey] was a young fella then. I knew he was up and coming. A doorman. Hard. He had that sort of air about him as a young man. Didn't drink, didn't smoke, didn't take drugs. Fit as a fiddle. Good boxer. The basic reading and writing weren't so hot. But he knew what he was doing. No fool. Extremely capable.'

Cavanagh and the Long Fella bonded over a love of West Ham and soon he was going to home matches with the Hunt brothers. They enjoyed his jokes on the way to the Boleyn ground, but Cavanagh was surprised at how the usually reserved Davey Hunt let himself go during those ninety minutes on Saturdays. 'No one ever got to the bottom of him. He was so deep. One time he could be so nice and inoffensive the nicest man you could meet. But under that was a man who thrived on violence. Nothing could stand in his way. He was invincible. If someone did try and muscle in he'd ruin them.'

In August 1986, Cavanagh's marriage started to fall apart
when his father-in-law was killed in a fight. Peter Morris
had gone to a pub to help a close friend looking to avenge
his daughter, whose husband had apparently assaulted her.
Morris was no push over and was said to keep an armoury
in his club. But younger and harder men had set on him
during the confrontation and he died a violent death.
The killing remains unsolved.[1] Morris' funeral attracted
the usual assortment of broken noses and three-quarter
length black leather jackets, including Davey Hunt, who
had just teamed up with Jimmy Holmes. It wasn't long
after that the two newcomers took over Galleons Reach
and turned the club into The Bancroft.

A deep depression descended on Sheron Morris after
her father's death. Cavanagh struggled to deal with it and
look after their two-year-old daughter so the marriage
eventually dissolved in 1989. By then, Cavanagh had
become very close to Hunt's brother, Raymond. 'He was
like a brother to me. We done everything together. He
was a good man. But he was gullible to a certain extent.
Instead of checking things out he'd go straight in.'

A good example was the events that followed a robbery
in June 1990 of $3.5m of American Express travellers'
cheques from St Pancras Station. The robbers had
originally approached Raymond thinking they would
ultimately be dealing with the Long Fella to fence
the travellers' cheques through his growing criminal

[1] The police investigating the Peter Morris murder in 1986 had brothers Billy
and Joey Stratford brought back from Portugal. They were never charged. Joey
Stratford was a part-time bouncer. A police report dated 3 September 1992
recorded intelligence from an informant that local drug dealers had enlisted
Joey Stratford along with David Hunt to sort out a problem with a drug cartel
operating in Spain and Holland.

network. But Raymond had decided to go it alone and was hawking the stolen items from a plastic bag he took around pubs in Canning Town. It wasn't long before detective inspector Peter Avery – the naked detective who Hunt had tried to turn – was alerted by one of his informants. Three months after the robbery had taken place, the Barkingside regional crime squad was lying in wait outside a house in Howard's Road, Newham. When the crime squad made their move, Sergeant John Redgrave went straight for Raymond Hunt who knocked the ginger giant unconscious with a ferocious punch. Redgrave soon recovered to help with the arrest of two of the suspected armed robbers.

The case came to trial in 1992 and the Hunt gang were at Southwark crown court to show support, and to jeer at the detectives about how Raymond had put 'the ginger one' on his arse. In general, the trial was a debacle for the police. There was a suspicion of jury tampering with one juror dismissed and the two main defendants walking free. Raymond, however, pleaded guilty in return for a light sentence. On his release from prison, Davey Hunt asked Cavanagh to keep an eye on his brother. The pair were given the Phoenix to manage, a new club in Plaistow which Hunt and Holmes owned through an offshore company. By this time, Cavanagh had become so close to the Hunt family that he often looked after their elderly and ill father who, like his own dad, was a 'shrewd and knowledgeable' character. Cavanagh sat with old Stevie Hunt at the family house in Canning Town watching the horse racing and nipping out to place his bets right up until his death in late 1993.

Cavanagh was one of the mourners who remembered the moment when Holmes pistol-whipped and stomped all over Mad Micky Behara at the funeral in Canning Town. Apart from that, Cavanagh was too busy with his own swindles to pay much attention when Holmes fell out with Davey Hunt and fled to the US. But when Holmes returned to the UK hell-bent on revenge, Cavanagh foolishly got involved in a way that changed his life forever.

Shortly after settling in California, Holmes asked Gary Oxley, his frontman in Soho, to pass Hunt a proposal for splitting their business interests.

The pitch amounted to this: 'Look Davey, you've had a good run out of me. I know you are making loads of dough but I'm out of it now. Just pension me off.'

For £1,000 per week, a fifth of the income from brothel and sex shops rents, Holmes said he was willing to manage the West End properties but sign them over to Hunt.

The response was emphatic. 'Tell that cunt he's not even allowed to phone this country.'

The belittling riled Holmes. He was recharged after six months in the Californian sunshine, but his head was still frazzled as he plotted to reclaim his Soho empire by any means necessary. A toe-to-toe confrontation with Hunt was out of the question. He'd never survive that. This was going to be a guerrilla war of hit and run, humiliate and evaporate. In order to win, Holmes needed the continued loyalty of Bernie Silver and Gary Oxley – unaware that the latter had already gone rogue and was secretly working for the Long Fella. Silver, however, remained faithful to his protégé. When Hunt had asked the Soho Godfather to sign over the leases held by Holmes, Silver refused. The Long Fella's reputation meant little to a man who'd seen off the Krays when the psychotic young twins tried to muscle in on his Soho empire.

Hunt was certainly put out, but by this time he'd already menaced Gary Oxley into switching sides and handing over Holmes' paperwork for the offshore companies that controlled the leases. Winton Investments Limited in the Isle of Man held leases and freeholds for The Bancroft and Phoenix clubs and properties in Brighton. Separately, Holmes had incorporated Earl Trading Limited using the alias 'Gerald Palmer' to control leases for 32-3 Great Windmill St and 27 and 29 Peter Street in Soho. Both these buildings were leased from Silver for prostitution and sex shops. Hunt particularly wanted to take control of the brothel at 2 Green's Court that Holmes had used as a lure to abscond with his £100,000.

The property company that owned the building was still in trouble with its bank and needed a quick sale of the freehold.[2] Oxley was told to start negotiations to buy it while pretending to be Holmes, who held the lease under a pseudonym.

Meanwhile, Hunt turned to Chris Williams, a pudgy property lawyer, to complete the Soho coup. Williams got a court order freezing the NatWest bank account where Holmes had deposited the stolen £100,000.[3] Hunt

[2]Raycastle Limited owned the freeholds of 2 Green's Court, Soho and 32 Preston Road, Brighton. They leased the properties to Holmes who held them respectively offshore in Earl Trading Limited and Winton Investments Limited. A receiver was appointed to Raycastle Ltd on 31 May 1995 and the company dissolved on 6 July 1998.

[3]Chris Williams acted for West Ham footballer Jason Wright, who was also friendly with Davey Hunt. Williams says Jason Wright suggested that Hunt instruct him to recover the £100,000 Jimmy Holmes had stolen. In a witness statement for Hunt's 2013 libel action against *The Sunday Times*, Williams said the cheques given by Hunt to Holmes were from Matthew Yallop or his company. The court order freezing Holmes' NatWest account was done on Yallop's behalf. Only £15,000 was left in the account.

and Williams then flew from London to the offshore tax haven of Jersey to meet Peter Michel in his cramped office. Michel came highly recommended by the businessman who had recently sold Hunt the land for his new waste disposal and scrap metal business in Dagenham.[4]

A slight and polished man, 48-year-old Michel cut his teeth acting for Formula One racing teams and the owner of a well-known restaurant chain. As well as respectable clients, Michel washed dirty money and evaded tax for organised criminals and crooked businessmen through offshore companies with dummy owners and trusts that acted as corporate veils. He also personally returned their cleaned money to the UK in his briefcase. Michel, though, didn't take to the muscled Hunt who he found thuggish, rude and, above all, frightening. Hunt, it was explained, needed an offshore company to secretly control the freehold for 2 Green's Court, which he intended to buy for £250,000 and continue running as a brothel.[5] Michel agreed and in June 1995 set up Jersey-registered Galleons Reach Limited with a local Midland Bank account. The company name was a reference to a point on the Thames where ships queued to get into the old East End docks.

[4]Joseph Chamberlain was a client of Peter Michel. Yalco Property Ltd, a company incorporated in Panama, initially held the freehold for 75-77 Chequers Lane. The 99-year lease was bought by Chamberlain's company Welbury Limited, incorporated in Jersey by Michel, and then transferred to Pluto Properties, another Chamberlain company. He then sold the freehold to Hunt for £90,000.

[5]In witness statements for the 2013 libel claim against *The Sunday Times*, Chris Williams and David Hunt claimed they were unaware in 1995 that Peter Michel laundered money for organised crime. Michel told the author he was unaware that Hunt was an organised crime boss when he agreed to set up Galleons Reach Limited. But he admitted acting for organised crime.

Six months later, Hunt bought the freehold on Green's Court by apparently borrowing £100,000 each from two friends based on nothing more than a 'gentleman's agreement'.[6] The remaining £50,000 he claimed had come from his 'savings'. Michel received most of the purchase price in cash and hid Hunt's ownership of the brothel from the taxman through a complex structure of trusts and bogus front men.[7]

Just before Christmas, Holmes quietly arrived back in the UK from California. He headed straight for his lockup in Brighton to recover more of the money from the drug deal that he had concluded before fleeing abroad in March. Holmes still had no idea that Gary Oxley was now working for his sworn enemy. On the contrary, he was assured that the Soho rents were being paid into a Midland Bank savings account in Jersey. However, when he flew to the tax haven the account was empty and Oxley nowhere to be found. Holmes rented a flat in Dublin as a base from where he could make hit and run strikes in Soho. He soon collared Oxley who confessed, claiming Hunt had threatened his life if he didn't hand over the offshore company documents. Shortly thereafter, 2 Green's Court was firebombed, the first message that guerrilla war had been declared in Soho.

Meanwhile, at a gambling club in Victoria, Holmes and Bernie Silver devised a parallel strategy to use the

[6]Bill Smith, a car dealer and Peter Pomfrett, a property developer.
[7]David Hunt's witness statement dated 15 March 2013. Peter Michel set up Galleons Reach Ltd using in-house trusts – Rroyds and Chimel – to administer the company. Michel misled the Jersey authorities by falsely claiming that someone Hunt had put forward was the ultimate owner. Michel told the author he set up Galleons Reach on the instructions of Chris Williams.

courts to retake the Soho properties from Hunt's control. Peter Donnelly, an old legal friend of Holmes, wrote to Chris Williams, Hunt's solicitor, asking him to hand back Green's Court. Remarkably, the response came that Hunt had no interest in the brothel but would like a 'face to face' with his former partner. Donnelly replied that his client was 'too anxious about his safety' to oblige.

That summer of 1996 Holmes embarked on a propaganda war by going to *Time Out* magazine. He knew how much it would hurt Hunt, who by now was trying to establish himself as a legitimate businessman, if he was publicly linked to the violent porn trade. At the time, the Long Fella was restructuring and expanding his empire in London and Essex using a mixture of fraudulently obtained loans from high street banks and crooked offshore arrangements. This accumulation of wealth and criminal standing annoyed Holmes but also presented fresh targets when the *Time Out* articles were finally published in July and August 1996.[8]

'I met fire with fire, and started hitting his apartments and houses with flyers. I went to where he lives and sprayed outside his home on his road, NONCE, GRASS, CUNT and all that. I dropped flyers all round his village saying he's a fucking drug dealing nonce and cunt. Really strong stuff because he was saying the same thing about me. People who I had done business with like Bernie Silver and had a really good reputation over the years with, he was saying he's a poof, a fucking queer cunt, this and that.

'He's never had it like that. I did it outside his bird's house and sat on the back of a bus and admired it through

---

[8]'Sex Shop Gangsters Move into Soho' 17 July 1996 and 'Racket and Ruin' 31 July 1996 by Tony Thompson, *Time Out*.

the window. I was a bit crazy to be honest. I still had that fire. Even though I couldn't confront him. What he wanted was for me to come out on the cobbles and smash the cunt out of me and say I told you. But I thought no I'm not going to fight like that, I'm going to fight the guerrilla fight.'

The printed leaflets drifted into the quaint Essex village of Great Hallingbury like poisoned confetti falling on Hunt's otherwise idyllic country life. Although not to the manor born, the lord of the Morleys manor was livid with the satirical content.

> DAVEY HUNT THE PIMP FEATURED IN THIS WEEK'S TIME
> OUT MAGAZINE. PAGE 12. READ THE TRUTH! BUY IT
> NOW AND TELL YOUR FRIENDS! ALSO RUNS SEX SHOPS
> SELLING GAY MAGS, LESBIAN MAGS, DILDOS, BLOW UP
> DOLLS, POPPERS. ASK NOW FOR A FREE BROCHURE. FREE
> HARDCORE VIDEO WITH EVERY PURCHASE!

Elsewhere in the Hunt empire, fax machines whirled as a personal message copied to his Soho business associates came through.

> TOLD YOU THAT I WOULD GET YOU OUT OF THE WEST
> END DIDN'T I ... YOU POOFED ME OFF TO EVERYONE.
> YES! I'M QUEER BUT I'M HERE.

Upping the ante, Holmes then wrote to Hunt at his solicitors admitting he was behind the *Time Out* articles and promising he would shortly be spilling the beans to a national newspaper about Hunt's involvement in various crimes and misdemeanours. 'I now unequivocally claim you to be a pimp, a drug smuggler, a kidnapper, an adulterer and to have carried out various mortgage and financial frauds as well as VAT and income tax evasion.'

Holmes dared Hunt to sue for libel and said he would defend himself.

'I am not worried about dropping myself in the shit,' Holmes wrote. 'Believe me, I want my day with you for what you have done to my health and my life. I can remember when I made you my partner you were still on the dole. Anyway, let's look to the future. I will show you for what you are not the image that you portray to the world.' The letter was signed 'your former friend and partner' and invited Hunt to send any legal response to Donnelly's office.

Days later Hunt's lawyer did respond. Again Chris Williams made the remarkable claim that his client had 'no legal, equitable or any other interest whatsoever' in Green's Court. The forgetful lawyer went on to stress how 'extremely close' the pair once were. Hunt, he said, accepted there were joint interests with Holmes in East End and Brighton properties and suggested they sit down to talk it out. But Holmes was in no mood to parlay. Instead, he wrote two extraordinary and emotional letters first to Hunt and then to his wife, which were sent to Morleys.

'As an enemy I respect and fear you but I have my stand to make ... If I can't have a share of what I created then no one can. I can strike at will as I have proved. The targets are sitting ducks. That last episode was just a taster,' he wrote. Holmes then laid out the pension he required to end hostilities for good. In the spirit of compromise he dropped his price from £1,000 to £400 per week to be paid into a bank account using the code word 'Sweetpea'. Knowing Hunt would need to save face, he also assured him absolute confidentiality if the terms were accepted. However, in the event no deal could be reached, Holmes was clear what would follow, and to underline it dropped a bombshell. He claimed he had AIDS. Whether this was a mind game or the truth Hunt could only wonder. Either way it was bad news.

'Dave, believe me I live with the threat of death hanging over me every day. Since I found out, my whole view on things have changed. I have no family, no friends and no real future. I have nothing to lose. I bear no malice towards you, you do what you think is right.

'I also have to say that prison holds no fear for me. When, or if, I restart action, any occupants in the buildings I will deem legitimate targets ... If you agree on a deal, Dave, please don't wank me off like before. I do fear you but I have to be able to face myself in the mirror. As much as you won't let up in your search for me nor will I let up with my attacks. The next attacks will be on the ground floors and basements. I don't give two fucks about the vermin inside. I have a death sentence hanging over me anyway. It doesn't matter to me if I serve it behind bars or on the streets.

'You took the best part of my life and now you want to take my life. I know that I'm only a poof in your eyes but I'm prepared to die, or go to prison for life over this. I've been dealt a poxy hand and I can't be pushed any further ... You need not worry if you top me, there are no hidden letters that can get you nicked. I'm not a grass ... Although, I still say you treated me shamefully and I did not deserve that. Whatever you may think about my sexuality I was one hundred per cent with you. Whatever will be, will be.'

The letter to Tina Hunt on 14 August 1996 was a lot
shorter and to the point. Holmes said he was going to
make a witness statement in response to a restraining
injunction her husband had sought against him for
flyposting the family home. There was some sympathy for
Tina, but her feelings were always going to be a casualty of
this guerrilla war. 'I have promised to tell the truth about
everything that myself and David have done as I can bear
it no longer,' Holmes wrote her. 'I'm afraid of David but
I'm going to tell the whole truth to clear everything up.
I'm sorry if my statement hurts you in any way. Jimmy.'

Two weeks later, Hunt responded in what appeared to be a
personal reply but had the mark of a lawyer's guiding hand. 'I
have never committed any crime so if you feel that you have
to go to the police as you threaten, then do so,' he began.

Hunt denied ripping off Holmes and brought up
the stolen £100,000 of which only £15,000 had been
recovered from Holmes' frozen NatWest bank account.
However, in the spirit of friendship and claiming he
too had been '100% loyal' Hunt offered to come to an
arrangement as long as Holmes no longer took the war to
his family. 'Originally you said you wanted £400 per week
and now you want half of Bancroft and half of the film as
well. Be reasonable and I am sure I can help you out,' he
wrote. The film was a reference to an investment in the
project to make a movie about the Krays.[9]

[9]David Hunt told the high court during his libel trial with *The Sunday Times*
that Canning Town armed robber Paul Edmonds had put together a group of
investors. Edmonds served time with Reggie Kray and Mickey Peterson who
Edmonds persuaded to change his name to Charles Bronson and promoted his
unlicensed boxing bouts. Edmonds was an associate of Hunt when Operation
Tiger was looking at the Long Fella. Edmonds was shot dead in November 1998
outside a pub in Plaistow.

Hunt's extraordinary letter ended with a promise and what looked like a dare designed to prick the ego of his nemesis. 'I give you my word that I am not looking for you. Please pluck up the courage to phone me.'

There was, however, no call, no meeting and no deal, just more war. In October, Holmes stormed the Soho properties, kicked out the hookers and porn merchants paying Hunt then changed the locks. Hunt retaliated by getting Oxley to re-take the properties. This was the cue for Bernie Silver, who owned them, to enter the fray. The Soho Godfather instructed his lawyers to write to Hughmans, the solicitors representing Oxley, knowing that he was merely Hunt's stooge. Silver feigned outrage that his properties were being used for immoral purposes and sought forfeiture of the leases. Hughmans disputed any connection with Hunt but mistakenly included an internal reference to him at the bottom of their reply. The exchange was a spectacular piece of legal dissembling but ultimately led to a possession order granted by the court in Silver's favour.

Hunt wisely backed off the Soho Godfather.

Over in Newburgh Street, a narrow, cobbled Soho alley, another front in the war was opening up. Holmes had been making threatening phone calls to his old friend, the bespoke tailor Mark Powell, at his new shop near Carnaby Street. Holmes was Powell's first Soho landlord. But along with Hunt they all drifted apart since those formative years in the late eighties when Powell also fronted Violet's.

It was Christmas 1996 and Powell's sartorial collection, with trademark gangster suits and overcoats, was on display. His new clients now included musicians Bryan Ferry and George Michael, film stars George Clooney and Harrison Ford, and TV personalities Jonathan Ross, Vic Reeves and Bob Mortimer. Holmes used to take fashion tips from Powell but now he wanted the £15,000 he claimed the tailor owed him. Powell already knew about the war with Hunt from the *Time Out* articles but refused to accept he owed Holmes any money. The dandy gangster didn't agree and suspected that Hunt had made Powell pay him the money instead. To enforce his claim, Holmes glued the locks of the Newburgh Street shop and, when that didn't work, he threw bleach over the new collection causing £5000 worth of damage then flew back to his Dublin bolthole.

Powell reported the incident to the police but decided not to press charges. Three months later, on Thursday 20 March 1997, his shop was firebombed. Alert neighbours saw a man pour petrol through the letterbox late at night and leave in a red Ford Escort whose number plate they passed to the police. The next evening Gary Oxley, now working openly for Hunt, took Powell to meet the Long Fella, whose capability needed no recital. In the back of a car, the tailor agreed to make a statement incriminating Holmes as the arsonist.[10] But just before he did so, the police informed Powell that the red escort had been traced to a man called – Gary Oxley. Powell was too frightened to say anything to the police. Let alone that in a few hours

[10]David Hunt denied during the 2013 libel trial against *The Sunday Times* that he had pressured Mark Powell.

Oxley was escorting him to a solicitors firm to falsely incriminate Holmes.

Powell's statement enabled Hughmans solicitors to go on the offensive and demand that the police arrest Holmes for the arson attack. Simultaneously, Chris Williams started libel proceedings against him. The pincer movement led Donnelly to call Williams on 3 April and suggest it was all an attempt to fit up Holmes for something he hadn't done. 'The timing of the letter between your firm and the allegations from Hughmans plus your client's connection with Mr Oxley is remarkable,' Donnelly pointed out. That said, Donnelly was willing to explore a settlement agreement, arguing that Hunt already had been repaid the stolen £100,000 in rent taken from Holmes's Soho brothels.

Williams agreed that the four of them should meet. 'Your client knows my client's word is his bond and my client's word is he will keep himself restrained both inside and outside the office ... My client thinks that your client is ill and would like to help. He's been a friend for many years. He's been godfather to his child,' he said over the phone with Hunt at his side. The Long Fella whispered into Williams' ear that Holmes was recently spotted at Waterloo station over the bank holiday.

'Did you hear any of that?' Williams inquired. 'Basically my client is saying he knows more of Mr Holmes' movements than Mr Holmes thinks. If he was concerned with getting at Mr Holmes he would already have done so.'[11]

---

[11]Transcript of phone call recorded by Peter Donnelly with Chris Williams and David Hunt on 3 April 1997.

But Holmes had no intention of a sit down with Hunt. The next day Donnelly's file was passed to the police, who went to see Powell. The tailor withdrew the arson allegation against Holmes and agreed to make two new witness statements about the pressure that had been applied to him by Oxley and Hunt.[12]

Unknown to Hunt and Holmes, their Soho war was being closely monitored by a squad of detectives working in secret to combat organised crime. Detective Inspector Jon Shatford ran the intelligence gathering operation, which had developed out of the bugging operations on the Silvertown strip in the early 1990s. Shatford and his team ran informants while monitoring phone taps and new bugs placed in the cars, offices and homes of their targets; the Long Fella was one of them.

Shatford's first approach to Holmes in January 1997 was rebuffed and talks broke down because the guerrilla gangster's demands in return for his help were, according to his own lawyer, 'unrealistic'.[13] But after Hunt's recent attempt to fit him up for firebombing Powell's shop, Holmes was now ready to break the fabled criminal

[12]The account in this chapter is taken from a police production order laid before the court by DC Andrew Millar requesting that Hughmans solicitors provide its file to the police on 6 August 1999. The account also comes from Peter Donnelly's file and an interview with Jimmy Holmes. On 28 November 2011, asked about his relationship with Holmes and Hunt, Mark Powell told the author: 'It's all rubbish, it's ridiculous, it's a long, long time ago ... To be honest I don't really know anything about the stuff that happened in that world. I just happened to be a person who was in Soho at the time and I knew people and that's the end of it. There's no other connection other than that at all.'

[13]Peter Donnelly's file note.

LEGACY

code and become an informant. He justified it because the Long Fella had 'sweet grassed' him first – a reference to Hunt's witness statement to the court when seeking an injunction against any further flyposting of his mansion. By July 1997, Shatford was regularly debriefing Holmes. It was the first time someone so close to Hunt was giving such high-quality inside financial information. Concerns about corrupt police tipping off Hunt meant the debrief was kept very tight. But Bernie Silver, who had worked with the police his entire Soho career, told Holmes that he'd heard about the arrangement and didn't care.

'I was doing business with Shatford,' said Holmes. 'Meeting him, talking. He wanted me to give up certain things. He half pumped me on a couple of murders, which I said I don't know anything about.' While he was happy to discuss his past, the kidnap and torture of 'the Bug' and Hunt's offshore businesses, Holmes clammed up like a cockney cockle when pressed about the unsolved 1989 murder of Terry Gooderham and Maxine Arnold in Epping Forest.

Shatford believed Hunt was vulnerable through his mistresses and his love of pigeons. Holmes disagreed. 'His weakness is his ego. He's a psychopath. He can't help himself,' he told the senior detective.

Armed with this information, in the summer of 1997, a plan emerged to use Holmes as bait to draw Hunt to a meeting at the Green's Court brothel. It was suspected that the crime boss would be unable to resist the opportunity to rid himself of his turbulent former partner in crime. Armed undercover officers would be in place posing as punters and prostitutes to catch him in the act.

Holmes was revengeful enough to take the risk. 'I could have got [Hunt] doing anything to meet me, to do me. He would have got a gun. I was willing to have a go at that. I thought, Fuck me! That's a good firm, a proper firm to have on your side. They aren't going to shoot me.'

For unknown reasons, possibly the high risk to life, the plan was abandoned. Shatford and his team, however, weren't going away. If Holmes was right, it was only a matter of time before Hunt's psychological flaw gave the detectives another opening.[14]

'Has Davey got anywhere near finding him?' Paul Cavanagh asked his friend Mark Wright in August 1997 over a pint. The pair were discussing the continued search for Holmes.

'No,' replied Wright, who was close to the Hunts through a love of West Ham and the car trade.

'D'you think he'd want me to have a go?' Cavanagh ventured, explaining how through his crooked insurance work he could access credit and other databases. It turned out that Hunt was interested and days later Cavanagh visited his Dagenham waste recycling plant hoping to earn some easy cash.

'Mark tells me you could find Jimmy Holmes. You're like a breath of fresh air, Paul. He's caused me loads of grief. What's it going to cost me?' Hunt asked.

---

[14]Donnelly wrote the following entry in his chronology of events for his client file. 'July. Discussions with police regarding proposed operation at Green's Court. Plan approved by Scotland Yard but aborted as a result of copy entries being received.'

Former DCS Jon Shatford said his 'recollection of this case is at best vague.' Letter 8 April 2013.

'Couple of hundred a week,' Cavanagh said tentatively.

'Oh! Fuck me! You can have that now. Come to the house Sunday and we can discuss the details over a Chinese.'

Cavanagh always found Hunt to be a top host but was sometimes baffled by the security at Morleys. He'd once stayed overnight and set the alarms off when he tried to leave early in the morning. 'It was like a disco in there, I didn't know whether to dance or cry,' he recalled.

That Sunday, while his wife collected the takeaway, Hunt vented at the embarrassment Holmes had caused him in the village, not to mention at home, and in Soho. By coincidence, Cavanagh was a cousin of Mark Powell, the Soho tailor caught up in the war.

'Jimmy's been spotted somewhere in Liverpool,' Hunt went on to explain.

Cavanagh nodded. He knew that if he ever found Holmes the dandy gangster was 'going for a walk'. The gruesome prospect didn't trouble him much because Cavanagh had little intention of putting that much effort into finding Holmes beyond a few database searches and a trip up north. In truth, Cavanagh's mind was elsewhere. He was trying to pull off an audacious insurance scam in Ireland that he anticipated would earn him a good share of a £750,000 payday. There was, however, one snag. Cavanagh was on bail for fraudulent trading involving an unrelated scam. With a trial set for early November, where he planned to plead guilty, he fully expected to be in prison by Christmas. All of which gave him little time to complete the Irish scam and stash his retirement nest egg for when he got out.

Over the following weeks from September into October 1997, Cavanagh made token enquiries about the whereabouts of Holmes. 'I knew people in Liverpool. I went up there to see me pals but they'd never heard of Jimmy. They knew people on the gay scene up there, because I'd heard he was a shirt lifter, but I don't know how true that was. He didn't strike me as one, but you never know these days.'

The tip didn't bottom out, but Hunt insisted he carry on and agreed to lend Cavanagh a Land Rover from Palmer's Prestige Motors in Chigwell, Essex. Michael Palmer ran the car showroom, which Hunt used as an office when he wasn't at his waste recycling plant. Stratford's detectives suspected the showroom was another front for drug money laundering.

Banking on the Irish scam coming good in the next six weeks, Cavanagh arranged to buy the Land Rover for £12,000 after he had finished searching for Holmes. But the news from Dublin was bad. Cavanagh needed an emergency injection of £10,000 to pay off a crooked insurance broker or the Irish scam was dead in the water. He didn't want to ask Hunt for a loan fearing it would cost too much of his share of the fraud. So without telling the Long Fella, Cavanagh sold the Land Rover to raise the money. However, when he flew to Dublin the local police were all over his associates so he turned round and came home deflated.

Now he had no nest egg, no Land Rover, no means of paying back Hunt and no clue as to the whereabouts of Holmes. To make matters worse he was also due in court in a few days to face the separate fraud charges. Instead of coming clean and throwing himself on the

Long Fella's mercy, Cavanagh made the worst decision of his life. He flew to Cyprus to hide away from Hunt and instantly became a fugitive from British justice. However, after only a few days in the Pathos sun, Cavanagh came to his senses and phoned Raymond Hunt for help.

'Fucking hell, Paul! Just tell Davey what happened and get the fucking Land Rover back,' Raymond counselled. 'I'll also speak to him and smooth it over.'

On Wednesday, 12 November Cavanagh returned to the UK hoping that the time he'd spent looking after Hunt's father would spare him a beating.

'Don't be frightened,' the Long Fella assured him on the phone. 'Come to the car showroom tomorrow morning and get the Land Rover back. I give you my word nothing bad is gonna happen to you.'

It was a long night wondering whether the word of a crime boss already losing face from the war with Holmes meant anything. Cavanagh went to bed reasoning that he'd be made to work off his debt, but woke up less convinced. He considered doing another runner then decided it was a bad idea. 'You don't want Davey coming looking for you,' he told himself while shaving then left home resigned to getting a beating. As Cavanagh approached the car showroom three large men were waiting for him outside. Every step in his suede loafers now felt extra leaden. He'd never known fear like it.

'You're bang in trouble, you are. Who did you sell the car to?' asked one.

Cavanagh arranged to meet the buyer at a nearby pub car park where it was explained that the Land Rover belonged to 'a proper person who had the right fucking hump'. The buyer wisely agreed to return the vehicle within days.

On the way back to the showroom, Cavanagh was nervous. 'What's gonna to happen?' he asked. 'Davey's given me his word.'

'If anything was gonna happen, you'd be coming down the road with us now,' came the reply.

'What should I do?'

'Go in and beg.'

In a backroom at Palmer's Motors they all sat waiting for Hunt to arrive. It was only then that Cavanagh noticed some voice messages from the night before. They were from his friend Mark Wright.

'Paul, whatever you do, DO NOT go to the car showroom tomorrow,' the message urged.

It was too late. Hunt had arrived wearing tracksuit bottoms and a grey sweatshirt.

'Why did you do it to me, mate?'

'I'm sorry, Dave. I needed the money as I explained to you over the phone.'

'I lent you the car,' Hunt insisted.

'Yes and I said I'll pay you and I will. I'm sorry.'

The discussion briefly turned to the arrangements for getting back the Land Rover, then Hunt's demeanour flipped.

'Right. I gave you my word I weren't gonna hurt you but you left me no choice, have you?'

'Fucking hell, Dave! I've known you a long time,' Cavanagh pleaded.

'Everyone knows about this and I can't have that, Paul. I said to my wife this morning, he's sat in here and goes and does that to me.'

Cavanagh begged.

'I'm not interested. Get up! Or I'll do you there,' Hunt
barked.

A resigned Cavanagh slowly rose to his feet. He offered
no resistance as Hunt approached with a boxer's sure
footedness, throwing a combination of hard and precise
punches to the lower body, especially the ribs.

After six or seven blows, it stopped. Cavanagh gasped
with pain and struggled for breath. At least it's over, he
thought. Then Hunt screamed, 'Give me a knife! Any
knife!'

Cavanagh froze as the Long Fella released the blade on
a lock knife. He'd passed the point of no return, his reason
vanquished by his nature. Surgeon-like, Hunt jabbed the
tip of the blade into the centre of Cavanagh's chin until
it touched the jawbone. Then, with a determined sweep
of his right hand, slowly drew the blade down over his
throat then up towards his victim's left ear.

Cavanagh heard a scraping noise then felt his skin flap
open. Hunt put both hands firmly on his shoulders and
spoke with an almost apologetic tone through eyes as
dead as a great white shark.

'Your punishment's over.' In the next breath he ordered
his minions to get Cavanagh to the local hospital.

'It's a bad one, Davey,' said one of those present as an
ashen-faced Michael Palmer entered the office holding a
chequered tea towel. Cavanagh pressed it against his face
and walked outside.

Little was said during the car journey to Whipps
Cross Hospital. Within thirty minutes Cavanagh was sat
alone in the accident and emergency room, trying not
to slip off the blood-soaked plastic seat into a welcome
unconsciousness. He'd given a false name to avoid an

arrest warrant, or at least buy some time. Later that night, when he came to on the ward, a doctor said he was lucky to be alive. Cavanagh's heart had stopped in the operating theatre while the surgeon stitched up his face. Whether his mouth would stay shut remained to be seen.[15]

[15]The account of the attack on Paul Cavanagh is taken from his affidavit dated 19 May 2015 and earlier statements to the police.

8

Blackjack

Detective sergeant Ray Ahearne would have been a good angler. Throwing out a baited line then waiting quietly for a bite suited his measured demeanour. By all accounts he carried himself this way at work where he was a fisher of men; an intelligence officer who identified criminals in crisis then turned them into informants.

Ahearne had served on the brash flying and regional crime squads from where, in 1992, he joined the National Criminal Intelligence Service, a new clearing-house for handling multi-agency requests for phone taps. When a job came up on an organised crime task force five years later, he happily accepted the invitation to join. The 3 Area Crime Operational Command Unit was working from an old police station in Ilford and covered Enfield in north London to Rainham in Essex. Resources were divided between taking out heroin-trafficking Turkish mafias and east London gangsters concerned with everything else. There were two proactive drugs wings, a surveillance arm and an intelligence cell.

Before Ahearne arrived in late 1997, an intense debate had raged within the intelligence cell about whether Davey Hunt should be the prime target. The Long Fella won

the day and was targeted by a new operation codenamed
Blackjack. Within thirteen years Hunt had risen to achieve
the highest designation in policing: a 'core nominal' – one
of the country's leading and untouched criminals.[1]

An industrious analyst on the intelligence cell was
responsible for charting the links between Hunt's
associates and his business and criminal interests. This
included sifting the intelligence Jimmy Holmes had
given during the recent Soho war. Meanwhile, detectives
bugged Palmer's Motors in Chigwell suspecting it was a
new front in the criminal empire. Hunt had bought the
freehold at 51-53 Chigwell Road for £160,000 in August
1996 with a £91,000 mortgage from First National. His
friend, Michael Palmer, fronted the business and put his
name on the door. Operation Blackjack soon discovered
that the crime boss was investing £300,000 in new high-
quality cars; money they could not account for from
analysing the Long Fella's income tax returns.

A covert camera outside Palmer's Motors beamed live
images to the secret police base in nearby Ilford, where
number plates and visitors were traced. Listening devices
inside the car showroom were monitored in real time and
mostly captured plans for the expansion of the Long Fella's
waste management and entertainment empire. However,
well-placed sources on Operation Blackjack claim that
the bugs also recorded Hunt's attack on Cavanagh that
Thursday in November 1997. It would appear that a
controversial decision was taken to ignore the assault

[1]The alternative targets were John West, Victor Falco and Iraj Parvizi, the man
who had allegedly infiltrated the Bank of England's monetary policy committee
by sweet-talking an insider's wife. Essex-based West, born in 1947, was
considered a 'fixer' for organized crime in east London, including the Hunts.

and protect the existence of the bugging operation in order to continue collecting more intelligence on Hunt's organisation.[2]

Doctors had kept Cavanagh in hospital over the weekend following the attack. It was only on Saturday that he found the courage to look himself in the mirror ahead of a visit from Mark Wright, the friend who'd left messages on his phone warning against going to the car showroom.

'No words can describe what I feel like. Cut and marked for life,' he told Wright, who struggled to look at the fifteen centimetre scar. 'I had his word as a friend. I wish I'd heard your message.'

The two men discussed their respective financial debts to the Hunts. Detectives had intelligence that Wright had borrowed money from Stevie and Davey Hunt who wanted it back to invest in a big contract with Railtrack, the conglomerate that owned part of the privatised British rail system.[3]

The Long Fella was also still chasing Cavanagh for the £10,000 Land Rover debt – the fifty-stitch scar, effectively £200 per stitch, clearly counting for nothing. 'I have a reminder every time I look in the mirror whereas for him it's just an everyday fucking occurrence,' he told Wright.

In the run up to Christmas, the trauma of the knife attack was getting to Cavanagh who'd been discharged and was drinking heavily to dull the nightmares. He

---

[2]Scotland Yard declined to comment on intelligence matters.

[3]A senior police source told the author in November 1999 that Operation Blackjack had contacted Railtrack to inform them of David Hunt's criminal credentials but their warning not to get into bed with the Long Fella fell on deaf ears. Paul Cavanagh claimed that Hunt told him in 1997 he wanted to invest the money owed by Mark Wright in Railtrack.

moved around cheap hotels to avoid Hunt until the beginning of 1998 when his girlfriend offered him refuge at her flat in Brentwood. None of these secret manoeuvres had escaped the attention of detective sergeant Ahearne, who was running a network of informants targeting Hunt and others. His source unit was one of the first in the Met to follow new guidelines for centralising the handling of informants. Previously, officers ran their own snouts and the opportunity for corruption – a share of the informant's payout, turning a blind eye to their criminality or rewarding them with seized drugs – was an ever-present temptation and problem. Under the new system, detectives had to hand over their informants to source units either completely or for co-handling.

Ahearne was running some twenty informants of varying quality, a quarter of whom were giving a wide range of information on Hunt and his associates that was being fed back into Operation Blackjack. Separately, the bugs and phone taps at Palmer's Motors picked up a lot of chatter about the aftermath of the knife attack on Cavanagh. It included Michael Palmer discussing how the gruesome assault was so bloody the carpet and flooring needed replacing.

By the start of 1998, Operation Blackjack had been going for almost two years without any result against Hunt, and the team were under financial pressure to wrap it up. The assault on Cavanagh became their best chance of putting him away. But first, detectives needed the victim to make a statement against the crime boss. Past experience showed this was unlikely to happen voluntarily. Three months had passed since the assault and Cavanagh hadn't gone anywhere near a police station. Luckily, Operation Blackjack had some leverage to persuade him to cooperate.

On 25 February 1998, Cavanagh was arrested at his girlfriend's flat for the fraud case he had avoided by fleeing to Cyprus. The arrest was really a pretext to persuade him to become a prosecution witness against Hunt.

'I won't beat about the bush. Why did Davey Hunt cut your face like that?' Ahearne asked pointing at the unhealed scar. Cavanagh played dumb but the wily detective, known as 'Grizzly' to his colleagues as much on account of his beard as his gruff attitude, pressed on.

'We've got intelligence that he's going to have another pop at you,' Ahearne shot back, which got Cavanagh's attention. In return for making a witness statement, he was offered witness protection and a good word with the judge on the fraud case.

'I know what you are on about,' Cavanagh replied, 'but I'd rather do my bit of bird and be able to look myself in the mirror.' However much he hated Hunt, grassing would only make it worse, he reasoned.

The judge gave him three years for the fraud, which Cavanagh used to get sober, fitter and on with his life. He was even coming to terms with the scar on his face and having to pay Hunt £10,000. On the outside, however, the Long Fella was concerned that the disfigured face staring back every day in his victim's prison mirror would eventually make Cavanagh want to tell all to the police. Hunt initially tried a friendly approach and, through Mark Wright, their mutual friend, the Long Fella sent Cavanagh a new pair of trainers. The gift was immediately given away to another prisoner not because Cavanagh was annoyed, but for aesthetic reasons. 'They were like something Ronald McDonald might wear,' he said.

The listening device in the car showroom revealed that a new plan was hatched to send Wright back to the prison but this time with a concealed tape recorder. But the idea was aborted and instead Cavanagh recalls Wright turning up at Hollesley Bay prison in Suffolk with Raymond Hunt. The visit was cordial and the pair left having been assured that his lips were as firmly sealed as the scar on his face.

However, that all changed in April 1999 following another visit from Wright, only this time he was alone and bearing no gifts, just bad news.

'Your girlfriend's taken up with another man, Paul. And the word is that Hunty's not finished and is gonna make an example of you when you get out in a few months.'

Cavanagh felt Wright was almost urging him to make a statement against the Long Fella as his only protection against another assault. The visit left him feeling depressed, if not suicidal.

'I've got nothing to live for,' he confided that afternoon in the prison Chaplin. 'I've been a total scumbag really.' A prison doctor prescribed a course of Amitriptyline, the strong anti-depressant, and sent Cavanagh back to his cell.

Operation Blackjack detectives were monitoring his fragile mental state and days later approached him to make a statement. On 23 April, Cavanagh crossed the line that so many feared to step over and named Davey Hunt as the man who had slashed his throat and almost killed him.[4] But that night back in his cell he woke with 'the

[4]Rather than admit that he sold the Land Rover to rescue the Irish fraud, Cavanagh falsely claimed in the same witness statement that three men to whom he owed money took the vehicle.

horrors'. The implications of standing up in court were sinking in. His first thoughts were to take his own life or maybe abscond from prison. But by the morning a new plan was forming. Over the next few days, word got back to the Long Fella that Cavanagh was willing to withdraw his statement for a consideration.

Shortly before 1 p.m. on 29 April, Palmer and Hunt waited in the car showroom for Cavanagh's call from prison. The Long Fella had his finger poised over the record button of a tape machine when the phone rang. Informed that he was being recorded, Cavanagh explained why he'd made the witness statement to the police and then asked for £7,000 to buy a false passport and disappear.

'Look, I don't want to see anyone down,' Hunt replied. 'Before I give you anything, Paul, you've got to speak to my solicitor.' And then, 'Don't make things any worse mate, do you understand? I never did nothing to you, did I?'

This was Cavanagh's cue and he duly agreed. But once again, on returning to his cell, panic set in. He didn't want to be a witness for the police but nor did he want to live life as a fugitive on the run. The drugs were messing with his mind. That afternoon Cavanagh called detective inspector Tim Smales to explain what he'd done. Smales already knew because Operation Blackjack was monitoring Cavanagh's prison phone calls and bugging Hunt's office. The fix was simple, the detective pointed out – make another statement saying he had contacted Hunt out of fear for his life.

Cavanagh agreed and as soon as the statement was signed on 11 May 1999, he was moved to a new prison. Two days later, Operation Blackjack detectives arrested the Long Fella and Michael Palmer. Although silent when questioned about the assault and the attempt to cover it up, prosecution lawyers felt there was enough to charge them both. Traces of smeared blood matching Cavanagh's was found on the chair leg of a desk in the car showroom. The chances of it being someone else's blood were one in eighteen million. A retired Metropolitan police detective was also charged with conspiring to pervert the course of justice. The bug in the car showroom had secretly recorded former flying squad detective, Derek Keene, agreeing to find out from serving officers if Hunt was under investigation.

'Definitely,' Keene reported back in return for a small cash payment.[5]

Operation Blackjack appeared to have achieved the impossible. One of the leading crime lords of London was in a high security jail awaiting trial. As word spread, many in Newham sighed with relief. For now, Paul Cavanagh was the talk of the East End underworld.

Davey Hunt's financial empire had grown spectacularly in the last decade. Yet the crime boss hadn't paid a single penny in tax on his hidden fortune. Financial investigators working with Operation Blackjack took an Al Capone approach and hoped to seize assets under a new law, the 1995 Proceeds of Crime Act.

In August 1999, while Hunt was on remand awaiting trial for the attack on Cavanagh, the investigators asked

---

[5]According to the Operation Blackjack case summary against Keene, during his interview he admitted the conversations with Palmer between January and April 1999 and accepted receiving payment but said he never made any inquiries with serving officers to see if Hunt was being investigated.

the Jersey authorities to access the accounts of Galleons
Reach Limited, his offshore company overseen by
crooked accountant Peter Michel. The detectives already
had financial records showing Hunt receiving £300,000
since 1996 from the Soho brothel in Green's Court. They
now needed proof that he was the secret owner of the
freehold and of Galleons Reach Limited in order to bring
an additional charge of 'living off immoral earnings'.

Detectives believed that documents in Michel's office
would also help prove their suspicion that Hunt was
laundering criminal funds from drug trafficking, fraud
and prostitution through the Jersey company, and had
used his waste recycling business to do it. The investigators
calculated that Hunt's Iron & Steel Limited had avoided
paying £150,000 in UK business taxes. A report
described how the business was 'stripped' of valuable
assets and put into administration only to re-emerge
phoenix like as three new debt-free companies.[6] Hunt
showed no link on paper to the new companies because
he'd hidden his ownership of the waste business freehold
through yet another offshore company, EMM Limited,
this time incorporated in the British Virgin Islands but
administered in Panama.

Central to many of these financial transactions was
Hunt's lawyer, Chris Williams. In an application for a

[6]Galleons Reach Limited (GRL) bought a £50,000 debenture that Barclays
Bank had over Hunt's Iron & Steel Ltd (HIS). This made GRL the biggest
creditor allowing it to put HIS into administrative receivership in June 1996
after less than a year of trading. GRL was paid back £60,000 from the receiver.
Hunt had already set up Hunt's Iron & Steel Holdings, Hunt's Iron & Steel
(UK) Limited and Hunt's Iron & Steel Contractors in February 1996. Two
nephews were listed as secretary and director of all three companies, which had
NatWest bank accounts.

court order to access his records, investigators pointed out that Williams had to be aware of who Hunt really was from the *Time Out* articles. The report also gave details of the lawyer's involvement in the purchase of the Soho brothel, the use of his client account for the flow of funds from Hunt's Barclays bank accounts and for the purchase of Palmer's Motors.[7] To further make their case, the court was told of information from 'a reliable source' that 'Hunt had invested £300,000 into this [car] business to purchase stock for the showroom. The business bank accounts regularly show large cash deposits and withdrawals and it is suspected that these accounts are used to launder the proceeds of criminal activity.'[8]

Separately, Hunt was expanding his waste management business by buying the adjacent wharf on the River Thames at Dagenham for £1 million. The bug in Palmer's Motors discovered that the money was paid into Williams' client account at the Allied Irish Bank in Ilford. Yet despite all this turnover and income, Hunt was still a tax ghost. He had cheated the Inland Revenue since 1982 by deliberately under-declaring his earnings. Operation Blackjack's financial investigators were concerned to

---

[7]Hunt bought the £160,000 freehold at 51-3 Chigwell Road with a £91,400 mortgage from First National PLC in August 1996. The £62,000 deposit came from Hunt's joint account with his wife at Barclays Bank and was deposited in the client account his lawyer Chris Williams held at the Allied Irish Bank in Ilford. The car showroom was rented to Michael Palmer at cost of the monthly re-mortgage payment of just over £1,000.

[8]According to the police report, some of those transactions were with Michel's Jersey trust companies that acted for Fleetfoot Holdings Limited, owned by Samuel Cook. He was charged with his father Robert in December 1997 in connection with a 500k kilos cannabis seizure. But due to his father's medical condition the prosecution discontinued the case. The Cooks used to own the freehold to Hunt's Dagenham waste plant, according to the police report.

discover that in 1996 the Revenue even allowed the crime boss to cut a sweetheart deal and pay just £30,000 in back taxes.

Hunt continued to make a fool of the timid taxman, as his offshore income remained hidden until Operation Blackjack started to unravel it and share those findings with the Jersey authorities.

It was the early summer of 1999 and Cavanagh was just weeks away from being released into the care of a witness protection team. Specialist police officers were going to look after him until Hunt's trial, which was set for November that year.

'Is it true?' asked Cavanagh's cousin, Joe.

'Have you made a statement against Hunt?' chimed in Cavanagh's best mate, Alan Twiddy.

'I weren't well when I made it,' Cavanagh told his disappointed visitors over prison tea. 'I know the rules. I'm frightened of repercussions and of what I've become – a fucking grass. I need you to help me get out of this. Go and see Hunt's people and ask what can be done.'

Once again, Cavanagh was losing his nerve about giving evidence. He never mentioned a figure but was hoping the Hunts would wipe clean his £10,000 debt if he withdrew the statement and disappeared with a bit of money in his pocket until the trial was abandoned. Joe Cavanagh had no fear of the Hunts. He was a hard man in his thirties who manned the doors of some lively East End pubs. Twiddy, whose nickname was 'Toofa' (a Gypsy term for cigarette), was much older and a fraudster. Not a fighting man like Joe, Toofa did the talking.

At a meeting on Wanstead flats, the Long Fella's representatives listened as Toofa laid out Cavanagh's proposition. Joe, meanwhile, was getting annoyed at Stevie Hunt, who was circling him like an attack dog. The two hard men snarled at each other while a deal was worked out. Cavanagh would receive £50,000 in compensation for the scar and for retracting his witness statement and disappearing. £35,000 would be paid up front and the balance when the Long Fella was released.

Cavanagh was delighted when he heard the news and offered his two intermediaries £5,000 each for their troubles. Toofa was put in charge of the cash, some of which he deposited into Cavanagh's Halifax bank account. The day came on 31 August when Cavanagh was released from prison into the care of witness protection officers who took him to a safe house in Nottingham. The officers stayed a few days then left Cavanagh alone with an electronic tag attached to his ankle. He had to be indoors between 7 p.m. and 7 a.m. or it would trigger an alarm at the security company monitoring the tag for the police.

With witness protection out of sight, on 3 September Cavanagh went to a nearby solicitor who faxed a full retraction to Hunt's lawyers in London. Later that day, he levered off the electronic tag and posted it to the security company with a note claiming that the police had pressured him to falsely incriminate Hunt. Detective Inspector Smales was livid when he heard the news and launched a manhunt for his witness, who by then had gone horse racing with Toofa in Scotland.

By late October, Cavanagh found a rented flat in the north of England where he tried to live a normal life. Only a few people had his new mobile number, so it surprised him when Smales called him out of the blue.

'Whatever you've done Paul, if you've had your pockets lined, we can cover it all in a new witness statement,' the detective explained.

But Cavanagh was too spooked to oblige and immediately abandoned the flat for a hotel. Toofa was sent from London to 'babysit' him as they bolted for the Cumbrian coast. Meanwhile, armed with the retraction statement, Hunt's legal team applied to have the prosecution thrown out. No witness, no case, they told the judge. Shortly after the court hearing, Stevie Hunt called Cavanagh.

'Have you spoken to that copper Smales?' he asked with a touch of menace. "Cos he's told the court you are coming back to give evidence.'

Cavanagh promised he was well and truly 'on his toes' and would stay that way until the Long Fella was free. By late November, the prosecution had no choice but to abandon the case against Hunt and Palmer. Keene, the former detective, was also formally acquitted.[9]

As soon as Cavanagh heard the news that Hunt was a free man he contacted Operation Blackjack to arrange his surrender knowing that the most he would get for breaking off his electronic tag and absconding was a few more months in prison. Cavanagh was also gambling that the police would not be able to prove the corrupt deal he had struck to withdraw his evidence against Hunt.

[9]Michael Palmer separately pleaded guilty with Steven Galvin to a fraud involving defrauding Lombard Finance of £42,000 for a luxury car. Bugs in the car showroom recorded the conspiracy. Palmer was jailed for 10 months in April 2000.

A police car arrived outside a McDonalds to take Cavanagh back to headquarters where he would be formally interviewed for perverting the course of justice. Officers' careers were on the line, he was told in the car. But Cavanagh didn't care. Soon he would be a free man with neither the law nor the Long Fella on his back. During the interview detectives asked about the large cash deposits into Cavanagh's Halifax Bank account, suspecting, correctly, this was evidence of perverting the course of justice. Cavanagh told them he had won the money gambling. But when the tape was turned off, he admitted retracting his statement for money.

'I was afraid that once I'd given my evidence witness protection would abandon me after six months and I'd be penniless and looking over my shoulder,' he explained on his way back to prison. The belated honesty, however, was worthless. Operation Blackjack was a busted hand.[10]

Cavanagh was released in January 2000 and tried to rebuild his life as a bookmaker away from London. The self-exile was a precaution against any reprisals. Hunt couldn't be trusted not to do something and there was also the chance some young upstart looking to make a name for himself would put a bullet in his head to impress the Long Fella.

Cavanagh was right to still be afraid. Unknown to him, the police had intelligence that while Hunt had been on remand awaiting trial a contract was put out to seriously

[10]The account of Paul Cavanagh's change of evidence is taken from his affidavit dated 19 May 2015. Paul Cavanagh's account of payments was corroborated by his Halifax bank statements and a source intimately involved in the negotiations with the Hunts who asked not to be named for fear of reprisals. Separately, Joe Cavanagh did not deny his involvement but politely told the author to 'Fuck Off!' Alan Twiddy had died when the author approached his family.

harm Cavanagh. In other words, while Cavanagh was negotiating to withdraw his evidence, the Hunts were still plotting to have him hurt or worse, just in case. A secret police report put it this way: 'Hunt had a contract for serious harm against [Cavanagh] even though he had withdrawn his statement, with Hunt wanting it to occur before [the Long Fella] was released from prison.'

Jimmy Holmes had also returned to self-exile in California after Hunt's release in November 1999. Holmes had refused any further co-operation with the police after being given a new handler he didn't like. Holmes smelled a rat when, at a cafe near Scotland Yard, the new man put a mobile phone on the table. Holmes suspected it was a recording device, a suspicion that increased when he was asked, without foreplay, to talk about the still unsolved murder of pub stock taker Terry Gooderham and his girlfriend Maxine Arnold in Epping Forrest in 1989.

'Nothing to do with me, that one,' Holmes replied, hiding his annoyance at the detective's bovine attempt to trick an admission out of him.

Straight after meeting the new handler, Holmes left for California cursing the police. 'Idiots. I didn't ask for money. I didn't want a change of ID. I said I'd sort out my own security. But they tried to drag me in on the [murder] conspiracy rather than be sensible. You can only do that once to someone.'

The double murder in Epping Forest had highlighted a corruption problem in Scotland Yard that eventually led to an astonishing secret report in 2002 concluding that Hunt had corrupted Operation Blackjack at the top.

It all started with the detectives trying to find out who killed Gooderham and Arnold. Instead, they picked up whispers that a group of Canning Town criminals were apparently getting 'help' from crooked cops. The previously described bugging operations on the Silvertown strip against Woollard, Sabine, Matthews and others added to the corruption concerns and ultimately led, in 1993, to the setting up of a Ghost Squad of anti-corruption intelligence officers.

The success of that operation, codenamed Othona, depended on remaining hidden from the rest of the force. So the detective inspector in charge of it faked cancer and appeared to retire from the police on ill health. MI5, the domestic intelligence service, and Customs' undercover unit helped the Ghost Squad to set up back stories and businesses, including a private investigations firm, to secretly test the integrity of suspect officers. Meanwhile, trusted detectives were recruited as 'sleepers' and posted to problematic police stations and specialist squads to identify pockets of corrupt activity or so-called 'lone wolves' and their criminal associates.

The Ghost Squad spied on officers and civilians for four years. In 1998, then Commissioner Sir Paul Condon went public with its findings. In a strategic speech to members of parliament during the crisis over the bungled investigation into murdered black teenager Stephen Lawrence, Condon launched a new squad of Untouchables to overtly investigate up to 250 corrupt cops his Ghost Squad had apparently identified. The Commissioner assured politicians that no stone would be left unturned and tame journalists, especially at the BBC, responded with glowing coverage that helped build the myth of a fearless Untouchables squad. Everyone behaved as though the nettle of corruption had finally been grasped so the police were somehow worthy of continued self-regulation.

In reality, over the next four years only the corruption that Scotland Yard wanted rid of was investigated, the rest was simply ignored or covered up. To do this, the Untouchables revived a discredited system of using supergrasses to secure convictions. In return for their tailored evidence, these slippery informants were rewarded with light sentences for their own criminality and corruption. Ultimately, the supergrasses badly conned and humiliated the Untouchables, who in turn covered this up to protect themselves. After spending tens of millions of pounds, the promised prosecution of corrupt officers and their criminal paymasters failed to materialise.

Outside of their own rapid promotion, the greatest success the Untouchables had was a sting operation codenamed Greyhound in April 2000. The targets were detective constable Martin Morgan and Bob Kean, a drug dealer, who was also his informant. The Teutonic-looking Morgan had served his twenty-year career in north and east London on the frontline of the war on drugs. He was effective, popular, brave and a fine footballer for the police. He was also greedy and extremely corrupt. Kean was a builder by trade who moved large quantities of cannabis and sought protection by providing high-grade intelligence on criminals and the IRA. Operation Greyhound was based on good intelligence and a creative use of bugging equipment that gave Morgan, Kean and their co-defendants no choice but to plead guilty to plotting the kidnap and torture of a money launderer who had run off with their dirty cash.[11]

---

[11]Ibid. On 7 July 2002, Martin Morgan and Bob Kean pleaded guilty and were jailed for seven years. For the full story see *Untouchables*.

In October 2001, while at last basking in some real success, Andy Hayman, the Untouchables' feckless commander, tasked anti-corruption officers with an odd assignment. They were told to secretly scope the extent to which organised crime had penetrated Scotland Yard, but in north and east London only. Hayman claimed the trigger for such a report was concern that murder inquiries in this corner of the force were being compromised. Others thought he was trying to empire-build off the back of the rare success against Morgan and Kean. His Tiberius Report, as it became known, was a snapshot based on old intelligence developed from operation Othona. In the preamble it was admitted that the compilers had no access to Essex and Hertfordshire police intelligence databases or those from the National Crime Squad, Customs and the National Criminal Intelligence Service.

Intelligence is not evidence, and some of the content merely repeated gossip that should have been omitted but instead was left to linger and potentially destroy or frustrate the careers of those the Untouchables didn't like or who had got the better of them during their recent 'war on corruption'. Internal politics played a part in Commander Hayman's commissioning of the Tiberius report, said one informed senior Scotland Yard intelligence officer, who went on to criticise it for at times joining low-grade and good intelligence to make 'conspiracy' where there was none. 'When it was read by senior officers it was thought that none of it was new or unknown and they wondered why Hayman had not done a similar exercise for [the rest of] London. So it was shelved,' the source explained. Either way, the conclusions were very bad news for Scotland Yard, which presumably is why its 186 pages

had such a limited distribution and was never supposed
to see the light of day.

The biggest police force in the UK was 'under serious
threat from infiltration' by Hunt's organised crime
syndicate, the report stated. Equally astonishing was the
claim that four senior officers in charge of Operation
Blackjack – which had been set up in 1996 to bring down
the Long Fella – were under suspicion for their handling
of informants believed to have supplied information to
the Hunt crime group.

More broadly, the Tiberius report identified seven other
crime groups in north and east London – the Adams and
the Bowers crime families being the most important –
who were able to infiltrate Scotland Yard 'at will' and
'continue to flourish and gain confidence in their ability
to evade prosecution.' The report further calculated that
forty two serving and nineteen retired officers along with
nineteen career criminals were 'associated with the corrupt
networks' serving these eight crime groups.[12]

The timing of the report was terrible. The UK police
response to the Al-Qaeda attack on 11 September 2001
in New York was already driving a shift of resources
away from fighting organised crime towards counter
terrorism and tracking home grown jihadists. In effect,
six months after the New York attacks, the Tiberius report
was asserting that criminals in Newham, Tower Hamlets
and Hackney – all potential Olympic boroughs with the

---

[12]Some of these detectives were on murder squads and at least three contract
killings remained unsolved because of their corrupt actions, the Tiberius report
claimed. John 'Goldfinger' Palmer was also named as heading one of the eight
crime groups or syndicates in the Tiberius report. Palmer was murdered in the
garden of his Essex home on 24 June 2015. The case remains open.

capital's largest Muslim populations – had corrupted
Scotland Yard at senior management level.

Hunt's syndicate was described as 'a feared criminal
force in east London for many years.' The Tiberius
report went on: 'The legitimate business enterprises
(scrap metal) provide a front for their criminal activities
which centre around the importation of class A drugs,
protection rackets and high-value vehicle crime. The
Hunt syndicate has developed an extensive criminal
empire, which so far has evaded significant penetration
from law enforcement. The syndicate has achieved this
invulnerability through a mixture of utilising corrupt
police contacts and the intimidation of witnesses brave
enough to give evidence against them.' Operation
Blackjack was said to be 'no better example' of this
problem. The Tiberius report was particularly concerned
about criminals using retired officers as corrupt 'conduits'
to those still serving.

It was no secret that retired officers are forever linked to
the police world through leaving dos, freemasonry, police
sports clubs and the world of private investigation where
criminals can become clients. Tiberius was particularly
concerned about Derek Keene, the former flying squad
detective who had been acquitted with Hunt and Palmer
in 1999.[13] He was secretly recorded at Palmer's Motors

[13]According to the Tiberius report, Derek Keene had walked into another major
organised crime bugging operation in 1995 against the Adams crime family in
north London. Police had bugged Pussy Galore, the Hatton Garden offices of
Solly Nahome, their chief money launderer. The report said Keene had parlayed
with Terry Adams, who offered to 'take out' the supplier of the ecstasy tablet that
had recently killed schoolgirl Leah Betts in Essex. Keene knew Betts's father, a
policeman, who was not aware of the gangster's offer. Adams, it was said, wanted
Keene to front a licence for the crime family's new club in Soho.

agreeing to find out through contacts at the local police football team if Hunt was a target.[14]

Another red flag in the Tiberius report concerned informants corrupting their handlers and then acting as 'conduits' of sensitive information to the criminal fraternity. The Untouchables secretly investigated detective sergeant Ray Ahearne during Operation Blackjack but found no evidence that would support disciplinary or criminal charges of corruption.[15] There were wider concerns about 'lax' supervision of informant handling by the detective superintendent who had brought Ahearne on to Operation Blackjack's source unit. There was also unease about the superintendent's relationship with the Hunts along with

---

[14]Palmer had also asked Keane to get dirt on detective inspector John Redgrave, the ginger giant, who had once run Hunt out of Canning Town. Martin Morgan was one of Redgrave's junior detectives. Redgrave was suspended in 1997 over separate corruption allegations that the supergrass later admitted were fabricated. See *Untouchables*.

[15]Ray Ahearne retired from the Met in August 2001 unaware that he had been suspected of misconduct. He felt his source unit had successfully recruited some twenty informants giving a range of intelligence on Turkish organised crime and Hunt's syndicate. Ahearne was not alone in thinking the task force was 'a victim of its own success,' as one former colleague put it. The whole set up at Ilford had created 'jealousy' and tension with other police squads and with Customs agents, it was suggested, and some of these targets were the very criminals also informing to Ahearne.

Such conflicts are not uncommon in the war on drugs where informants are a currency for achieving promotion, appeasing a police force's political masters and securing continued funding for a particular operation or specialist squad. Handling such slippery customers, however, can easily lead to spurious misconduct allegations against frontline officers, as a canny informant will seek to exploit inter-agency rivalry to stay out of jail. Yet without them, police work was impossible.

his replacement.[16] Certainly, there was evidence of Hunt and his associates trying to find out what the police were doing against him during Operation Blackjack. But it is also important to bear in mind that Hunt spent nine months in prison in 1999 awaiting trial for the attack on Paul Cavanagh and undermined that prosecution by paying off his victim, not the police.[17]

Detective Inspector David 'Mac' McKelvey had no knowledge of the astonishing secret conclusions of the Tiberius report when, four years later in May 2006, he decided to take on the Long Fella, but from reading other reports on Davey Hunt, Mac knew corruption could be a problem for the Newham crime squad.

At the age of forty-five, Hunt had survived everything Scotland Yard had thrown at him and emerged more cunning, stronger, richer and as violent as ever. He now controlled the Olympic borough through its shadow economy and justice system – a crime lord of the rings in waiting and, if the secret Tiberius report was correct, someone with a long and corrupt reach into the police force responsible for Olympic security.

[16]Operation Blackjack was set up under detective superintendent Gavin Robertson, who brought Ahearne onto the unit. The Tiberius report raised concerns about a quartet of Blackjack detectives and their dealings with the Hunt syndicate. All four former detectives vigorously deny the allegations and no charges were ever brought. When approached for comment for this book, Robertson's lawyers said: 'Throughout thirty-two years of service as a police officer our client did not receive a single complaint alleging dishonesty. Since his retirement he has not been approached by any police officer from any police force alleging dishonesty, corruption or indeed any other impropriety.'
[17]Paul Cavanagh said he never experienced any corruption during his contact with Operation Blackjack detectives.

In the briefing room at Stratford police station, Mac told his assembled detectives that he was imposing new security measures and only those with the necessary clearance would have access to the CRIS report of the new operation, where all sensitive details of witnesses and strategy were logged in real time. Outside of Hunt, he told the Newham crime squad, the greatest threat to their safety came from inside the police.

PART THREE

Let the Games Begin

9

Judas Pigs

After the Long Fella and his men pulverised Billy Allen's minders during the court hearing in February 2006, the legal battleground for control of the Silvertown strip moved to the secure surroundings of Kingston crown court in southwest London.

When the trial reopened on 19 June, this time it was the Newham crime squad escorting Allen to and from court. He was their witness in a case being built against Hunt and Chic Matthews for blackmail, threats and grievous bodily harm. That operation was codenamed Epsom. A second operation codenamed Houdini was investigating the Aladdin's den of stolen goods found on the disputed land. There was no jury to intimidate at Kingston crown court – just a no-nonsense judge who knew a villain when he saw one and immediately laid down the law.

'The reason why the case has been held at this court is to provide maximum security to deter anybody from thinking that what happened on the last occasion could be repeated,' Judge Collins warned the parties. 'I have not been told how much the land is worth, although common sense suggests it is likely to have substantial development potential because of its location. But it is clear that in this action the stakes are high.'

What unfolded over the next two days read like a gangster film with a who's who cast of villainy: five crime families with subplots of blackmail, murder, police corruption, grasses, double crosses and drugs. Chic Matthews sat on one side of the court with his eldest son 'Chicky' Matthews junior, who was forty-four. Their allies, the Hunts and the Bowers, were nowhere to be seen but waited silently in Canning Town for news.

On the other side was Allen, the convicted fraudster and his Canning Town cousin Terry Sabine, the convicted drug trafficker. Since 1982, the Sabine family had used a part of the land at 1-7 Brunel Street for their car valeting business and a pallet yard. In return for a percentage of the development deal that Allen was working on, Sabine was willing to swear that the Matthews had not been on the land for twelve uninterrupted years. It was a bold move for 45-year-old Sabine to go against the Long Fella, who he also considered a friend. But then again, money has no loyalty.

Chic Matthews gave an entertaining performance from the witness box. Allen's dad, he said, was a 'good friend' who had allowed him to use some of the land as overspill for his scrap metal business across the road. When Jimmy Allen was brutally murdered in 1986, Matthews claimed he lent Billy £100,000 while the will was sorted out. But Billy did a runner so Matthews moved onto the land as collateral in 1987. Shortly afterwards, he told the judge, corrupt police stitched him up over a drug factory on the Silvertown strip that had nothing to do with him. Allen also ended up in prison, for fraud, Matthews delighted in informing the judge, and Chicky Matthews junior took over and started a storage business on the land. Matthews omitted to tell the judge that the Newham crime squad had recently raided the storage business and discovered over £1 million of stolen goods from multiple lorry hijacks across the UK.

When Allen's barrister asked Matthews if he had any paperwork to prove the £100,000 loan, he said it was a 'gentleman's agreement' paid in £50 notes from a pot of money that he kept at home and had 'earned' from doing unspecified business.

'That is not true … why did you not go and look for [Mr Allen] to get your money if you had lent him so much?' Jane Giret QC persisted.

'I couldn't find him, he's slipperier than an eel,' Matthews explained.

'He went to your daughter's wedding.'

'No he did not, dear … He's a liar. Mr Allen is the biggest liar God put breath into. His nickname's Billy Liar … I gave him that [£100,000] out of respect for his father who was a very good friend of mine.'

'You weren't there when your daughter got married because you were in jail weren't you?' Giret inquired.

'That is right. In prison, put there by Mr Allen… The evidence I have got that Mr Allen is a police informer… He ain't going to like that, dear… He sent me to prison… He gave false evidence to bribe police officers. I went to prison for ten years. I spent five years and three months in prison before I went to the appeal court and been proved innocent. You do not want to hear me say that.'[1]

[1]Kingston Crown Court 20 June 2006.

At this point, Matthews handed the judge a transcript of the anti-corruption squad's 1993 interview with former detective Rodney Whitchelo, the man who tried to blackmail Heinz. The transcript stated that Billy Allen was a police informant on the drug factory operation against Matthews.

None of this deterred Allen, who gave a polished performance from the witness box. He denied borrowing £100,000 from Matthews but admitted defrauding Barclays Bank by using the land as collateral to raise money. Judge Collins reminded everyone that as he has been bankrupt since 1991, Allen's assets – including the land – were in his trustees' hands. Allen assured the court that he was working to pay off all his creditors.

Rarely does a judge overseeing a land dispute have to decide between such opposing colourful characters, but in the end the whole case turned on the evidence of one man, Alan Penny, who Billy Allen had also ripped off using the land as a lure. Penny told the court how he thought he'd bought 1-7 Brunel Street after the murder of Jimmy Allen. But Billy ran off with his £35,000 deposit, so Penny took a charge against the land and moved onto it in mid-1987 followed by the Matthews family. All was looking good for their camp until Penny accepted that, in a 1994 letter to the trustees, he had recognised Allen as the owner of the land and therefore possession was not uninterrupted for the required twelve years. The case was over. Allen had won.

'You will have possession forthwith,' Judge Collins told him. In the same breath, Matthews was ordered to pay two thirds of Allen's legal costs and make provision for his profits claim. While the legal teams argued over money, old man Matthews slipped out to the toilet followed by Mac's men. As soon as he was zipped up, detective

'The Long Fella', Davey Hunt, in 2013 outside the High Court where he lost his libel claim and was found by Mr Justice Simon to be a violent organised crime boss.

'Avant-garde' gangster, Jimmy Holmes, posing for his book *Judas Pig*, a 'love letter' to the Long Fella.

Billy Allen, the property developer who pitted his wits against the Hunts and Matthews in a turf war for control of the Silvertown strip.

© Dave McKelvey

Mac on Chicky Matthews junior's motorbike, found during the search of London City Storage in March 2006.

Chicky Matthews junior was jailed in January 2019 for handling items stolen in 2010 from Chatila, a jewellers. The haul was found in the ceiling of his office at London City Metals by detectives investigating the Hatton Garden safe deposit heist. Chicky claimed he was storing the items for family friend, James Tibbs.

Bernie Silver in his heyday. The 'Soho Godfather' stood up to Hunt's move on his porn empire.

Mark Powell, Soho tailor to the stars, was caught up in the guerrilla war between Holmes and Hunt.

© Stuart Wilson/Getty Images

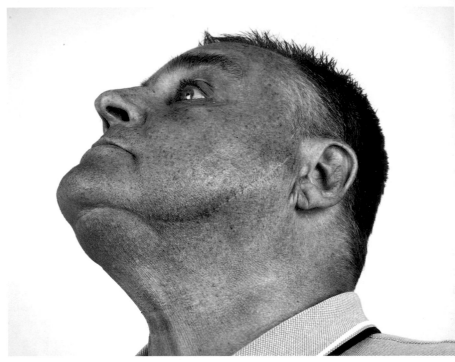

Paul Cavanagh reveals the scar Hunt gave him in 1997. 'I have a reminder every time I look in the mirror whereas for him it's just an everyday fucking occurrence.'

Police suspected 'TOWIE Godfather', Mark Wright, was a double agent informant for the Hunt organised crime group, which Wright denied.

The disputed land on the Silvertown strip in 2013. It is still abandoned after a turf war involving five local crime families and the Newham crime squad.

Hunt's twenty-acre mansion in Bishop's Stortford that he bought in 1993 for £600,000 while working as a part-time doorman and scaffolder.

Hunt's Waste in Dagenham formed a joint venture with demolition firm and Olympics contractor, Keltbray.

Whistleblowing Newham Parks police constable, Pelé Mahmood.

Newham Labour councillor Mike Law (left) receiving a bravery commendation in March 2005 at the ceremony where Pelé Mahmood accused the council of racism and corruption.

Retired anti-corruption and undercover detective Ash Siddique (right) with Prime Minister Theresa May in 2015 at the mosque he now runs in Barking, East London.

'They called me bent so I've come as a banana.' DCI Dave McKelvey attending an interview with the anti-corruption squad in October 2008.

Taxpayers and fans took a hammering after the Olympic stadium was awarded to West Ham United F.C. in 2013, following a bidding process marred by corporate espionage. Hammers co-owners, David Sullivan (left) and David Gold (right), flank London mayor, Boris Johnson, Baroness Karren Brady and Newham mayor Sir Robin Wales.

Newham mayor, Rokhsana Fiaz (centre) lays a wreath on Armistice Day 2018 alongside West Ham United F.C. owner David Gold (left). She called for an inquiry into 'culture and practices' at the council over its part in the stadium deal.

constable Darren Guntrip arrested him for blackmail and
witness intimidation of Allen.

'That cunt? I can't believe you're still listening to him.
He killed his mother, his father and beat his step-daughter
within an inch of her life. I did eight years in prison
because of that cunt,' Matthews remonstrated.

At the police station, he continued his rant against
Allen, this time on tape. 'The man's got a vendetta against
me for some reason. He knows I know he killed his
father and he knows I know who done it so he wants to
get me out of the way… got me ten years in prison… I
was proved innocent and taxpayers' money was used to
give me a fortune. It's fucking ridiculous and they still
keep listening to him.'

Matthews denied making any threats by text or phone,
sending a funeral wreath or using heavies to bash up Allen's
minders. He then suggested Allen had probably paid both
sets of heavies to fight each other so he could blame him.
When to it came to Davey Hunt, Matthews didn't just
deny any association or deal with the Long Fella over the
land, he gave a remarkable reason why.

'I wouldn't have any deal with Mr Hunt because he killed
one of my best friends. [Allen] killed his father. They're
matched together and I wouldn't even talk to people like
them. You know, I've got a bit of pride in my own ways
and faults. I wouldn't spit on him if he was on fire.'

Although Matthews wouldn't say who Hunt had
allegedly killed he happily named the man he claimed
Allen had hired to kill his father. 'The man who done it
was Kenneth Kenny. He's dead now. Someone shot him
in the head in [Romford] hospital car park.'[2]

---

[2]See footnote 5, page 33.

In Matthews' eyes, Billy Allen was still a police informant and he cheekily asked Guntrip if 'Billy Liar' was feeding him any titbits. 'I know you're not allowed to say nothing, just look at me and wink.'

The exchange alarmed the detective because he had earlier found a piece of paper in Matthews' coat pocket with his name on it next to the initials of the police watchdog. Guntrip had spent the last few months painstakingly tracing all the stolen wine, clothes and jewellery found at London City Storage and was building what he thought was an unassailable case against Matthews' son. The discovery of the paper suggested that the crime family were rolling out an old trick of making false allegations of corruption between the police and Allen to undermine any prosecution.

At 9.30 p.m., the other detective in the interview room went to the front desk where Chicky Matthews junior was in an agitated mood waiting for his father to be bailed.

'You're protecting a killer. [Allen] killed his family,' he shouted out.

'Regardless, sir, we have to investigate,' the officer replied dryly.

'You fucking mug, you're all cunts.'

'Your dad will be out soon,' said the now unnerved officer.

'Where's that cunt Guntrip? If he was a fucking man he'd take his badge off and fight me outside.'[3]

Over the summer, Guntrip sent the Operation Houdini case papers to the Crown Prosecution Service for a

[3]Statement of PC Neil Godwin 21 August 2007.

decision on whether Chicky Matthews junior should be charged with handling stolen goods.

Meanwhile, detective constable Paul Clark was trying to secure witness statements from Allen's minders, without which there was no chance of successfully prosecuting Davey Hunt and old man Matthews for blackmail and the assault at court. The key was Danny Woollard, Allen's main minder and a leading East End gangster in his own right who knew the Hunt family when Davey was just a boy. It was not out of any observance of the fabled underworld 'code' – one must not grass – that stopped Woollard from making a statement, it was the fear of being killed if he did.

Nevertheless, he agreed to meet Mac, Guntrip and Clark at his Essex home on 20 September 2006 and explain what had happened at court seven months earlier in February. Woollard was willing to be taped but said he would never sign a witness statement. But before the recording began the three detectives had to pull themselves together after falling into uncontrollable laughter when Woollard's wife walked into the sitting room with the teas followed by the pet Alsatian.

'We knew that Woollard had a thing about using the dog to perform sex acts,' explained Mac, who recalled laughing so hard that he broke the antique chair he was sitting on.

When composure returned, Woollard, still unaware that he was the butt of the joke, told the three detectives his story.

'I was pissing and shitting blood for about two weeks. I went blind in one eye within about three weeks and had four abscesses in my brain. Ended up having two operations three or four weeks afterwards and I was in hospital for about eight weeks.'

Woollard said his involvement started after the incident in Whitehall when a representative of Matthews made a throat slitting motion while driving past Allen on the eve of a court hearing in July 2005. Allen asked him to put a protection team together, and there were no more incidents. Then, days before the hearing in February 2006, Woollard said he turned down £100,000 to walk off the job so that Allen would be too frightened to continue his claim allowing Matthews to win the land by default.

Woollard recalled taking a call from the Long Fella. 'Davey Hunt said I'm working for Chicky Matthews junior. I've put £600,000 into it and I would like you to come work for us. The actual words he said was, if you pull away, they'll pull away. So I said, no I can't do that.'

Hunt, he claimed, offered him '£1 million' to stop being Allen's minder. Woollard refused but felt he had struck an agreement with the Long Fella that there would be no violence at court and whoever won the land dispute would give the other some money. It therefore came as a surprise when Hunt and his gorillas with knuckledusters bashed the daylights out of him during that court hearing in February. 'If I knew they were going to be twenty handed I wouldn't have walked in with only my prick in my hand. It's a proper liberty believe me,' he told the now composed detectives in his living room.

'What would they do to [Allen] to get the land?' Mac inquired.

'They'll kill him if they have to,' Woollard responded, adding, 'they offered me £1 million to get him out of the equation. They could of had him killed a lot cheaper than that, you know what I'm saying.'

'Why do you think Hunt sided with Matthews?' Mac asked.

'Money. He's greedy ... Right through the thing, we tried to do it with no violence. He's supposed to be a businessman. I don't know where he gets his brains from, you know.'

Woollard was probably exaggerating about the money he had been offered to walk away. But the explanation he gave Mac for not making a witness statement against Hunt had a chilling authenticity, especially out of the mouth of a man suspected of murder and armed robbery. It put the task facing the Newham crime squad into sharp perspective.

'I'll help you as much as I can,' Woollard told the three detectives. 'But I've got a family. I've got to live in this area and I'll be frightened of repercussions for my family ... I don't really want a war, because if he done it to my family I would have to do it to his family, if I was still alive.'[4]

Still determined to bring Hunt down, Mac came up with a plan to prick the Long Fella's ego and lure him onto the Silvertown strip where it was hoped his violent nature would reveal itself in front of hidden cameras and undercover police officers. Allen would be the bait and his cousin, Terry Sabine, the messenger.

Mac's idea was that Sabine would casually tell Hunt that Allen now had protection from some heavy eastern European gangsters in return for giving them a percentage of the land development he was planning with HSBC bank and an Arab sheikh to build a mini world trade centre. Hunt would never stand for that, it was imagined, and

[4]When the author phoned Danny Woollard on 7 April 2010 he agreed to talk about anything but what happened at court. He never called back.

would personally threaten the upstart foreign gangsters unaware they were really undercover police officers. This evidence would shore up the case against the Long Fella for blackmail and threats because Allen's own credibility was always going to be a problem in getting any prosecution off the ground.

Mac floated the plan during a power point presentation to a team of senior Scotland Yard intelligence chiefs, which began with an explanation of the criminality so far uncovered:

London City Storage comprises of 41 containers and two Portacabin offices. During the search police recovered stolen property valued at over £1 million. [It] consisted of shoes, cigars, alcohol, clothing and goods from various prestige stores, including Harrods and Harvey Nichols. The property has been identified as stolen by means of burglaries and lorry diversions. Stolen jewellery valued at approximately £250,000 was recovered from a safe. The jewellery had been stolen by means of a burglary at Gresham Street, EC1 (Hatton Garden). The premises having been attacked over a weekend period, the sophisticated alarm system being deactivated and the safe having been 'picked' by a professional 'safe breaker'.

Matthews [junior] is clearly involved at the highest levels in the theft of substantial amounts of stolen goods from lorry diversions, 12 separate loads having been identified. Since November 2004, Caxton Street and Silvertown Way have been the venue for over 100 lorry diverts of valuable goods. Offences in Essex and Hertfordshire have also been identified with goods recovered.

It is now clear from the intelligence gathered that
this hierarchy consists of individuals with a history
of criminality and violence. There are clear links back
to Soldier 3 and the associations made at that time.
Offending includes extreme acts of violence, murder,
blackmail and intimidation. This organised criminal
network run crime in east London and surrounding
counties. They have a distinct structure with foot
soldiers acting on their behalf carrying out acts of
violence in support of the organisation's criminal aims.

At the head of this organisation is David Hunt ...
[He] has evaded justice over many years by corrupting
police and the judicial system. He is seen by many
as untouchable. It has been historically impossible
to support criminal cases against him with private
witnesses, most of whom have withdrawn their
evidence through threats of violence or have simply
disappeared.

Information suggests that Hunt has already made
approaches to the Bowers family, currently serving a
sentence of imprisonment, to purchase the Peacock
public house. Terence Adams, the head of the
infamous north London criminal gang, has apparently
already made efforts to purchase adjoining properties,
including Twilights nightclub. This is supported by the
recent stop and search of Steven Bryant, a lieutenant
and close associate in that gang.

Mac's outgoing borough commander at Newham backed
the plan. 'His team, although young in service, have
proved their ability to support such operations with
considerable success. This is not a long-term infiltration
and will be regularly reviewed ... These individuals are

recognised by both the public and criminal fraternity as the 'godfathers' of crime with a mafia style network ... It is time that the criminal empire built by Hunt and his associates is dismantled,' said an accompanying report.

However, it was not to be. The deployment of undercover officers to the Silvertown strip for such an open-ended period of time was considered too manpower-intensive. Mac was further taken aback when the director of intelligence said the Hunts were 'too dangerous' for Scotland Yard to take on. Policing priorities had certainly changed since the 7 July 2005 jihadist attacks on London, the day after the Olympic bid was won, when resources and manpower shifted into counter-terrorism. Some wondered if this redeployment was done at the expense of fighting organised crime and was giving the gangsters a free pass in the run-up to the Games.

Mac, though, wasn't deterred. In late September, his boss at Newham authorised a three-month surveillance of Hunt as a prelude to his arrest.

The Long Fella had become very security conscious after the nine months he'd spent on remand at HMP Belmarsh in 1999 for slashing Paul Cavanagh's throat. Nowadays, he would walk out of restaurants at the smallest hint of a police presence and changed his phone regularly. But Davey Hunt was also a creature of habit. He got up early, tended to his pigeons in the twenty acre grounds of his Essex mansion, the Morleys, then drove his Bentley to the waste management plant in Dagenham or to Peak's gym before heading home in the afternoon to his family. It made him a lot easier to follow. The police helicopter with a long-range camera also helped the Newham crime squad keep tabs.

While Hunt was followed around London and Essex, Mac contacted a new agency set up to tackle the UK's leading criminals. He wanted the Serious Organised Crime Agency (SOCA) to take over the operation. It was a reasonable move but one that would annoy senior officers back at Scotland Yard because it made them look ineffective.

SOCA had been set up in April 2006 as the latest effort to create a British-style FBI. It combined police and customs investigators – who had no love and a lot of mistrust for each other – with Revenue and Immigration inspectors and the National Criminal Intelligence Service. Former spies from MI5 and MI6 were drafted in to add an oversight function and bring fresh thinking to crime fighting. SOCA was supposed to deal with Level 3 organised crime groups. These were defined as 'loose networks' of capable criminals, some bonded by blood, with 'a cluster of subordinates, specialists and disposable associates.' After a secret briefing from Mac in early November 2006, a SOCA analyst began pulling together all the available intelligence on the Hunt crime family under the codename Operation Delux. An early assessment noted that they were 'too big' for Scotland Yard.

On 6 November, Mac briefed his team that the time had come for the Long Fella and his older brother to be arrested for threats, blackmail and grievous bodily harm. He delighted in emailing senior intelligence chiefs back at the Yard that SOCA was now on board. The next morning the Newham crime squad knocked on the door of a large detached house with a gravel drive in Hornchurch, Essex. Stevie Hunt let them in and then sat impassively on his living room couch reading the newspaper with his feet up throughout the search of his immaculate family home. Downstairs, detectives found mortgage agreements and development plans associated with his rental business, Property Investments UK Limited.[5] Upstairs were trophies of success: a signed shirt from West Ham and England footballer Joe Cole, a signed pair of world heavyweight champion Joe Frazier's boxing shorts, photographs with British middleweight champion Nigel Benn and a silver knuckleduster in the bedside drawer.

Over in Great Hallingbury, Mac was waiting for Davey Hunt to get a fair distance from the Morleys before making a hard stop on his Bentley at a bend in the country road. Another car blocked it from behind while detectives rushed to the driver's side, one of them brandishing a pickaxe handle threatening to smash the window if Hunt didn't open up. The Long Fella calmly complied. And, while being cuffed, he politely requested that the detectives wait thirty minutes until his children left for school before searching the house. Mac agreed and sent Hunt to join his brother for questioning at Dagenham police station. It was notable how long it took detectives to drive from the large wrought iron gates at the entrance to the Morleys to the front door, where Hunt's wife asked them to think about her white carpets and remove their shoes.

Tina Hunt, the daughter of a retired police officer, was as polite and calm as her husband during the search

[5]During the search in November 2007 detectives found business cards for Christopher P Carle, business development manager for Property Investments UK Limited and co-director since 2003. Eight years later, Carle was found dead at home in March 2011. An inquest recorded a verdict of suicide by hanging and heard 56-year-old Carle had mounting debt, poor health and problems over access to his daughter. (*Epping Forest Guardian* 24 June 2011). However, his brother posted on the internet that Carle had borrowed money from Stevie Hunt that he couldn't pay back.

and even revealed the location of a safe in the upstairs
bathroom. Inside were wads of cash, jewellery and a
letter from an inmate called Franny that mentioned
police corruption. It meant nothing to Mac, who ensured
the letter was forwarded to the anti-corruption squad.[6]
He then drove from Hunt's mansion to a notorious
country club in Abridge, Essex that the Long Fella had
bought for £3 million.

The Epping Forest Country Club was, for much of the
nineties, an infamous hangout for the violent, high
on their own supply Essex drug gangs and glitterati
from the worlds of sport and light entertainment. It
once had a more discerning clientele. In the seventies,
England and West Ham United captain Bobby Moore
bought it with Sean Connery as a private members'
club called Woolston Hall. But the venue fell out of
fashion and at the turn of the decade Peter Pomfrett,
a local property developer, picked it up cheaply and
made it into a riotous, cash-spinning, clubbing goliath
for Essex.

Billy Allen was a close business friend of Pomfrett
at the time and Allen remarked that Pomfrett was no
gangster, just a developer with a few local 'councillors
in his pocket.' However, through the nightclub game
Pomfrett started mixing with the leading criminals who
were bringing in ecstasy, cocaine and cannabis through
the largely unguarded Essex coastline.

---

[6]Mac said he was later told that the anti-corruption squad had lost the Franny
letter. Hunt's eldest son, David junior, told detectives during the search of the
Morleys that Joe Calzaghe's boxing belt was a personal gift to his father from the
world super middleweight champion.

The Country Club and Pomfrett soon caught the attention of the police, especially after the triple murder of three drug dealing regulars. The December 1995 shooting of Tony Tucker, Pat Tate and Craig Rolfe, the so-called Essex Boys, has entered gangster folklore as the defining crime of the ecstasy era. The men – a gang of steroid-using bullies and drug abusers who used the Epping Forrest Country Club as their office and playground – were the victims of a contract killing. A debate still rages over whether the police acted corruptly to put away the wrong shooters, and who in the Essex underworld put up the contract.

The drug violence at the Epping Forest Country Club continued after the departure of the Essex Boys and the security running the door became embroiled in tit-for-tat murders and further allegations of police corruption.[7] Such heaviness was way out of Pomfrett's league, but through a mutual friend, car dealer Michael Palmer, he was introduced to Davey Hunt. It was Pomfrett who Hunt claimed had loaned him £100,000 on a 'gentleman's

[7]In October 1999, Darren Pearman, a member of a firm of Caning Town drug dealers, was stabbed and died following a massive fight with bouncers at the Epping Forest Country Club. Ron Fuller, one of the bouncers involved in the fight, was shot dead the following year.

The 2002 Tiberius report on Scotland Yard corruption in north and east London found that officers were moonlighting for a security company that was the target of an organised crime unit investigation. Two officers, Julian Connor and Simon Pinchbeck, were reported to have lobbied the detective inspector running the operation to suggest that security boss Kevin Camp was a good man and didn't need the attention as he was pitching for a big contract. The Yard started a corruption operation into Connor and in January 2001 discovered he was also making inquiries about Lee Manning who had been stabbed at the Epping Forest Country Club. Topguard Security, Camp's company, had the door contract for the club at the time.

agreement' to help buy the Soho brothel at Green's Court in 1995. A year later, Palmer was in business with Hunt in the car showroom in Chigwell, Essex where Paul Cavanagh's face was later slashed.

The police suspected that Hunt was a silent partner in the Epping Forest Country Club, if not on paper then through some informal arrangement with Pomfrett, whose name kept cropping up on the police bugs inside the car showroom. The club was eventually closed in 2002 under police pressure and competition from other Essex venues. Pomfrett, then forty-nine, wanted to sell up and retire having netted £25 million from an international VAT fraud.[8]

The Long Fella always wanted to own the club outright, which he saw as a 'great cash business'. And in August 2005, Hunt's (UK) Properties Limited bought it and the surrounding golf course for over £3 million, which was paid to Bullwood Limited, Pomfrett's offshore Isle of Man family trust. Hunt had big plans to restore the venue to former upmarket glory – a restaurant and members room – with a fancy club and bar that kept the cash rolling in. Pomfrett had neglected the golf course but Hunt restored it, realising that as well as getting off their faces, patrons also paid well for another type of round. This latest asset in Hunt's empire was renamed Woolston Manor Golf and Country Club, and when the Newham crime

[8]On 6 September 2007, Peter Pomfrett was required to make a statement about the £100,000 loan because Hunt's offshore company Galleons Reach Limited was under investigation by the Jersey authorities. Pomfrett was also under investigation for the VAT fraud and on 23 January 2008 was jailed for ten years reduced on appeal to eight. On 9 December 2013 he was ordered to repay £3.3 million or serve a further seven years in prison.

squad raided it after arresting the Long Fella that day in November 2006, detectives found forty cases of stolen Bollinger champagne which was traced to a recent lorry hijack.

A 36-year-old woman, said to be Hunt's mistress, was arrested at the club and taken to Dagenham police station. Kelli Love was no gangster's moll. She'd had an enterprising career as a legal executive at an east London solicitor's firm where hard work, people skills and cunning made her a formidable defender of criminals in need.[9] As well as part-time manager of the golf club, Hunt had given Love the lease for his Soho brothel on very favourable terms. She was a cut above the women the Long Fella usually consorted with, and the Newham crime squad made sure that his wife knew about it. [10]

[9]Kelli Love previously worked for solicitor Erica Peat who represented detective constable Paul Goscomb. He was suspected of corruption along with his former Stoke Newington colleague Martin Morgan. Goscomb had just come off the organised crime task force responsible for targeting David Hunt in Operation Blackjack. Goscomb was discharged at trial and faced disciplinary proceedings. (See *Untouchables*)

[10]Operation Blackjack passed financial intelligence on Hunt's offshore companies and Soho interests to Westminster Council and the Inland Revenue. The council moved to compulsory purchase 2 Green's Court after a shooting incident at the brothel in January 1999. There had been 55 crime reports including firearms, blackmail, threats to kill and murder in the previous two years. Hunt claimed he was unaware of the prostitution and promised renovation works to convert the building to a residential property. The council agreed to back off but the property remained a better-looking brothel under a new lease Hunt gave to Kelli Love. She paid some of the rental income to Galleons Reach Limited (GRL), his Jersey-based company. The Inland Revenue asked Hunt about the relationship between the Jersey company and Hunt's Iron & Steel in the UK. He admitted he was the beneficial owner of GRL and in 2003 reached a second sweetheart tax deal. This time Hunt offered to pay £70,000 in back taxes from 1995 to 2002 for the offshore company and a £30,000 fine. The taxman accepted his terms.

With just five years of service, 31-year-old constable Paul Clark was the least experienced member of the Newham crime squad but had been given the prize of interviewing two of the most significant and menacing crime figures in the UK. The opportunity was part of Mac's style of mentoring young crime fighters by letting them learn on the job. Clark, it would be fair to say, was both elated and shitting himself at the prospect.

Stevie Hunt made no comment during the interview at Dagenham police station. But just before it started, he speculated about what might happen to Billy Allen, the complainant. 'He'll probably end up hanging over a gate with something in his head. He has lots of enemies. It won't be me. I'll be having dinner with my solicitor in Bermuda,' a police log recorded him saying.

Davey Hunt was even more intimidating and Clark would never forget the menace that the Long Fella exuded while he swabbed the inner walls of his mouth for DNA. Before the interview started Hunt had prepared a statement in which he claimed never to have met or spoken to Allen but confirmed his presence at court in February. This, he said, was at the invitation of Matthews, a family friend, but Hunt denied any involvement in violence or threats. He also denied any knowledge of the stolen champagne found at Woolston Manor.[11]

Clark decided he was going in hard with the Long Fella.

---

[11]Kelli Love had done the same during her interview and detectives would shortly receive a statement from another 'family friend' of the Hunts who stepped up to take the blame. In a statement dated 10 November 2006, Tommy Carr, a manager at Woolston Manor, claimed that four months earlier, coincidentally just after the lorry hijack, he bought the Bollinger and other alcohol for cash from an unnamed man who appeared at the golf club.

'You're a murderer, aren't you Mr Hunt?'

'No comment sir.'

'That's what Chic Matthews called you. A murderer. He said he wouldn't spit on you if you were on fire because you had killed his best mate?'

Hunt looked annoyed but still made no comment allowing Clark to press his advantage further and read out a passage from Paul Cavanagh's witness statement.

'You slashed this man's throat and paid him to withdraw his evidence, didn't you Mr Hunt?'

'No comment, Sir,' he repeated, no doubt on the advice of his solicitor from the central London firm where Kelli Love also worked.[12]

After a few more questions, Clark concluded the interview and turned off the tape. This, he claimed, was the moment that the Long Fella opened up.

'I've only been nicked because of who I am. I know you lot have got the hump with me.' It was a comment that Clark interpreted as a reference to the failed Operation Blackjack.

Returning to the court incident, Hunt said, 'When we show our faces it stops. It's all about respect. A deal was done. No violence just let the case run and then they bring heavies. What can I do? They brought it on. When I give my word I stick to it.'

That night, Mac was in his local pub with members of a community action group who met regularly to discuss planning decisions for the area. He had slipped out to make a call and on his way back into the pub bumped

[12]David Phillips and Partners

into a neighbour who was clearly drunk and struggling to find his phone.

'You whacked Davey Hunt today. It was you, wasn't it?' the neighbour slurred.

The comment alarmed Mac. He had always suspected that his neighbour knew the Hunts through the car business and this seemed to confirm it. Mac's team had deliberately not identified themselves by name or police station as a protective measure against any possible compromise. They used their warrant numbers instead, although one detective had slipped up during the raid on Woolston Manor and mentioned Mac's surname in front of Kelli Love.

'Are you saying I've got a problem?' the detective asked his neighbour, who immediately downplayed his comment and left with his wife. It was now 9.30 p.m. and Mac spoke to a member of his team who said the Hunts had not long been bailed from Dagenham police station. He then called his superintendent who arranged for a police car to remain outside his home. Over the next forty-eight hours Mac documented his concern that the Hunts knew where he lived and would approach him at home with a corrupt offer to compromise the case against them. The report was sent to the new borough commander at Newham and Scotland Yard's anti-corruption squad, the Directorate of Professional Standards (DPS).

The DPS has several arms, the most covert of which was at the time called the Intelligence Development Group (IDG) or, as regular officers called it, 'the dark side'. It operated in the shadows, collating intelligence from informants, phone taps and probes on potentially corrupt officers which was stored on a standalone database, the CLue2 system.[13] The IDG ran a check on Mac and the Hunts. There was ample intelligence on the Long Fella going back to the mid-eighties. Mac's entry included a number of occasions when he had reported corruption allegations to the IDG. There was also the old intelligence on the saga over the apology he'd received from a senior officer for blocking his transfer to the Flying Squad.

The IDG concluded that there was 'no proof' to support any concerns about Mac's integrity. But it found the potential threat of compromise was real because the Hunt organised crime group had 'targeted officers who have investigated them in the past.' The IDG report said: '[SOCA also] had concerns around possible corrupt officers in the Metropolitan Police Service and other forces as well as solicitors involved with [the] Hunt brothers.'[14]

They had been released on bail while prosecutors considered whether there was sufficient evidence to charge them with blackmail and threats against Allen. Clark wanted to secretly record the brothers when they next reported to the police station in case they made any more threats or incriminating comments off tape. In the application for authority he wrote: 'The [police] should act to prevent the honest people within the community

[13]Some IDG intelligence went back to the original operation that came out of the probes put into various business premises, including Terry Sabine's Portacabin, on the Silvertown strip during the early nineties. The quality of intelligence held on the CLue2 system ranged from an A1 rating – an 'always reliable' source whose information was 'known to be true without reservation' – which usually meant a phone tap or a bug, to D5, where the source was regarded as 'unreliable' and the information 'suspected to be false or malicious'
[14]IDG report 9 January 2007.

from being victim to the intimidating tactics employed by this subject and his criminal associates. People within this community fear this subject and are afraid to ask police for assistance ... The geographical area where this group of individuals are currently operating fall within the Olympic development zone. There is a real risk that they will bring high levels of organised crime to the fore in the coming years whilst the sites are being developed ... Having a major criminal organisation in close proximity to the Olympics development site could have an adverse economic implication for the UK economy.'

The application was refused by the new hierarchy at Newham who felt the crime squad should be more concerned with less ambitious targets, such as burglary and robbery more in line with Sir Robin Wales' policing priorities as mayor. It didn't help that Mac had just been transferred on promotion as a detective chief inspector to Enfield in north London. He was allowed to keep control of the Hunt and Matthews cases, but was not given any extra resources when, in late November 2006, the Crown Prosecution Service charged Chicky Matthews junior with conspiracy to handle stolen goods and conspiracy to steal. Junior was remanded to prison where his phone calls were monitored and revealed his concerns about the evidence.

Meanwhile, in December support came from the Regional Asset Recovery Team (RART), which was concerned with money laundering and clawing back the proceeds of crime from serious villains. They wanted to look at the Hunts and the Matthews. Mac admitted to RART that the financial investigators at Newham were unable to scratch more than the surface of the two families' finances.[15] The boss of RART responded: 'These sort of people were it seems to me to be the very people the Proceeds of Crime Act and the money laundering legislation associated with it were made for.' Mac replied that it was 'nice to find someone at last who is interested. I've held numerous briefings to no effect,' he wrote.[16]

When Kelli Love was arrested at Woolston Manor, detectives searching her desk found a book called *Judas Pig* by Horace Silver, published in 2004. It soon emerged that this thinly veiled account of life with Davey Hunt was

---

[15]The police believed that Stevie Hunt was involved with fourteen pubs and nightclubs across Essex and the Matthews had properties in Dubai, Spain and had recently purchased a £1.8m building in Canning Town, none of which appeared to tally with the published company accounts.

[16]RART's covert investigation into Davey Hunt led to Jersey where his accountant was being prosecuted for money laundering. Peter Michel had set up Galleons Reach Limited in 1995 for Hunt to own his Soho brothel offshore. Between 1993 and 2001, £5.6 million in cash was made available to fifty-two of Michel's clients. He bought them properties and laundered dirty or taxable cash by 'layering' it in and out of a pooled client account. He also administered companies for art dealers and those in the music and construction businesses. Michel would submit false invoices to reduce their profits and therefore the tax payable in the UK. He then provided the clients with their untaxed cash. This was done as part of what the prosecution called a 'standing arrangement' for delivering clean cash in a briefcase to clients in England. Michel charged 95p per £100 plus his flight for moving in total over £1 million in cash from Jersey to London this way. He pleaded guilty to four of ten counts and was jailed for six years. Almost £10 million was confiscated as the proceeds of his crimes.

In 2009, Michel successfully appealed his 2007 conviction. The appeal court expressed 'deep dismay' about the nature and number of interventions by the trial judge in Jersey. However, they said the evidence against Michel was 'overwhelming'. He had almost served his sentence and declined a retrial. He never 'rolled over' against his clients. A Jersey cop who investigated Michel said he was 'too frightened'.

the work of Jimmy Holmes, whose *nom de plume* mixed a childhood nickname with a nod to his Soho mentor.

Since fleeing to the US, the avant-garde gangster alighted on a literary plan to get Hunt imprisoned or killed by revealing some of their allegedly joint exploits at the expense of others. After three years writing, Holmes snuck back to the UK to deliver the manuscript with revenge in his heart and clarity of purpose in his mind. The book title refers to a sow that hunters use to infiltrate a herd of wild pigs so they can find and kill them. The book was intended to be the sow that led the police and vengeful villains to Hunt's door. Holmes later described *Judas Pig* rather sardonically as 'a love letter from me to him.'

Mac had asked Clark to find Holmes but there was no trace of him until the discovery of the book. On 3 January 2007 the virtually retired gangster called the Newham crime squad detective in response to a message Clark had left with his publisher. Both men were very cagey at first for different reasons. Clark didn't know if it was really Holmes or someone from Hunt's mob. For his part, Holmes still mistrusted the police for trying to trap him ten years earlier into telling them what he knew about the still unsolved murder in Epping Forest of Terry Gooderham and Maxine Arnold. Holmes came straight to the point.

'What's it about?'

'I'm looking at David and his brother.'

'What for?'

'GBH, witness intimidation and blackmail.'

'I'm surprised he's still at it with the money he's got. What do you want from me?'

'To meet.'

'No way, the last time old Bill tried to stitch me up.'

Clark tried another approach. 'Your book claims Mr Hunt was responsible for several murders. Can you give me some names?'

Holmes thought about it then claimed to Clark that Hunt had once admitted shooting a well-known Canning Town face in 1982 and was forever worried about his DNA being found.

Clark thanked Holmes for his time, knowing that as soon as he hung up, the dandy gangster was in the wind.[17]

[17]Nicky Gerard was the son of Kray henchman, Alfie Gerard. Nicky was said to be a contract killer who murdered Tony Zomparelli in 1974 for killing Ronnie Knight's brother. Nicky Gerard was murdered in Canning Town on 25 June 1982. Tommy Hole and his son Kevin were suspected but only Tommy was charged and acquitted of the murder. Kevin Hole was jailed five years later with his father-in-law Chic Matthews senior for the drug factory in Canning Town and killed himself in prison. Tommy Hole was shot dead in December 1999 in Newham. Matthews was rumoured to be behind the hit because he and Tommy Hole had argued over compensation for Kevin. Another rumour was that Tommy Hole was the victim of a revenge shooting for getting away with the killing of Nicky Gerard. Jimmy Holmes told the Newham crime squad that Davey Hunt admitted taking up the contract to kill Gerard because he had once run him out of a party when he was a teenager. Hunt was never arrested for the murder. Clark sent his DNA to the police laboratory at Clapham police station but it was lost for two weeks. When it was relocated there was no match with any DNA found in the Gerrard case. Hunt denies any involvement in murders.

10

Estocada

In late January 2007, the 'dark side' of Scotland Yard's anti-corruption squad received an extraordinary tip-off that the Long Fella had asked a corrupt officer to 'lose' the police file on one of his associates, a former Sniper.[1]

The tip had three specific elements. Firstly, that the corrupt officer was called Dave; secondly that he was a chief inspector at Romford police station due to retire in fifteen months; and thirdly, the file had to be lost by 7 February.

The 'dark side' or Intelligence Development Group (IDG) were immediately alerted and, for no discernible reason, instantly fingered detective chief inspector Dave McKelvey as their man. The simplest of checks would have shown that Mac was not at Romford and was not due to retire. Further research would have revealed that it was one of his cherished cases under threat of compromise.[2]

---

[1] Billy Jacobs.

[2] Financial enquiries arising out of an investigation into Paul Monk had led to Billy Jacobs, a former Sniper and friend of the Hunts. These were the case papers that it was said had to be lost.

Newham crime squad detectives had arrested Paul Monk for the importation of almost one ton of cannabis from Spain. The former Canning Town lorry

Internal documents show the IDG was still strongly
pushing the line that Mac was likely to be the Long Fella's
man on the inside. But detective inspector Jason Tunn, the
anti-corruption officer tasked with developing this theory,
wasn't convinced. Tunn soon identified the officer at
Romford and discovered that he was potentially vulnerable
to a corrupt approach because of his connections in the
Essex pub trade, where the Hunts were very active.[3]

In July 2007, Tunn submitted a closing report that gave
Mac a clean bill of health. It was the second time in the
last six months that he'd been secretly investigated and
exonerated. Clearly, though, someone or some faction
within the anti-corruption squad was predisposed to
thinking Dave McKelvey was at best not right, and at
worst, corrupt.

While all these secret manoeuvres in the dark were taking
place, Mac, Guntrip and Clark had to deal with some

---

hijacker had disguised the drugs in dehumidifiers and bricks, which detectives
seized from a lorry parked in an Essex industrial estate. But Monk's first
trial was abandoned when SOCA revealed that Kevin Cressey, a well-known
criminal, was following jurors to make corrupt or threatening approaches.
Cressey had form for working with corrupt detectives. John Donald, a regional
crime squad detective had offered to lose the case papers in Cressey's own trial
in the early nineties. The criminal agreed but also approached BBC Panorama
journalists who secretly filmed Donald asking Cressey for money. The
documentary broadcast in September 1993 led to a major corruption probe.
(See *Untouchables*).

Mac persuaded the judge to order jury protection for Paul Monk's retrial.
Monk was jailed for nine years in March 2007. While on parole he fled to Spain
in 2013 but was brought back and jailed in March 2017 for 18 years following
another massive drug importation.

[3]The officer retired unaware of the DPS's interest and without any related
disciplinary or criminal charges against him.

surprising developments of their own. Chic Matthews had
immediately appealed the June 2006 ruling rejecting his
adverse possession claim. His solicitor was now claiming
that the Newham crime squad had been 'deliberately
impartial' against his client. The strong inference being
made to the appeal court was of a corrupt relationship
between the police and Billy Allen that went back to his
role as an informant against Matthews during the drug
factory operation in the nineties.

The criticism prompted Mac to take the highly unusual
step in February 2007 of writing directly to the lead judge
who was about to hear the appeal. Lord Neuberger was
left under no illusion that good evidence of organised
crime had been discovered at the Matthews family's
storage business on the disputed land; that Allen only
came forward after the police raid on that business; that
a separate force took the threat to Allen's life seriously
enough to issue a formal Osman warning and finally,
that neither Chic Matthews or his son had made a formal
complaint.

Nevertheless, in March 2007, the appeal court
overturned the previous decision by the Kingston judge
and accepted that Matthews *was* entitled to adverse
possession, although the three judges said they were left
with 'the strong impression that neither side has told the
whole story.' Allen said he felt 'fucked wholesale' by the
decision and immediately lodged an appeal to the Law
Lords, the highest court in the country.

Matthews, meanwhile, had another result a few weeks
later when in late March the Crown Prosecution Service
said there was insufficient evidence to prosecute him or
the Hunt brothers for intimidation, blackmail and threats
over the land. Prosecutors felt, not unreasonably, that

Allen's criminal record, the lack of CCTV evidence of the actual fight and a refusal by Woollard and his men to make statements made a successful prosecution unlikely.

When Mac heard the news he wrote a melodramatic entry in the log. 'It is now clear that Hunt and his criminal network have effectively won the day and stand not only to avoid prosecution but also see a substantial profit from the adverse possession proceedings ... We've made every effort to identify the significance of this case to senior management and failed. There is little that can be done.'

The Newham crime squad still had the Aladdin's den case against Chicky Matthews junior for the stolen items found in containers at 1-7 Brunel Street. That evidence, they believed, was unassailable. But it too was about to fall by the wayside in some very murky circumstances that left the strong impression a much darker agenda was at work.

In late February 2007, Billy Allen passed Mac some, if true, alarming information from one of his Canning Town contacts. It concerned a meeting that had apparently taken place on a boat in Spain. Rumours were circulating that Hunt and the notorious armed robber Micky McAvoy were there to discuss the assassination of two unidentified individuals. A man called Carl Robinson was said to have taken up the contract for £1 million and the person telling Allen all this was afraid that he was one of the targets for having introduced the property developer to Danny Woollard. Allen consulted Terry Sabine, who believed that at such a high price the targets were more likely to be senior members of the Adams crime family from north London who, he said, had fallen out with the Hunts over the Silvertown land.[4]

Mac tried to verify the claim of a contract to kill by speaking directly with Allen's source and also with Woollard, who added his voice to what now looked like an echo chamber of criminals repeating the same information. Mac was sceptical and recorded in a log that the £1 million price tag seemed 'excessive and unusual'.[5] He had no reason to believe the alleged contract posed any danger to him or his men, especially Guntrip, who was busy preparing for Chicky Matthews junior's trial, which was due to start in late September. However, all that changed when new intelligence came in from someone unconnected with the Allen circle.

The source was a man who appeared to be plumbed into the heart of Hunt's operation. Eastwood (a pseudonym) was a jump-up merchant and burglar who'd recently been arrested in Newham. As a long-standing police informant he wanted to trade bail for information on a massive drug deal that he claimed was about to go down by the Long Fella's waste recycling plant in Dagenham.

[4]There was a ring of truth to the idea of an inter crime family feud. A detective targeting the Adams had recently briefed Mac that paperwork found during a raid on a firm of Essex accountants linked Tommy Adams to the Silvertown strip. Separately, the police suspected that Steve Bryant, an Adams family enforcer, was behind the recent attempted murder of one of Hunt's men over a £250,000 debt. He was never charged with the offence.

[5]Police intelligence, said Mac, confirmed that Micky McAvoy was living in Spain after his release from a 25-year prison sentence for the 1983 Brink's-Mat gold bullion robbery. And 30-year-old Carl Robinson, a target of Scotland Yard's specialist Trident and Murder Suppression teams, was linked to firearms, drugs, kidnapping, attempted murder and contract killing.

Mac passed the information to Shaun Sawyer, the director of intelligence at Scotland Yard, and other relevant senior officers.

Detective constable Paul Clark was unable to debrief the prisoner and SOCA didn't want to show their interest in the Hunt gang, so it was agreed that Mac would take down whatever Eastwood had to say. It was a lot. Over a two-hour debrief in front of two other detectives, Eastwood claimed that a large cocaine shipment was arriving imminently in Dagenham and offered to introduce an undercover officer to the players. The prisoner also claimed that drugs were stored in a pigeon loft on Hunt's jetty near the recycling plant and in a secret hole under the trampoline in the gardens of his mansion.[6] The level of detail helped persuade Mac of Eastwood's credibility. 'He had no idea that the [detective] sitting in front of him and who he was telling all this to had been to the Morleys and the waste plant. He didn't know who I was.'

Eastwood's second big claim was that Hunt had corrupt police contacts, some of whom he nurtured at Woolston Manor Golf and Country Club. The informant partially identified two by their first names and where they worked. A third was fully identified and said to tip-off Hunt about any police raids. Eastwood, however, saved the best for last, a bombshell that would have repercussions far beyond what he could ever have imagined. Mac scribbled furiously as the informant unpacked the following story. Hunt, he claimed, had put up a £1 million contract to kill three corrupt police officers who had taken his money but failed to assist over a Turkish heroin deal.

Eastwood identified the hitman as Carl 'the Dread' Robinson, who he claimed was under time pressure to complete the contract killing and was staking out one of

[6]This allegation was never investigated or otherwise corroborated.

the targets who worked at Stratford police station and
drove a Silver 52, 53 or 54 Plate Ford Mondeo. The other
two police targets had moved from Stratford but their
location was known, Eastwood claimed. Mac felt a 'cold
shudder' as he left the police interview room to call Clark.
    'Are you at home?'
    'No, we're still on the search Guv.'
    'Have you been driving a silver plate Mondeo?'
    'Yeah. A 53 plate, why? How's the debrief going?
    Mac asked Clark to pass the phone to his sergeant,
Jim Madden, who was explained the unfolding situation.
Returning to the interview room, Mac asked Eastwood if
it was possible that the contract was not on three corrupt
police officers but on three honest ones who'd taken on
Hunt? Eastwood couldn't say but later took the detectives
to an address where he said 'the Dread' stored his weapons
and pointed out his Range Rover. Though alarmed that
the Newham crime squad might be the real targets, Mac
calmly updated Shaun Sawyer, the Yard's director of
intelligence, about the chilling development. 'It appears
that this relates to three police officers. There is specific
intelligence about potential targets. There are also links
to named corrupt officers,' he wrote requesting an urgent
meeting.[7]
    Mac and Clark were looking for reassurance. Either
way, three corrupt or honest officers could be under
threat from a known hitman and a violent crime boss.

---

[7]Mac also sent SOCA a report on Eastwood. It prompted his old handler to
call and counsel caution because the informant's reliability had been recently
questioned. Mac later found out that Scotland Yard had mounted an operation
in April 2006 to foil a supposed plot to kidnap the children of model Katie
Price and singer Peter Andre based on Eastwood's information, but it had come
to nothing.

Surely someone in the upper ranks would take control of
such a situation, they thought, but no intelligence chief
would make the time. Meanwhile, as with all the other
corruption allegations connected with the Hunts and
Matthews, Mac reported what Eastwood had said to the
Directorate of Professional Standards (DPS). The matter
was passed to an ambitious new detective inspector at the
anti-corruption squad who would soon become Mac's
nemesis.

Ashfaq Siddique is a man of many faces. Until recently,
he had been a core sergeant at SO10, the undercover unit,
where some of the Yard's darkest secrets are locked away.
Siddique had excelled at infiltrating dangerous criminals
in the UK and abroad since joining SO10 in 1992.
However, his departure from the undercover unit was an
unhappy one.

The experience of being arrested and released without
charge in 2002 for the murder of his niece's boyfriend
rankled with the undercover officer, who sued Scotland
Yard for racial discrimination claiming detectives
wrongly assumed it was an honour killing. His claim
also spoke of wider racism in the police and the loss of
trust his father, a Muslim community leader, now had in
Scotland Yard and the government's anti-radicalisation
strategy. The Yard initially fought the discrimination
claim but suddenly settled in 2006 and paid Siddique
a large sum of money. However, he never returned to
the undercover unit after admitting lying to his boss.[8]

---

[8]Siddique's 16-year-old niece had run away to Bournemouth with Rexhap
Hassani, her 21-year-old boyfriend, in 2002. To get time off to search for her,
Siddique lied to DCI Martin Smith, his SO10 boss, and to colleagues, that his

Perhaps as a show of trust, Siddique was instead allowed
to transfer to another highly secretive unit, the anti-
corruption squad.

Before his arrival at the DPS office in Ilford, Siddique
served briefly at Stratford in early 2006 when Mac was
still there. The two men weren't friends, but on his way to
seeing him, Mac felt he would get a sympathetic hearing
from the anti-corruption officer because of his own recent
experience with senior management. Siddique certainly
listened, and at the end of the meeting told Mac to have
nothing more to do with Eastwood because the DPS were
going to debrief him. On his way back to the Yard, Mac
felt a little better until a senior officer called to say he
should fill out a formal Osman warning of a threat to life
for himself, Guntrip and Clark. It felt insulting that no
one at the Yard could even be bothered to risk assess the
situation independently.

Mac turned for advice to a very experienced organised
crime detective who, like so many, was now working in the
counter terrorism command. Detective superintendent
Clive Timmons had previously worked on the Hunts
and Carl 'the Dread' Robinson. They were 'individuals
capable of immense violence ... sophisticated and difficult
criminals,' he emailed Mac. 'I am privileged to be a senior

---

niece had been in a car accident. In his defense, Siddique said he lied because
DCI Smith had allegedly made racist comments behind his back and therefore
was unlikely to be sympathetic.

Another sensitive issue was Siddique's alibi for 15 November 2002, the day
Hassini was kidnapped, asphyxiated and his bound body dumped in a Newham
wasteland. Siddique told murder detectives that at the time he was in a SO10
safe house in east London and then turned his phone off during dinner with a
female officer. Mushtaq Ahmed, the brother of Siddique's wife, was eventually
jailed in October 2003 for killing his daughter's boyfriend.

detective in the organisation who has the misfortune of classing you as a friend. Our staff are our most valuable asset ... Until the intelligence is proved, disproved or discredited I feel there is a clear obligation.'

The senior management's lack of reaction made Mac reflect on how the organisation viewed him after twenty-five years of loyal service, from a young constable with his own surveillance van to a detective chief inspector still caring about cases that had grief rather than promotion written all over them. In Mac's mind he was a vocational detective. The organisation, however, seemed to see him more as a loose cannon.

'I sometimes hark back to the old days,' he wrote to Timmons. 'I have no doubt 10-15 years ago the regional crime squad or the task force at Ilford would have immediately been all over these individuals and had them in custody by the morning. I find it very sad and depressing that this is what we have come to! I've spoken to Ash Siddiq[ue] on the dark side and some of his boys. Why do they remind me of the Dementors from Harry Potter with their air of menace ... Anyway I am now going to bed having had no sleep for two days.'

Gold groups are usually set up at Scotland Yard when a matter poses a serious risk to the force's reputation. On Friday 21 September 2007, eighteen senior officers from a range of specialist departments – Trident, the Projects Team, Specialist Intelligence Section, witness protection and the anti-corruption squad – sat around the table to discuss their McKelvey problem. SOCA was briefed separately. Mac was delighted when he found out about the meeting, and hoped to finally explain the complex background to the intelligence that he had first received from Allen's sources and now from Eastwood. But instead he was excluded.

Commander Rod Jarman chaired the Gold meeting. It was an ominous sign because he usually handled cases where an officer was under internal investigation by the DPS. The minutes recorded little of what was discussed, but it was clear that the main decision was to question Mac about his relationship with Allen and why he'd ended up debriefing Eastwood. Suspicion, it seemed, was already being seeded by the DPS that he may have exaggerated the threat to life. The interview took place later that day and was not what Mac expected. Two junior DPS officers aggressively questioned him and appeared to have already formed the view that Allen and Eastwood should have been treated as informants.

Mac was fully aware of the rules for handling informants, which had been brought in during the nineties since many scandals involved corrupt relationships between these tricky individuals and the detectives who recruited, ran and paid them. To prevent this and to protect officers from compromise, source units were created on every borough or specialist squad. These sensitive postings were staffed with officers trained in recruiting and running informants but who had nothing to do with the operational side of policing. In other words, the source unit handlers extracted information from their informants and passed it on for the operational teams of detectives to work up into arrests. This 'sterile corridor' was supposed to protect prosecutions from challenges by the defence that informants had been prompted or induced to secure convictions or for other corrupt purposes.

Victims of crime often gave information, which did not automatically make them an informant as long as they

weren't 'tasked' to find out more. There were provisions
within the rules for this type of police relationship with a
victim of crime, which is what Mac, Guntrip and Clark
believed they were observing in their well-documented
dealings with Allen. In the case of Eastwood, there were
provisions for officers to conduct a one-off 'intelligence
debrief' with a prisoner willing to give information,
usually soon after the arrest. However, the DPS officers
were determined in their belief that those rules had been
broken. Additionally, Mac's two inquisitors accused him
of 'telling too many people' about what Eastwood had
said. He insisted that only senior officers and SOCA
were made aware because officers' lives were potentially
at risk.

Towards the end of the testy interview, Mac refused
to hand over Allen's contact details but agreed to pass
on the request to meet. The DPS already had access to
Eastwood, but still hadn't debriefed him. On the way
back to work, the anger bubbled over and Mac called
Siddique to complain but instead found himself sobbing
uncontrollably to the point he terminated the call and
came off the motorway. It hadn't taken long for a once
confident detective willing to take on Hunt to end up one
now crying alone on the hard shoulder.

Over the weekend, Mac, Guntrip and Clark told their
wives about the possible threat. It was hard to give them
any concrete answers about the risk because it still hadn't
been assessed. Mac was too angry or anxious to sleep. He
could feel the support of his organisation slipping away,
and with it his sense of self. On Monday, his GP prescribed
sleeping pills and anti-depressants. Meanwhile, Guntrip
met with the two barristers about to prosecute Chicky
Matthews junior in one week's time for the Aladdin's den

of stolen items found at his storage business and asked for an adjournment of a few weeks. The prosecutors saw genuine anxiety in Guntrip's delivery when he told them there was intelligence of a contract to kill him, Clark and Mac. They naturally asked for confirmation from a senior officer and when it came the trial was adjourned until the last week of October.

Meanwhile, at a Gold group meeting on 25 September the DPS continued to raise its 'concerns' about how Eastwood and Allen had been handled. At this stage, commander Jarman still didn't see it having any impact on the Matthews trial. However, that view was to radically change over the next six days, thanks to the secret and misleading machinations of the DPS.

By September 2007 a fixed view had formed among senior managers at the DPS that Mac had corruptly handled a number of informants. But where had this view come from, as it was wholly at odds with evidence in the DPS's own files?

Eight months earlier, in January 2007, the DPS had conducted a thorough investigation concluding that Mac 'correctly' passed Allen's information to the borough source unit. More recently, the source units at Newham and the one at the DPS were also consulted and both agreed that Allen was not a Covert Human Intelligence Source (CHIS), in other words an informant, and therefore it was within the rules to deal with him as a witness of crime.

Also, by this time, the DPS had examined the relationship between Mac and Allen partly at the behest of SOCA. The agency wanted to ensure that Delux, its new operation against the Hunts, wasn't the fruit of a

poisoned tree and asked for a health check on Mac. In late
January the DPS had told SOCA there were 'no issues'
with his integrity.[9]

Yet on 1 October 2007, anti-corruption chiefs launched
an investigation into Mac, Guntrip and Clark over their
handling of Allen and Eastwood – the inference being that
they were working corruptly for Allen and had invented
the contract to kill to assist him in some unspecified way.
In case the DPS was wrong about this, it also launched a
parallel investigation into whether the trio were alternatively
really working for Hunt. All the bases were covered, which
on the 'no smoke without fire' principle ensured that Mac
and his two colleagues were now damaged goods.

Siddique was put in charge of the investigation
codenamed Kayu, but with oversight by the highest levels
of the DPS. It could not have escaped those in charge
that going down this route put the Aladdin's den trial
in immediate jeopardy and any other trial involving the
Newham crime squad.

The DPS also briefed the Gold group that the threat
to life was nothing of the sort and didn't even meet
the lowest level to spark a risk assessment. The strong
impression allowed to linger was that Mac had 'monkeyed
up' the threat to life for some still as yet undefined but
more than likely corrupt purpose. It was an extraordinary
impression to push because the DPS had by then

[9]Statements of SOCA officers Paul Owens (30 October 2008) and Steve
Robinson (12 December 2008).

DI Jason Tunn fully reviewed the handling of Allen and Nick Dennett, an
employee of Newham Council, by DCI McKelvey and DCs Guntrip and Clark.
Tunn spoke with the source units at Newham (DI Boyce and DSU Newlands)
and the DPS (DI Clarke). His investigation (Operation Ralftech) concluded in
July 2007 that the guidelines had been correctly observed.

debriefed Eastwood, who confirmed the same details about the contract to kill. Therefore, the worst that could be said was that Mac had a mistaken but genuine belief about who the targets were.

But for some unexplained reason the Gold group was unaware the DPS had spoken to Eastwood so, believing there was no threat, it disbanded – leaving senior DPS managers to continue making decisions in the dark. Even Siddique recorded in his log that senior managers, up to at least deputy assistant commissioner level, were not including him on all decisions impacting on operation Kayu. Nevertheless, two weeks before the Aladdin's den trial was due to start in October 2007, he and his bosses were of one mind that there were 'serious concerns' about Mac's handling of Allen.

It was a view that was hard to justify with no new facts, especially when the facts that the DPS did possess pointed the other way. So why pursue it when the stakes – undermining a major organised crime trial – were so high?

Scotland Yard has long operated a highly discriminatory attitude towards its staff. There are those who get crucified over little or nothing and those they choose to protect or ease out of the organisation without fuss, no matter how compelling the evidence of corruption. The DPS had clearly decided Mac was going to be nailed to the cross. They discovered that a joint bank account with his wife had a £75,000 surplus. The inference of corruption was allowed to linger until the bank explained it was a home improvement loan and they had 'no concerns'. Similar financial checks on Guntrip and Clark raised no red flags.

But with days to go before the Matthews junior Aladdin's den trial started on 25 October it was now being suggested at the top of the DPS that Mac and Guntrip had crossed the line and were acting criminally by perverting the course of justice in deliberately mishandling Allen and manipulating intelligence to assist him. Operation Kayu was no longer just a disciplinary investigation but a criminal one that could result in prison for the three detectives.

Senior DPS management were aware that when shared with the prosecution this view would almost certainly lead to the abandonment of a major organised crime trial. Yet before Siddique began a series of secret briefings of the two barristers prosecuting Chicky Matthews junior he wrote in his decision log on 22 October that there was 'no evidence' the three detectives were in a corrupt relationship with Allen.

In contrast, the presentation given to Tim Cray QC and Angus Bunyon had the air of a matador in the *tercio de muerto,* the death stage of a bullfight. A good *estocada,* when the matador plunges his sword between the bull's shoulders directly into the heart, should result in a quick kill. A bad *estocada* leaves the animal floundering and the crowd's bloodlust unsatisfied. Siddique's lethal sword was an eight-page memo and its presentation on 24 October was a quick kill that left the Matthews case for dead and the three Newham crime squad detectives bleeding out.

The memo's opening paragraph said Mac had been 'an officer of concern' to the DPS 'for a number of years'. This alone would raise the anxiety levels of any prosecutor. But it went on to document six recent incidents that made it impossible to carry on. The prosecutors had no way of knowing that those incidents were wrong, inaccurate, exaggerated or misleading. The first incident suggested that Mac had corruptly 'influenced' an investigation into a police colleague accused of a homophobic attack. In fact, he had attended the station as the detained officer's Police Federation representative and acted legitimately and without complaint.

Next, it was suggested that the Eastwood intelligence of a threat to police officers was 'manipulated' to secure the adjournment of the Matthews trial. The prosecutors were not told that DPS's own source unit believed Eastwood had been properly handled.

Then there were the concerns over a failure to disclose the true relationship between the Newham crime squad and several sources of information including Allen who, like Eastwood, should have been treated as informants, the memo suggested. Again, both the DPS and Newham source units did not agree but the prosecutors were not told this.

Although pointing out that operation Kayu was still in its 'infancy' with 'numerous enquiries' to pursue, faced which such a memo that would have to be disclosed to the defence, the two prosecution barristers were left with no choice but to abort the trial. They simply had to take the DPS memo at face value and the logical conclusion was that the main police officers could no longer be put forward as witnesses of truth. On Thursday 25 October 2007 the prosecutors told the judge they were offering no evidence against a grinning Chicky Matthews junior.

'It's all over. They've got the wrong man', the formally acquitted scrap metal dealer predicted, walking past Guntrip on his way out of court. 'The [police] will be in the dock.'

Mac took the week off after the trial was abandoned. On Monday 29 October he lay in bed, too emotionally exhausted to get up. He hoped to be signed off sick with depression by his doctor later in the morning. The phone rang but he couldn't find the energy to answer. However, noises from the front of the house drew him to the window where he saw a group of DPS officers led by Siddique. Half-shaven and in his bathrobe, Mac let them in then shuffled in a daze to his sitting room where he was formally suspended. While the DPS searched the house, he read the official notification saying he was under investigation for perverting the course of justice. Even if his actions turned out not to be criminal his 'unprofessional style of policing is unacceptable,' it said.

In shock, Mac handed over his warrant card, police phones and radio. The denuding moment feared by police officers the world over stripped him of all he had held sacred. When an officer came into the sitting room with a collection of imitation guns, Mac told them they were taken out of the loft to protect his family. 'There's some night vision goggles in the car I use to check the garden for intruders,' he volunteered.

'It's good you are going sick,' Siddique told him. 'Use the time to be with your family and go to the gym and lose weight.'

Mac's wife rushed home, distressed, and put on a united front for the DPS. 'He's a good husband,' she told Siddique, 'and a good detective. I only go on at him because he works too much.'

Meanwhile, at Newham police station, Paul Clark was feeling the same shock as the DPS informed him he was now on restricted duties. It took an enormous struggle not to voluntarily surrender his warrant card and turn his back on his young police career that had already cost him his marriage. Clark had been separated from his wife and

two children for a year, and when not sleeping at Stratford
police station would schlep to his parents' house, a long
train ride away. Now his career was forever blighted.

Darren Guntrip had joined the police in his thirties.
He was still hurting from the collapse of the Matthews
trial. He had put the case together almost singlehandedly, while holding down a recent promotion to the
Flying Squad. 'If I had not wanted the trial to go ahead
I would not have spent eighteen months gathering over
500 statements from 174 witnesses, working night and
day in my own time for no pay in order to get this matter
to trial,' he told his accusers.

As an additional humiliation, after the DPS searched
his desk he was transferred off the Flying Squad to a
research post and put on restricted duties. Days later,
Danny Woollard spotted Guntrip's slumped shoulders
and beckoned him over to his car. 'I hear you're in the
shit, son,' he said to the 41-year-old detective.

From the brief conversation that followed, Guntrip
realised that many in the East End underworld now
believed he had taken a pound note to throw the trial.

'We've all had a few quid in our time,' said Woollard
benevolently, 'I don't blame you.'

The Crown Prosecution Service is supposed to review the
caseload of all officers suspected of serious misconduct
and corruption in the evidence chain to see if any other
trials might have to be dropped. However, only one
other trial involving the three now-tainted detectives
was subsequently abandoned. It, too, involved major
organised crime, the Silvertown strip and a raid on a plot
of land where compelling evidence of luxury cars stolen to
order for overseas export had been discovered.

Danny McGuinness, the defendant in this second trial, was a Newham council contractor who, since his arrest, was threatening to expose a nexus of freemasons, crooked cops, gangsters and council employees wrapped around a very nasty murder in the Olympic Borough. From the outset, Mac had felt an unusual drag slowing down the investigation of McGuinness. Pressure came not just from inside the police but also from the council. And weeks after the Chicky Matthews junior trial was abandoned in October 2007, the DPS also caused the McGuinness trial to be discontinued.

In the midst of his creeping despair, Mac searched for clues among the case papers and a once sharp memory now dulled by anti-depressants that could shed light on the questions torturing him: Why us? Who had I upset? A recollection started to emerge about an unusual incident that had taken place more than two and a half years earlier in March 2005 during a police award ceremony. 'At the time I didn't understand the significance of it, of the characters involved and how it would affect my life.' But the more he chewed on the incident, the more he came to realise that Scotland Yard and Newham council were united by a corruption problem that they had to bury in the run up to the Olympic Games. Furthermore, it dawned on him that the case his team of detectives had built against Danny McGuinness was threatening to unpick the cover-up.

11

Document 522

Pervaz 'Pelé' Mahmood looked like a man with the world on his shoulders as he waited to collect his police award for bravery. It was Friday afternoon on 4 March 2005 and the sports club was full of bantering police officers and officials from Newham council assembled for the borough commander's commendation service. Mahmood was a 'no-nonsense' veteran of the council's Parks Constabulary, which tackled anti-social behaviour, meaning anything from the antics of hooded youths on bikes to moving Travellers off council land.

Mahmood felt his childhood had equipped him for the job. Every day in 1970s Canning Town was about dodging the gauntlet of racist bullies on his way home from school. But sometimes an Asian boy just can't avoid a beating; even one as nimble as Mahmood, who was nicknamed Pelé after the Brazilian footballer. His father had come to the East End from Pakistan in the late fifties and spent most of his working life at the Ford plant in Dagenham. He eventually saved enough to buy a house near Rathbone Street market, brought his wife over and filled it with kids.

Pelé was good enough to try out for West Ham United's youth team but his father forbade a football career to protect his son from the violent racism then plaguing the beautiful game on and off the terraces. So, after a stint as a market trader on his uncle's clothes stall, and as a driver for disabled children, Pelé joined Newham council first as a security guard and two years later transferred to the Parks police when it was set up in 1998.

The unit came under the council's enforcement division, which had a £1.5m budget and was run by former local police officers who answered to Sir Robin Wales, the mayor on a mission to clean up Newham. His Parks police dressed to look like real cops and acted as if they had real police powers, when they possessed no more right to make an arrest than any ordinary civilian. Most of those they stopped and searched didn't know this. A few councillors at the award ceremony were concerned that these so-called 'plastic bobbies' were overstepping the legal mark in a push to make Newham safe and attractive to the International Olympic Committee, whose decision on who got the 2012 Games was just four months away.

The awards were, in part, a public relations offensive, although Pelé's citation was in genuine recognition of his bravery for stopping an assault by a group of men without backup. It was agreed that he could make a short speech after the citation was read out. Pelé started by thanking the Newham police for supporting him over the last seven years. Then, eyeballing his bosses in the enforcement division, he said: 'However, the Parks police is no place for ethnic officers because the management is racist and corrupt.'

The room of mostly police officers erupted in cheers and laughter as Pelé headed for the door while his words ricocheted around the room. One of his bosses was able to intercept him on the way out.

'What was that all about?'

'It wasn't a publicity stunt,' Pelé fired back. 'It was from the heart. My conscience is clear.'

The Newham crime squad were watching the drama unfold from their table. They too were up for an award. The punking of the council had given the alcohol-free ceremony a much-needed boost. 'I didn't even know what the Park's police was,' said Mac. 'We were all laughing.'

At another table, 46-year-old Labour councillor Mike Law had the opposite reaction and was wondering what to do about it. 'Go after him,' urged his wife, who had come to see her Jujitsu-trained husband receive an award for disarming a man with a knife.

Law caught up with Pelé in the car park. He told him about his background in security and how he had 'drifted' into local politics when Sir Robin Wales suggested he become a councillor. The mayor had brought him into the Labour party three years ago but they were no longer allies, as he was one of the few councillors to raise concerns about the Parks police becoming Sir Robin's personal storm troopers, Law explained.

'You're all part of the system. How do I know you'll take me seriously?' said Pelé.

All Law could do was insist his was an independent voice in a Labour stronghold without any effective opposition and he would champion Pelé given the chance. Within a few weeks, the councillor had

interviewed sixteen Parks police officers about the two
principal allegations: corruption and racism. Local
businessmen, it was being alleged, paid bribes to secure
council contracts and a culture of cronyism was also
rife in the enforcement division based on being white,
ex-police and a freemason.

Law tried to raise these damaging claims with Sir Robin
but their meeting, he said, was cancelled. Instead, on the
advice of Asian contacts in the Greater London Assembly
and Scotland Yard, he wrote to Sir Ian Blair, the police
commissioner. A few days later, Law bristled when the
council's chief executive and deputy separately warned
him to back off. They were not accused of corruption
but whatever had happened was on their watch. 'You're
getting into very, very nasty territory,' Law recalled the
deputy telling him.

Undeterred, the councillor went to see Jim Fitzpatrick,
Labour MP for Poplar and Canning Town and gave him
his file of allegations. It incensed Law that Pelé Mahmood
had been suspended immediately after the award ceremony.
Furthermore, those he so publicly accused of corruption
and racism were now investigating themselves while the
suspect contractor relationships continued. Allegations
of racism were particularly sensitive in a borough with
such a high Muslim community. The 5 May 2005 general
election was only weeks away and many constituents
were already angered by the dishonesty behind Tony
Blair's war in Iraq. Newham council was already aware
of the problem in its enforcement division because eight
claims of racial discrimination – with payouts tied to
non-disclosure agreements – had been secretly settled in
the last eight months.

At 7 p.m. the next day Fitzpatrick texted Law with news. He said Wales was 'fuming' but there would be an independent inquiry led by Amanda Kelly, the former head of the council's legal department. She convinced Law of her independence and on 23 May he made a witness statement outlining the allegations of 'corruption, poor management [and] favouritism' in the enforcement division. The rebel councillor warned Kelly to be under no illusion about what she was going up against. The sixteen whistle-blowers, he wrote, had been warned by their bosses about the futility of complaining because 'councillors [were] in their pockets [and] orders had come directly from the chief executive and the mayor.'[1]

Pelé felt good downloading his concerns to Kelly in her makeshift office at Newham town hall. He described how John Page, a retired senior police officer, ran the enforcement division like a fiefdom and favoured two contractors: Drakes, owned by Charlie Butler and DM Security, run by Danny McGuinness.

Both of these men were burly freemasons plugged into the Newham underworld and contracted to remove abandoned, untaxed and stolen cars for destruction at the council pound as part of the general clean-up of the borough. Pelé recalled times when he had reported

[1]The account of the award ceremony and its immediate aftermath is based on interviews with Pelé Mahmood (17 March 2009/11 June 2018) and Mike Law (5 and 12 March 2009, 13 June 2018). In an email exchange with Jim Fitzpatrick on 23 April 2018, the MP said: 'I have vague recollections of several discussions with former Cllr. Law about a number of complaints he had about Newham council but nothing specific.'

Drakes for clamping properly parked vehicles and McGuinness for stealing car parts, only to be told by his bosses to mind his own business. The two contractors also provided a secondary service of removing Traveller and Gypsy caravans off council land. Pelé told Kelly that these so-called land invasions were the most profitable 'fiddle'. Parks would be left unlocked so the caravans could set up camp. The Parks police were sent in but 'mysteriously', he said, the Travellers only moved on when Butler or McGuinness arrived.

Butler had once explained to him how the scam worked. The council paid him £1,200 per caravan, so he would pay £200 to each caravan owner to park up, £400 was kicked back to the enforcement division boss, and the rest he would split with McGuinness.

John Page 'swanned around like he was untouchable', Pelé told Kelly. But the enforcement boss was 'a forward-thinker' and already had a successor groomed for his planned retirement in 2012. Getting on in the enforcement division meant being a yes man, a freemason and an ex-police officer, Pelé alleged. Some ethnic minority Parks police officers could barely speak English or understand the law, he said, but they were employed because it effectively race-proofed the unit while ensuring the white management remained unchallenged.

Like Law, Pelé also warned Kelly that she was taking on something bigger than John Page. 'The basic truth of the matter was this management team were not only racist bullies but were also very corrupt. John Page and his deputies were dealing with convicted criminals who they were awarding council contracts to … Charlie Butler personally told me that he was giving kickbacks to the management team from the money he was earning from the council. Both Charlie and Danny [McGuinness] were well known criminals with nasty tempers who got things sorted ...'[2]

After several hours, Pelé left Kelly's office feeling unburdened. He headed home to await the backlash.

A second whistle-blower from inside Newham council came forward to the Kelly inquiry and corroborated Pelé's kickbacks-for-contracts allegations. Nick Dennett went further and claimed there was a direct relationship between the contractors and the mayor's inner circle. When Dennett joined the council in 1999 as a street enforcement officer he told Kelly the management culture was and remained autocratic and unfair. His bosses were freemasons and some saw him as an oddball and know-it-all as a former City Police and Royal Military police officer with a law degree. He explained that the enforcement division had grown out of the mayor's dissatisfaction with the local police not taking on anti-social behaviour and low-level crime in Newham. John Page was allowed to operate as he saw fit to deliver what his political masters wanted.

Dennett was prone to depression and felt bullied from time to time. Matters escalated, he believed, when he started asking questions about Danny McGuinness and Charlie Butler, the two heavily-built and extensively tattooed contractors with a reputation for violence and getting things done. Dennett was puzzled as to how the two men could get rid of Gypsies and Travellers. They were, he told Kelly, the panacea to all the enforcement division's problems. However, there came a time when

[2]Pelé Mahmood's witness statement 24 July 2012.

Butler appeared to have fallen out of favour because
the contractor once arrived at the council's central
depot livid after learning he'd lost car removal work
to McGuinness. He called Page 'corrupt' and was
threatening to kill him.

Dennett felt unsupported when he tried to raise these
issues within the council. More so, he claimed, after it
became known he had spoken to the Kelly inquiry.[3]

Amanda Kelly finished her report in September 2005,
after the summer of celebration that the Olympics were
coming to London for the first time in fifty-seven years.
She had experienced a lack of cooperation by the managers
in the enforcement division who had also claimed to
have lost officers' notebooks, which were vital to proving
allegations of racism towards Muslim staff and members
of the public. Kelly felt that any racism in the Parks police
needed to be addressed immediately given the rise in racist
attacks on Muslims following the recent 7 July bombings
in London by home-grown jihadists.

More generally, she concluded that the mayor's Parks
police had 'drifted' beyond its remit into 'a private police
force' with 'an almost total absence of management
systems and procedures' and 'a lack of managerial
competence.' The whistle-blowers' perception of a
'culture of favouritism', she said, was supported by 'the
many family and other relationships' in the enforcement
division. This included masonic bonds. Kelly was
concerned that unlike elected members, council officials
didn't have to declare membership of the freemasons, yet

[3]Nick Dennett declined to be interviewed. All quotes are taken from his 2012
employment tribunal witness statement and related sources.

made most of the decisions. Her conclusions undoubtedly scuffed the mayor's Teflon coating. But Sir Robin Wales could withstand them because the more damaging ones, those straying into potential criminal misconduct, were parked in a secret appendix not widely disclosed to elected councillors. Conor McAuley, who was chair of the Labour Group at the time, claimed the executive was also prevented from seeing the full report.

The council's Internal Audit department had reviewed the procurement practices in the enforcement division and reported to Kelly that the evidence was 'tantamount to corruption.' In her report, she found 'almost a complete lack of controls in the procurement process'. Specific contractors, Kelly went on, were used on the basis of 'custom and practice' leaving the council vulnerable to corruption. John Page had claimed to Kelly that he inherited some customs and appeared to put the rest of the blame on 'pressure from the mayor and members to deliver on anti-social behaviour.' Kelly, however, was having none of it and criticised Page for failing to put his house in order and for importing some questionable arrangements of his own. The lack of controls and management failures, she said, were 'exacerbated by the scale of the payments to some contractors and possible relationships between staff and contractors.'

As an example, Kelly reported that John Page and his number three, Dave Gosling, had gone on holiday to New York in March 2004 for St Patrick's Day and stayed at the same hotel as McGuinness. Both said it was 'pure coincidence' and denied that the contractor had paid for them. Separately, Kelly found that Gosling had received two motorbikes from another contractor who won his

contract without any tendering process.⁴ The holiday
to the Big Apple made the enforcement division appear
rotten to the core and Kelly suggested that Page face a
discipline investigation, where someone might even
contact the New York hotel and ask who paid the bill.
However, the council had other ideas and a secret deal
was reached with Page and others to exit by the back door.

Chris Wood, deputy chief executive of Newham
council, announced their departure on 20 September. No
details were given of their severance package. Two weeks
later, Dave Burbage, the chief executive, announced to
the people of Newham that the Kelly report had found
'grounds for optimism'.

Pelé Mahmood couldn't see much beyond darkness.
The fight had taken its toll on his mental health and he
had been briefly hospitalised. It didn't help, he said,
that an internal council communication was doing the
rounds falsely claiming the police had once arrested
him for trying to murder his daughter. Nevertheless, the
Kelly report emboldened Pelé and three others to sue for
racial discrimination and victimisation. Newham council
resisted, but on the steps of the employment tribunal
suggested a secret settlement. Pelé was offered the most
money – £80,000 – to walk away, but was the only one
who declined. 'It was never about the money but getting it
out in the open,' he told the council and pressed ahead with
his claim, which he won.

⁴Dave Gosling told the author that he left the council in July 2005 after twenty
years and was never interviewed by Amanda Kelly. He said he knew of Butler
and McGuiness as contractors but had no real personal dealings with them. He
refused to comment on whether McGuinness paid for the New York holiday.
John Page died in 2017.

Victory, as ever, came at a cost. The career he excelled at was ruined, he was on anti-depressants and 'the stigma of mental illness' would follow him to other jobs, he told himself.[5] Conversely, back at the council's enforcement division little had changed since the Kelly report. Senior managers had left, certainly, but remarkably, going into 2006 Danny McGuinness was still the council's main contractor.

Newham was the first council in the country to exercise new powers to remove untaxed and abandoned vehicles, and at one point up to 2,000 vehicles were being removed every month, many of them by McGuinness.

In the first few weeks of 2006, Mac and his crime squad were asked to tackle the problem of abandoned stolen cars – the Silvertown strip was a particular 'hot spot' – as part of a wider £15 million Home Office initiative, Operation Scrap It.

Detective constable Darren Guntrip was guided towards Nick Dennett as a council employee with an ear to the ground. But he had left the council's enforcement division because of problems with McGuinness and was now at the commercial property division. Dennett gave what information he could but, separately, a source inside DM Security revealed that McGuinness used a Parks police warrant card to steal high-quality cars to order and

[5]Pelé Mahmood won his discrimination case against Newham Council in 2008. Paolo Rodrigues had previously settled for £55,000 and Mick Houghton for £45,000. Pelé said he wanted to go back to work, but changed his mind on discovering that Stewart Walls, a colleague who the tribunal fined £5,000 for racial discrimination, had been reinstated.

some of the vehicles bound for Ghana were stuffed with dirty money belonging to Canning Town criminals.

McGuinness was close to the Bowers and a police report at the time had outlined concerns that Hunt's organised crime group was involved in 'the export of stolen prestige cars out of the UK.' The inside man also claimed that McGuinness sold stolen car parts to buyers that included a masonic lodge of ex-police officers working for the council.

Guntrip set up an observation point overlooking the council yard that McGuinness was allowed to use on the Silvertown strip. Days later, on 6 February 2006, the police arrested him with a large wad of cash and a load of stolen vehicles in the yard. McGuinness also had a Parks police warrant card in his name and two liveried pickup trucks that looked like police vehicles.

'This'll never get to court,' the forty-nine-year-old told detectives as they led him away in handcuffs. 'You'll see.'

Back at the police station, McGuinness made no comment until the tape was turned off, when he continued to hint that he had police and council officials in his corner. The following month the crown prosecution service charged him with the theft of over one hundred cars. Like a town crier, McGuinness let it be known through his network of friends that he was going to expose the kickback culture of 'brown envelopes' if the case against him ever got to court.[6]

The noise must have reached the office of Newham borough commander, Mick Johnson, who sent for Mac and Guntrip. 'We thought we were going to get a pat on the back but instead walked into a shit storm,' Mac recalled.

[6]Interview with Danny McGuinness 16 and 22 December 2015.

'What have you done? Why didn't I know about this operation?' Johnson began.

'Why would you need to know Sir? It's car crime.' Mac replied.

'You've embarrassed me in front of my partners,' Johnson insisted.

Guntrip was surprised by the reaction as Johnson didn't normally hand out bollockings. 'It was one of those days you never forget,' said the detective constable. 'We came out of there shell-shocked.'

Mac had an additional insight into Johnson's reaction. 'It was clear he had been approached at a very senior level ... We walked out of there thinking what have we done wrong, this was a great job.'

That McGuinness was still working for the council when he was arrested was a clear indication of the protection he enjoyed despite the findings of the Kelly report. The old procurement process, which she found so prone to corruption was simply allowed to carry on.[7] The prosecution of McGuinness threatened to unpick all that plus the secret and highly questionable deal that allowed the enforcement division chiefs to leave quietly by the back door. It was a deal that Mike Law was starting to view as hush money.

[7] After the Internal Audit department told Kelly in July 2005 that its inspection found the procurement practices in the crime and anti-social behaviour division were 'tantamount to corruption', she recommended it be inspected in one year's time to monitor her suggested reforms. But no inspection took place by Internal Audit for another seven years until after the Olympics had finished. That Internal Audit report in August 2012 (by Martin Harvey, who was the same audit manager in July 2005) said that 'given the seriousness of the position in 2005' the management response seven years later was 'poor.'

The rebel councillor was so disgusted by how his own party appeared to be burying the scandal that in protest he crossed the floor and joined the Tories for the last quarter of his four-year term. News of his unease reached the lawyer representing McGuinness who asked to see him.

Janice Brown was a well-liked criminal defence lawyer who came from Silvertown. Her sister Lyn was a former Newham councillor and deputy mayor who, sources in the Labour party claim, owed her rise to the patronage of Sir Robin Wales. By 2006, Lyn Brown was the new Labour MP for West Ham and a powerful supporter of the borough's interests in Westminster. The Brown sisters had grown up with the Bowers brothers and were particularly close to their youngest sister, who died in a hit-and-run incident when she was a teenager.

When McGuinness was arrested in February 2006, it was the Bowers who suggested he use Janice Brown. The lawyer had previously represented Chic Matthews in the drug factory trial; David Hunt in the pigeon fanciers gala dinner assault case; and Paul Bowers in the £1 million Gatwick robbery planned from the Peacock gym.

At their meeting, Janice Brown gave Law a flick of the defence McGuinness was going to run. She said her client had been 'sanctioned' by the council to sell some seized cars and that corruption and freemasonry were features in the case. Shortly afterwards, Law was invited to the House of Commons to meet Lyn Brown. The MP was keen to know what dirt he had but Law was reticent about showing his hand. '[Lyn] asked for everything I'd got on the Parks police scandal,' said the rebel councillor, but he refused to hand over the file.

Instead, the dossier was shown to his new party and Law tried, without success, to get former London Tory mayoral candidate Steve Norris, and Boris Johnson, the future one, interested in what was going on in Labour Newham. It was quickly apparent that 'there wasn't a cigarette paper between the parties' and no interest in raising the spectre of corruption after London had won the Olympics bid. In effect, Law had run up against a new united front across party lines to put on the best show possible. The New Labour government and its favourite mayor, Sir Robin Wales, were already playing nice with the loathed socialist mayor of London, Ken Livingstone. Just as Lord Sebastian Coe, the former Conservative MP now in charge of organising the Games, had to get on with Labour politicians at Westminster.

Law was right to believe that reopening a corruption scandal in the key Olympic borough was not a priority when there was so much money and political capital to be made in the six-year countdown to London 2012. He had no idea how much wider the spectre of corruption in the council's enforcement division had spread, including into Scotland Yard.

The 'dark side' of Scotland Yard's Directorate of Professional Standards was already aware of the corruption involving Newham council contractors months before Pelé Mahmood made his accusatory speech at the award ceremony in March 2005. A secret operation had been looking at Charlie Butler's relationships with police and council officers when the 55-year-old was suddenly shot outside his house in October 2004.

Butler was kept on a life support machine for eight months until his death in June 2005, by which time the Kelly inquiry was in full flow. The anti-corruption squad never shared the incredible intelligence it was amassing about the council contractor with her inquiry. Instead, the 'dark side' operated in complete secrecy from a covert base in Epping to prevent any compromise from Butler's extensive network of friends in the police and the freemasons, including those in the council. The prime suspect for Butler's murder was a seasoned detective who it was initially believed had organised the assassination to stop him exposing a cell of corrupt police colleagues.

Detective constable Chris 'clubber' Cubitt was immediately suspended and arrested when Butler was shot but gave a no comment interview to the murder squad, who worked from the same Barking police station.

The senior officer in charge of the murder inquiry thought the arrangement was unworkable and asked for an outside force to take over, but Scotland Yard disagreed. However, when threats and intimidation from within Barking police station, where Cubitt was well-liked, reached intolerable levels, the murder inquiry moved to the anti-corruption squad's secret base in Lippett's Hill, Epping.[8] The murder inquiry was made more sensitive because Butler was a police informant and Cubitt had been his handler. Both men were also senior freemasons and associated with other serving and retired police officers and Newham council officials through the masonic brotherhood.

The corruption and murder detectives now working the case together had a theory that Cubitt had fallen out with Butler and started a chain of events that led to his murder. Butler was said to be the keeper of £180,000 stolen by a

---

[8]The corruption probes into DC Chris Cubitt and Charlie Butler was codenamed Wolfsburg and Nesaru under a steering group chaired by DCS Jon Shatford. He was the intelligence officer who debriefed Jimmy Holmes in 1997 over his Soho fall out with Davey Hunt.

corrupt circle of police officers two decades ago. However, in 2004 the money went missing. Those looking for it kidnapped and tortured a young man and delivered him to Butler's house where he was interrogated further before being let go. A witness came forward to say that before his death Butler was complaining that Cubitt, who he was calling 'that fat cunt', was trying to 'stitch him up'. The witness, a neighbour, said Butler talked about 'going to see some top bloke at Scotland Yard' to expose corruption involving drugs, people trafficking and robbery.[9]

As the murder and corruption inquiries went into 2005 and then 2006 the working hypothesis hardened that 'exposure of long-term historical police corruption' was a possible motive for the murder of Charlie Butler. Old intelligence existed that the Newham council contractor had in the past tried to use his alleged role in stashing the £180,000 as leverage to get out of trouble and told people that if he went down, corrupt officers would go down with him. In bottoming out such an explosive claim, murder detectives encountered obstruction from a powerful masonic network in Newham. It was quite possible this was the same network that Amanda Kelly and whistle-blowers, Pelé Mahmood and Nick Dennett, were coming up against.

A confidential police report on the Butler case said 'the power and influence of Freemasonry upon this investigation, particularly in respect of matters relating to Cubitt, were alarming and should be a cause of concern to the Metropolitan Police Service.'[10]

[9]Statement of Jennifer Long read out in the murder trial.
[10]Closing report dated 19 June 2010.

When piecing together his life, the murder inquiry learned that Butler had fallen out with fellow contractor, Danny McGuinness. This chimed with what Mahmood and Dennett told the Kelly inquiry about how Butler complained that the enforcement division was favouring McGuinness for certain contracts that used to be his. The murder inquiry discovered that McGuinness had been an informant for Newham police. A well-placed police source explained that McGuinness was 'binned off' (de-registered) after eighteen months because his handlers realised that all he wanted was protection for his corrupt activities. The main thrust of the information he provided was about his business rival, said the source. 'He was Charlie Butler's partner at first. A lot of what he was gushing about was Butler, blaming him for everything. He was looking for a bit of protection, a leg up [if he got in trouble]. He never came up with much. He gave as little as he could. He was looking for a bit of cover, protection.'

Separately, Cubitt had a reputation in the Barking office of being a wheeler-dealer able to source cheap car parts. This dovetailed with what the source inside DM Security was claiming, namely, that McGuinness traded in stolen car parts including supplying a circle of freemasons in Newham.

The murder squad interviewed McGuinness but never pursued him as a suspect. Their focus also started to shift away from Cubitt when information came in that the motive for the murder might be sexual abuse within Butler's family. Two men who emerged as prime suspects paid to shoot Butler for abusing his stepdaughter were arrested in January 2007, the same month Cubitt's suspension was lifted and he retired from the police after thirty years' service.[11] Cubitt was no murderer but the closing report into the case described him 'as dissolute and wholly treacherous, an intimidator, bully and abuser of his position of trust.' The assessment was likely coloured by threats Cubitt was alleged to have made towards the detectives investigating him for murder and corruption, who in response had security measures installed at their homes.

The closing report also remarked that although Cubitt was not involved in the planning or shooting of Butler, his 'fear of exposure' and that of his 'acolytes' in the police for alleged past corrupt activity *was* a realistic motive. The Police Federation didn't see it that way and on his retirement gave Cubitt a lifetime recognition award for representing officers under internal investigation, a role which accounted for some of his continued

[11]DC Chris Cubitt was suspended but never charged with any criminal offence. He did not respond to an interview request.

The murder investigation first looked at David Austin and Douglas Johnson in September 2005. They were arrested in January 2007 and stood trial on three occasions for the murder of Charlie Butler.

The first trial was abandoned because the Law Lords banned the use of anonymous prosecution witnesses as unfair to defendants. The government rushed through a law reintroducing their use but allowing defendants the right to know the witnesses' identities. The second murder trial at the Old Bailey ended with a hung jury. Judge David Paget QC said on 25 March 2009: 'Charlie Butler by all accounts was not a very nice man who may have had many enemies lurking in the background. One possibility lurking in the background is the possibility of police corruption. He was apparently associated with a corrupt police officer. It is possible that someone associated with that corrupt police officer wanted him out of the way. There is also evidence that Butler may have sexually abused his step-daughter.' In the third trial, where the prosecution put forward sexual abuse as a motive for the murder, the jury returned guilty verdicts in March 2010. Austin and Johnson were given minimum sentences of 30 years each.

popularity among colleagues since his early days at Stoke Newington.[12]

The secret corruption intelligence about Cubitt, Butler and McGuinness was deemed far too sensitive to be put on HOLMES, the largely unrestricted police computer system for managing murder inquiries. Instead, paper copies of the file were put into a ring binder called 'Document 522'.

On 24 April 2007, DC Guntrip received an email marked CONFIDENTIAL and HIGH importance from a senior manager at Newham council's enforcement division. Nigel Mould, a former police officer, wanted to 'urgently discuss the status of the forthcoming [McGuinness] trial', while his boss [Ian Walker] and a chief inspector on Newham borough wanted a separate meeting 'to discuss the wider borough issues and implications.'

Guntrip was mindful of the bollocking he and Mac had received from their borough commander after arresting McGuinness on the Silvertown strip. The detective was also struggling on limited resources to prepare the prosecution case against Chicky Matthews junior over the Aladdin's den. As he read Mould's email, Guntrip's interest piqued when the council manager said he was also 'greatly concerned' by a very recent phone call from a former enforcement division colleague who worked under Page from 1998 to 2002. 'John [Tisshaw] asked me about the case and stated that he had been contacted by the [McGuinness] defence as a witness for them. I made no comment other to affirm that I was a prosecution witness,'

[12]DC Chris Cubitt was DI Dave McKelvey's police federation representative during his dispute with DCS Sharon Kerr in 2003 over his failure to get into the Flying Squad.

Mould wrote. Tisshaw, he said, had been seconded to the
Home Office funded 'Operation Scrap It' from 2003 to
2005 and was responsible for the 'primary contract with
Drakes and the secondary one with DM Security.'

Mould went on: 'This is hugely significant and will have
a direct impact on the case if the defence are indeed asking
Tisshaw to act as a witness … This simply reinforces my
increasing concerns about this investigation, its potential
ramifications, whether you can confirm to [my boss] that
all strands have been covered and that you are fully aware
that Newham, the department of the environment and
rural affairs, the Home Office and potentially all the other
London boroughs may be drawn into this?'

One of the pressing concerns was what to tell the
judge and jury about why McGuinness was allowed to
operate as a contractor after the Kelly report in September
2005 and until his arrest in February 2006. The council
planned to say that all the contracts McGuinness had with
Newham were out to tender at the time of his arrest and
he was therefore 'working out of contract.' However, the
question still remained why he was working at all since
Pelé Mahmood blew open the scandal in March 2005.

Mould was relieved to hear from Guntrip that the
council's concerns about the trial might shortly evaporate.
McGuinness had recently persuaded a judge to dismiss
the case on a legal technicality, but the prosecution was
appealing.[13] The relief at Newham council was short-lived

[13]On 2 March 2007 a judge ruled the prosecution hadn't established that the
council owned the vehicles allegedly stolen and cannibalised or shipped to
Poland and Bulgaria by McGuinness. The contractor, the judge said, may have
acted in 'a less than honourable way' and breached the trust of the council but
there was no contract laying out what DM Security could and could not do.

as the prosecution successfully appealed in July 2007 putting the trial back on track for later in the year. It was in these intervening autumn months that a cabal of senior officers at the anti-corruption squad set a course of action that ensured the Matthews and McGuinness trials were derailed.

Internal documents show that in the six days after the formal abandonment of the Aladdin's den trial on 25 October 2007, anti-corruption detectives liaised with their counterparts looking into the Charlie Butler murder. Detective inspector Ashfaq Siddique, the officer in charge of Operation Kayu, whose poisonous presentation to prosecutors had killed the Matthews trial, also wrote a decision log entry on 31 October suggesting wrongly that Mac had leaked intelligence from Butler, which resulted in him being shot.[14]

Shortly thereafter, the case against McGuinness was abandoned, much to the surprise of his barrister, James Mulholland, who felt the prosecution had previously fought 'tooth and nail' to keep the trial on track. 'We were never given a satisfactory reason,' said the barrister.

Mac and Guntrip, meanwhile, were treated to an insider's explanation for these extraordinary events. Prosecution sources, they said, privately indicated that

[14]Shortly before Butler was shot in October 2004, DC Cubitt had passed intelligence to a group of detectives, including Mac. The information, he said, came from Butler, Cubitt's old informant, and involved the alleged location of a gun. Mac did nothing about it because he was studying at the time for his DCI exam. However, after the shooting, Cubitt contacted Mac wondering if the two matters were connected. Mac made a statement to the Butler murder inquiry describing the sequence of events. A source on that inquiry confirms this and that there was nothing to suggest that Mac had leaked any intelligence that got Butler shot.

corruption concerns in Newham council were the real reason for the McGuinness trial being aborted. The contractor, it was felt, wouldn't get a fair trial unless Newham council enforcement manager John Page and others were also prosecuted. But by this time they had left the council with secret deals, and no one wanted to unpick that.

12

The Dementors

In November 2007, not long after the Aladdin's den trial of Chicky Matthews junior was aborted and Mac had been suspended, anti-corruption detectives from Operation Kayu finally interviewed Billy Allen, the man they believed had corrupted the Newham crime squad.

He and Mac had always got on well, Allen told them. They'd not only bonded over what they could each get out of each other – for Mac it was the Hunt organised crime group, for Allen it was his land – but also over personal tragedy.

Allen's now six-year-old son was born with acutely deformed feet and spent most of his life in and out of hospital. 'He never complains,' Allen would tell Mac, who sympathised as he'd had a similar birth defect after his mother took the drug Thalidomide while she was pregnant. But through corrective surgery Mac's legs had straightened, which gave Allen reassurance about his own son's future and created a bond between them. It was not what Operation Kayu wanted to hear. They were looking for evidence of a corrupt relationship not an endearing story of the crippled child and the cop. Allen also made it clear to them that there was nothing untoward about his relationship with other members of the Newham crime squad. They had treated him fairly and he only had respect for them, he insisted, adding that the throwing of the Aladdin's den trial was a travesty of justice.

Back at the Directorate of Professional Standards (DPS), a decision was taken to carry on, at all costs, and find something that would justify their actions in causing the Matthews and McGuinness trials to be abandoned at a cost of millions of pounds to the public purse.

By the start of 2008, a new senior investigating officer had taken over Operation Kayu and was reviewing some of the actions his predecessor, Ashfaq Siddique, had used to justify his lethal memo. Detective chief inspector Simon Rose wasn't entirely convinced about the case being built against Mac, Guntrip and Clark but on 7 January 2008 he wrote that there was 'substantial support within the DPS for the line that this takes as long as it takes.'

Siddique was leaving the DPS for another sensitive post, this time running informants at Islington borough. He lobbied, though, to retain responsibility for dealing with Mac because of his detailed knowledge of the case. Rose agreed even though it would cause tension between them. For example, at some point Rose discovered that anti-corruption detectives under Siddique had debriefed Eastwood a whole month before the Matthews trial was aborted and, what's more, that the prisoner confirmed all that he had told Mac about Hunt, drug deals, police corruption and a contract to kill three officers. The revelation begged many questions, most notably, why weren't the prosecuting barristers told this and instead led to believe that Mac had 'monkeyed up' the intelligence for some corrupt purpose?

Rose insisted that Eastwood be re-interviewed to hear it for himself. Once again, the prisoner repeated what he first told Mac and then the Operation Kayu team under Siddique. Rose next sent his men to see the informant who had first tipped off the Newham crime squad about the stolen copper at Matthews' scrap yard, which in turn led to the discovery of the Aladdin's den. The anti-corruption detectives returned to the DPS office with no evidence to suggest corruption.

It was the same story when in February 2008, Rose's men went to see Nick Dennett, the Newham council officer who had beef with McGuinness. Dennett thought they had come to discuss corruption in Newham council. His mood soon turned angry when the DPS detectives explained that the McGuinness trial had been abandoned because they believed the Newham crime squad, not the council, was corrupt. Nothing could be further from the truth, Dennett told them. Guntrip, he said, was the only officer who had listened and tried to do something about the whole rotten state of affairs.

Dennett went on to explain how McGuinness had made death threats against him soon after the contractor was arrested in February 2006 with the stolen cars. Guntrip had offered to put Dennett in the witness protection scheme but he refused because he wouldn't inflict such restrictions on the liberty of his wife and children, who instead moved away from the family home. Dennett continued working in Newham but wore a bulletproof vest paid for by the council. He felt victimised from then on for having spoken out about McGuinness, first to the Kelly inquiry and then to the Newham crime squad. Dennett was also depressed and drinking heavily to fill the void of returning to an empty home. He attributed his subsequent mental breakdown to the council's failure to protect him as a whistle-blower.

'Have you or your family had any history of depression?'

'No,' Mac told the police psychiatrist, barely able to acknowledge the irony that it was 16 February 2008, his twenty-sixth anniversary of joining the police, and he was now being assessed for his fitness to be formally interviewed about corruption.

'What about homicidal thoughts?'

'No, none.'

'Have you ever thought about harming yourself?'

Mac paused.

'Yes. Twice in the last five months,' he said welling up. 'The first time, I sat on Ingatestone station for about half an hour. I was going to throw myself in front of a train. It was only when I thought about my kids that I stopped. Then just before Christmas I was off my head. It was night and I was driving on the wrong side of the road at high speed hoping for an on-coming lorry to crash into. I was on meds but I couldn't sleep. I'd tried everything and had no idea what was going on. I thought I'd been fitted up. The DPS had no contact with me about what was going on, they were doing nothing about the threat and there was other things going on.'

'Like what?'

'I was walking the dog and three men were there with guns in a van. I called Essex police five times but nothing. I ended up chasing the van in my own car to a golf course in North Weald across the fairway. The police eventually took over and recovered the weapons and nicked them.'

'How are you feeling now?'

'I'm fine. I want to be interviewed. I need to get this over with.'

Mac had said the same thing to Ashfaq Siddique nine days earlier when they clashed over the limited amount of disclosure that the anti-corruption officer was offering ahead of the interview. Before storming off he told Siddique, 'You know me Ash. I've spent twenty-six years working my bollocks off. I've never had a day off sick. I always worked long hours to get the job done. I took this Hunt job everywhere in the Yard and no one wanted to deal with it. I briefed senior officers and no one wanted to know. Well, I tell you what. You can stick your fucking job up your arse.'

In one respect Mac was lucky to have friends a rank above him willing to stand up to the powerful DPS. One of them, a superintendent who had himself been the subject of unfounded suspicion, wrote to Mac's borough commander describing the 'unbearable self-doubt and feelings of betrayal and isolation' a detective experiences when the organisation turns on them.

'He has always accepted that his style of policing and his forceful personality are not to everyone's taste,' the friend wrote. 'But it has, over many years, been very much part of the reason he and the team he has been involved in have been so successful ... And he now feels disowned by a service he has put first for twenty-six years above the interests of his family and personal life because of his wholehearted vocational attitude to lawfully taking on and convicting some of London's toughest career criminals.'

Mac, he warned, had talked about suicide and whether his children would be better off without him. They still didn't know the truth. Every day since his suspension four months ago, Mac would leave home as if he was going to work and stay away all day, partly not to take his anger out on his wife. Typically, he couldn't tell her what he was feeling because he felt she wouldn't understand, not being from the police world. There was also the shame of putting his marriage and family last for an organisation that had now turned on him and searched his home; that his work had brought a threat to his family's door that was not taken seriously by those who should know better.

The police psychiatrist was worried about the effect being interviewed by the anti-corruption squad would have on Mac. 'You can interview him in short periods but if you are going to charge him today I think he is a suicide risk,' Siddique was told.

'I'm not charging him today,' the detective replied.

'OK. But when he learns the full case against him I feel there's a high risk he will harm himself. He hasn't taken his medication this morning. He's not sleeping.'

'He was relaxed this morning in the canteen,' Siddique replied. 'He even joked about the blow up the last time we met when he stormed off. He said he was later found naked on the M11!'

'I think he shouldn't be interviewed until he has treated his depression and they should consider voluntary or involuntary admission to hospital,' the psychiatrist recommended.[1]

---

[1]The account is taken from an interview with Dave McKelvey (6 November 2015) and the witness statements of Dr Spencer Phillips (15 February 2008), DI Ashfaq Siddique (17 February 2008) and DCI Simon Rose's Decision log (14-17 January 2008)

In the back of all their minds was the recent suicide
of a detective under investigation for far lesser offences,
who had hung himself at home after several interviews
during which he had made clear his suicidal thoughts. It
was the same anti-corruption office in Ilford and Forensic
Medical Examiner's office for the police that mishandled
the mental welfare of the now dead officer, whose inquest
was coming up in a few months.[2]

Rose was already concerned about any repeat with
Mac if the interview timetable was pushed. In January
2008 he'd written in a decision log, 'This is not worth
someone dying.' It was therefore logical that the advice
the psychiatrist was now giving to Siddique a month later
would be heeded.

Tension between Rose and Siddique over their different
assessment of the evidence of corruption was another
factor. Rose did a summary of where Operation Kayu had
got to after sixteen months. He now believed that many
of the key assumptions made about the conduct of Mac

[2]Timothy 'Tommy' Payne, a police officer based at Edmonton, hung himself at
home on 12 November 2006. He was under investigation for selling duty free
cigarettes to officers and others. The inquest was held in June 2008 and recorded
a narrative verdict that his arrest, suspension, the freezing of his assets and several
interviews by the anti-corruption squad had 'a profound effect on his mental state'.
The coroner went on: 'He was convinced he would lose his job and go to prison.
He felt guilty that his friends and colleagues had been implicated. Mr Payne was a
proud and private man who felt humiliated and singled out. He became paranoid
and his appearance changed. He became the shell of the man he was. All of this
contributed to this tragedy.' While in custody, Payne had spoke of his intention
to kill himself. There had been a previous attempt and a note. Yet he was not
referred by the police doctor to the local mental health crisis team on his release, no
adequate written welfare plan was in place and the anti-corruption squad did not
'communicate certain important facts about Mr Payne which would have led to the
interviews being stopped.' The coroner ordered changes to procedures as a result.

and Guntrip did not ring true and '[Operation] Kayu caused [the Matthews trial] to be stood out until it was abandoned.' Rose discussed these matters with his superiors who decided that Mac should no longer be interviewed for criminal offences but disciplinary ones only. The decision did not sit well with Siddique who successfully reversed it before moving to his new job.

Several months later and no further forward in pinning any criminality on Mac, Rose appeared concerned there would be backlash when the proverbial hit the fan. On 24 April 2008, he wrote in his decision log: 'I want top cover at Association of Chief Police Officers level for the direction we take at this crossroads ... The enquiry continues to be a painful unresolved issue in the office.' Rose commissioned an external review of whether there had been any mishandling of sources by the Newham crime squad. In other words, the main issue that had led to the Matthews and McGuinness trials being abandoned.

SCD 11, the central intelligence unit for all specialist squads at Scotland Yard, was given the job. Its conclusions were devastating for those whose actions had forced the two trials to be thrown – Allen, Eastwood and Dennett had been handled within the rules. This should have been the *estocada* moment for Operation Kayu and led to the exoneration of the three detectives. Instead, the senior management at the DPS, whose hands were dirtied by this affair, decided to affect a slow retreat but make it look like victory. Mac, Guntrip and Clark would be kept on the hook of anxiety and career limbo for months to come.

It is this abuse of power – when the police can investigate itself – that is so problematic. Rather than accept that

Operation Kayu was a failure, as no criminality could be proved, the DPS decided it was going to pursue the three detectives for disciplinary offences, where the standard of proof was lower and the anti-corruption bosses were judge and jury in their own cause. Nevertheless, Mac was relieved when in July 2008 his suspension was lifted, he was allowed back to work on light duties and to associate with Guntrip and Clark. The trio knew they had not acted corruptly with Allen or Hunt, but the effect of being suspected of such treachery was too much. Clark, for example, had taken a career break and was seriously considering not coming back to the police.

In September, Mac took a two-week rest at the police hospital in Goring for mentally damaged detectives before his discipline interview in a month's time. Rose had decided that Siddique would not be called back to conduct the interview. 'I am concerned that objectivity is maintained and whilst Ash had good knowledge of the original intell[igence] the position and circumstances have changed,' he wrote tellingly in a decision log. 'There are two emails I have received from Ash after he was notified of the recent changes and I believe he is very upset at the recent developments.'

The day of Mac's disciplinary interview finally arrived on 3 October 2008, almost a year after his home was searched and he had been suspended. The detective chief inspector walked into a small utility room next to his office at Edmonton police station and pulled down the blinds. Among all the tracking and listening equipment, he reached into a plastic bag and pulled out a bright yellow costume borrowed from a friend. It slipped neatly over his jeans and polo short with a hole for his face to poke through.

A colleague walked into the room and burst out laughing then took a photograph of Mac holding the written response he had prepared for any questions the anti-corruption squad may have about Allen and Eastwood. Though he had a big grin for the camera, behind it was a broken and depressed man, seething with rage that a star chamber within Scotland Yard's most secretive and powerful department was tearing his career – and sanity – to shreds. The Dementors from the DPS had sucked out all the happiness he had for policing.

While the photo did the rounds of the police station, Mac slipped up the stairs to the sixth floor where his federation representative and his 77-year-old father, George, were waiting. The DPS had refused to allow his solicitor to sit in on the interview and wanted a mental health worker present. Mac refused as he was going to discuss sensitive police matters so a compromise was reached that his father would attend.

When the federation representative saw Mac on the sixth floor landing he shook his head.

'It'll only wind them up.'

'Good,' Mac replied. 'They called me bent so I've come as a banana.'

Mac had fantasised about coming to the interview, in one of those blow-up cowboy-on-a-horse outfits and responding 'Neigh comment' to every question. But in the end, the banana suit won the day. Mac strolled into the public affairs office for some banter with the secretaries and press officers. Police and civilian staff came in and out as word spread that 'the DCI's wearing a banana suit for his interview with the funny firm,' a derogative name for the anti-corruption squad.

The federation representative walked into the press office and pulled Mac aside.

'The DPS have seen you. They are ready. You can't be interviewed like that, they will just say you are mad and call it off Dave,' he remonstrated.

Mac desperately wanted to be interviewed, not sectioned. Upon reflection, his point was made, his disdain shown, so he unpeeled himself in a side office.

The interview didn't get off to a good start. When matters strayed away from disciplinary and into criminal territory Mac told the two anti-corruption detectives to arrest and cuff him or stop their line of questioning. They refused. So he upturned the table and walked out. In his written response to the allegation of 'monkeying up' the Eastwood intelligence, Mac said: 'What possible motive could I or any of the other officers have in wanting to make this up? The suggestion is ridiculous and insulting. I have spent nearly twenty-seven years fighting crime, serious, organised and violent crime. I do not scare easily. I have historically been subject to threats as part of my job and been assaulted. Unarmed I have faced armed suspects without "flinching". My team at Stratford had caused the Hunt organised crime network more disruption and damage in the months we investigated them than all of [Scotland Yard's] Specialist Crime Directorate or SOCA had ever done. This "threat to life" is something completely different. David Hunt is one of, if not the most powerful criminals in the south of England. He had the motive and means to put together the contract. He employed one of the most dangerous individuals to carry out that contract,

Carl Robinson, a feared assassin. Both know my address. How can the MPS possibly believe that no threat exists? It is incredible.'

When the interview continued on a discipline only basis, it came as a relief. Mac had answers to everything, but it left him feeling depressed. As an insomniac, he often bashed off 'ranting emails' to the DPS in the early hours of the morning. It helped clear his head and let him sleep. At three in the morning on 7 October 2008 he'd been thinking about why prosecution barristers had been misled and only the Matthews and McGuinness trials were abandoned. No longer did Mac believe that he was the victim of a 'vendetta' by senior officers who didn't like his style. It must be something worse, he told himself. At 3.35 a.m. he pressed send on an email with his new theory. 'Hunt's network of corrupt officers' may have penetrated the anti-corruption squad too.

Until he sat through the interviews, George McKelvey had no idea what his broken son had been up against. It frightened him that Mac had kept all the horror and pressure from his family.

In November 2008, George raised the matter with the Labour government as a supporter of Tessa Jowell, his local MP, who was now the Olympics minister.

His letter was also addressed to Sir Ian Blair, the police commissioner, and copied to Prime Minister Gordon Brown, home secretary Jacqui Smith and the newly-elected Tory mayor of London, Boris Johnson.

'The story I listened to would make any taxpayer very angry to know that police officers doing their jobs are put at such risk and then treated so poorly ... The investigation must have cost millions ... Please can you help to bring some pressure to bear to complete this investigation ... David is very unwell and has become worse.'

Rose eventually saw the letter and advised the commissioner that there should be a 'more conciliatory' response. Any disciplinary hearing against Mac, he warned, was going to be 'a circus'.[3]

[3]Decision log of DCI Simon Rose 19 November 2008.

PART FOUR

Legacy

13

Promised Land

Crime boss Harold Shand, played by Bob Hoskins in the uncannily prescient masterpiece, *The Long Good Friday*, looked every bit the captain of industry cruising along the River Thames that fictional summer in 1980. The speech he was about to deliver read like something written for Margaret Thatcher, the recently elected prime minister, but was instead intended to rally a group of crooked cops and local politicians essential to his new business venture in London's Docklands:

> I'm not a politician. I'm a businessman with a sense of history. I'm also a Londoner and today is a day of great historical significance for London. And I believe that this is the decade in which London will become Europe's capital. Having cleared away the outdated, we've got mile after mile and acre after acre of land for our future prosperity.

As his private yacht headed east under Tower Bridge, Shand waxed nostalgic about life on the great waterway

that once moved goods from the darkest corners of a
faded empire:

> There used to be 80 or 90 ships in here at one time. They
> used to queue up to get in all the way up to Galleons
> Reach. This used to be the greatest docks in the world
> at one time. No other city in the world has got right in
> its centre such an opportunity for profitable progress.
> So it's important that the right people mastermind the
> new London. Proven people with nerve, knowledge
> and expertise.

Shand is the creation of crime reporter-turned-
scriptwriter, Barrie Keeffe. The film chronicles the violent
mobster's attempt to cash in and legitimise his criminal
empire during the Tory-led first phase of Docklands
development in preparation for a fictional Olympics.
Almost three decades later, in 2008, life was imitating art
in the rise of Davey Hunt and his plan to dry-clean a
criminal empire and cash in on the second phase of the
Docklands redevelopment and Olympic regeneration
under a New Labour government.

Waste management has long been a lucrative front for
organised crime. With four years to go before the Olympics,
the Long Fella was touchy about any suggestion of being
a crime boss. In 2008 there was hardly a whiff of gangster
about him. Hunt was, to use the common parlance of
villains in need of makeovers, 'a legitimate businessman'.

The Serious Organised Crime Agency (SOCA), however,
didn't agree. For several years it had been developing an
understanding of the Hunt network under Operation
Delux; looking at the blood family, the assets, the associates
and the type of crime involved.

SOCA had collated intelligence linking the Hunts to a 200 kilo cocaine importation through Colombian connections and up to two tons of cannabis per week in lorries from Spain. Palmer's Motors, where Cavanagh almost died, was considered a den of criminality and a laundry of dirty money. The Long Fella was also said to have assisted Patsy 'bolt eyes' Clarke, convicted of handling the stolen Brink's-Mat gold, to launder his money in Spain. On one occasion French customs had stopped £800,000 at the border.

Like many British criminals, Spain still held an attraction for Hunt, but he knew the real action was to be had back home with the unprecedented opportunities presented by London hosting the Olympics. SOCA could see it coming. The agency's UK risk assessment for 2008 had a new section on 'Criminal activity associated with the London 2012 Olympics', which predicted that the Games would present 'serious organised criminals with a range of money making opportunities.' It said that 'in the run-up to the Games, the large number of lucrative contracts for construction, services and sponsorship are likely to attract the interests of serious organised criminals, who may attempt to corrupt or extort money from those involved.'

After London won the bid, two bodies were created to see the project through. The London Organising Committee of the Olympic and Paralympic Games (LOCOG) under Lord Coe's leadership had responsibility for implementation while the Olympic Delivery Authority (ODA) oversaw construction of the venues. The 'neglected post-industrial landscape' of Newham was one of five boroughs 'riddled with contaminants; suffocated by invasive plant species; scarred by dumped shopping trolleys, and dominated by giant overhead electricity pylons' that the ODA made its mission to transform and 'make Britain proud.'

'Legacy' was the buzzword of London 2012; a commitment not to repeat the same mistakes that left former host cities with 'white elephants' without any social, environmental or educational benefit to the local population when the Olympic caravan moved on. Despite the global financial crisis, which started to bite in 2008, the London Olympic development was the biggest demolition programme in Europe with more than two hundred buildings knocked down and others erected. Some, such as the media centre, were big enough to house five jumbo jets standing wing tip to wing tip.

On the campaign trail to becoming the first Conservative mayor of London, Boris Johnson had talked up the Games as a never-again, not-to-be-missed business opportunity for UK plc. The Long Fella, whose own politics remain a mystery, was, as ever, ahead of the curve. In April 2008, he had formed a joint venture between his waste management plant and a leading demolition group of companies whose owner donated heavily to the Tories.

Brendon Kerr left school in Belfast at fifteen to be a carpenter's apprentice. In his twenties he left Belfast for London, where after a few construction gigs in 1989 the Ulsterman joined Keltbray, a niche demolition company, as project manager. Fourteen years later, the 37-year-old was chief executive and owner of the company, turning over £50 million a year.

Under the first five years of Kerr's leadership, Keltbray doubled its turnover and demolished sites in the City to make way for innovative skyscrapers such as the Gherkin and the Shard. Meanwhile, it demolished and helped rebuild Arsenal Football Club's new Emirates stadium and then came the Millennium Dome, directly across the Thames from the Silvertown strip. By 2008, the cigar-chomping Kerr was rewarded with work on the centrepiece of the London 2012 Games – the Queen Elizabeth Olympic Park Stadium in Stratford.

Kerr needed a nearby plant that could handle his dirt. Hunt's Waste in Chequer's Lane, Dagenham, just eight miles east of the stadium, was perfect. The seven-acre recycling plant could also be accessed by barge along the Thames, as the Long Fella had already acquired the jetty at the end of Chequers Lane for £1 million and built some new offices to oversee operations.

Hunt's waste business had grown to become one of the biggest in Europe through hard work and, according to a London rival, threats not to bid for contracts that the Long Fella wanted. Hunt had bought the ninety-nine-year lease for Chequers Lane in 1994 using crooked Jersey-based accountant, Peter Michel. Three years later, Michel set up an offshore company to hold the lease. He incorporated EMM Limited in the British Virgin Island because there was no requirement to identify the ultimate beneficial owner, which meant Hunt could hide from the UK taxman. For an extra layer of secrecy, EMM was administered by Mossack Fonseca, a Panama-based law firm that set up offices in Jersey to meet the demand for BVI-registered companies.[1]

---

[1] Mossack Fonseca would later be dragged out of the shadows when 1.5 million of its files were hacked and published by a platform of journalists as 'The Panama Papers'.

Hunt's (UK) Properties Limited held a second lease for Chequers Lane and Hunt rented the whole site to a company involving his best friend and a businessman regarded by SOCA as a major organised crime figure.

Phil Mitchell, a pugnacious 46-year-old, was a school friend and one of the regulars who went with Hunt to watch West Ham play. Mitchell had been arrested in 1999 in relation to the slashing of Paul Cavanagh, but was not charged, and had turned up at the central London court the day Billy Allen's minders were annihilated. The Newham crime squad, bizarrely, found a photograph of Mitchell on Hunt's bedside table when they raided his mansion over the court fight. Mitchell was going to be arrested but the matter was dropped for lack of evidence around the time that Hunt started negotiating the joint venture with Keltbray.

Edward 'Teddy' Barham owned the Barham group, a waste company operating from Chequers Lane. SOCA regarded 56-year-old Barham as a 'Level 3' organised crime figure, which meant, like Hunt, he was in the premiership division of criminals targeted by the agency. SOCA noted that, 'During 2006 there appears to be an emerging association between Hunt and Barham, a Level 3 drug trafficker with a previous conviction for heroin offences ... Hunt and Barham now share a number of business addresses.'[2]

Keltbray conducted no due diligence when getting into bed with Hunt and Barham and, in April 2008, Keltbray Hunt Limited was incorporated. Kerr told the trade press he was 'thrilled' with the acquisition, but wouldn't

[2]Teddy Barham declined to comment.

say how much he paid for the Barham Group.[3] 'Hunt's Waste have been recycling waste from their headquarters in east London for nearly a decade. It is our plan to work together to build on the successful business performance achieved to date, and to strengthen the Keltbray Group delivery ability to clients by offering them access to a recycling hub.'

For Hunt it meant a rebranding using Keltbray's ubiquitous logo on his tipper trucks that shuttled between the building sites of London. Meanwhile, the new Keltbray Hunt brochure spoke of key 'working partnerships' with the UK's major engineering companies, Canary Wharf, British Telecom, the National Grid and the NHS. With the stroke of a pen, Hunt had arrived at the big boy's table and was hitched to a company and a CEO loved by The City.

The joint venture immediately secured a second Olympic contract to prepare the site where 10,000 competitors would live during the Games. The £1 million contract for the Athletes Village involved removing non-hazardous waste and returning it recycled to the construction site next to the Westfield City shopping centre that was also going up in Stratford.

---

[3]Keltbray's statement to the author on 17 July 2018 said: 'Keltbray Hunt Ltd, now named Keltbray Environmental Ltd (KEL), was formed in 2008. The shareholders were Keltbray Group (Holdings) Ltd 51 per cent, Philip Mitchell (PM) 16.3 per cent, Lawrence Lillie (LL) 16.3 per cent and Edward Barham (EB)16.3 per cent. The assets of a waste recycling business owned by PM, LL and EB were transferred into KEL for a consideration paid by Keltbray Group to PM, LL and EB. The opportunity arose through contact with LL. The business operated from a site in Dagenham and two leases were in place for the site with EMM Ltd and Hunts (UK) Properties Ltd. Mr Hunt had a connection with these companies. We do not carry out due diligence on entities we rent properties from, it is usually the other way around.'

Kerr became a director of the new company along with Mitchell. The Ulsterman retained a 51 per cent controlling interest and effectively bankrolled the joint venture, although the new company had access to an overdraft facility with the Royal Bank of Scotland. Mitchell, Barham and an associate held the remaining shares and under the terms of the agreement Hunt's EMM Limited received around £500,000 per year for the lease.

Kerr's joint venture with two leading organised crime figures took place while the demolition tycoon was cosying up to the Conservative party under David Cameron. What he wanted and what he got in return for his generous corporate and personal donations remains unclear. But over the coming years, Kerr, who *The Sunday Times* Rich List estimated as being worth £40 million in 2008, made regular donations (totalling £100,000) to the Tories and £70,000 to the office of Dr Liam Fox. The MP for north Somerset was a senior member of Cameron's shadow cabinet at the time and would later come out as a leading Brexiteer and international trade secretary in Theresa May's government. The connection between Kerr and Fox remains a mystery because the demolition tycoon and the politician simply won't explain it.[4]

Chic Matthews' victory over Billy Allen for the Silvertown strip was short-lived for two reasons. The septuagenarian gangster died a year later in March 2008 and a government agency was about to start buying up all the plots in private hands to develop the site as a 'high-priority project'.

[4]Keltbray said: 'Mr Kerr's political donations are all documented and accounted for and made in line with his political affiliation.' Liam Fox did not respond to emailed questions.

The government's vision was to build a 'landmark feature' in Canning Town that announced the entrance to the regenerated royal docks – two sixteen-storey residential towers on the north and southern tips of the strip linked by smaller blocks. The London Development Agency (LDA), a government body, was given a £20 million budget to compulsorily purchase those parts of the strip that weren't already owned by Newham council or London Underground.

From on high, the 2.4 hectares of land is shaped like a makeshift blade and that was exactly the sort of intimidating vibe it gave off to visitors. A Newham council official told the LDA the strip was 'an eyesore'. The LDA's consultant went further and said the site was 'an extremely poor, even hostile environment, especially at night' and noted that prospective developers feared to tread there unaccompanied.[5] DHL, the courier service, had already stopped delivering to the area, but would still drop off packages to war zones such as Afghanistan and Iraq.

Homebuilders Redrow, the council's preferred bidder, had an initial plan to build more than 600 residential units and some commercial ones, but the company pulled out after the global financial crash.[6] 'Despite emergent developer activity in the area and the strategically important and sustainable location, the private sector has failed to assemble the site or show any real prospect of developing the land in a comprehensive manner that might maximise its potential,' the consultant explained in his report.

[5]Report by GVA Grimley for the LDA December 2006.
[6]Interview with the LDA 4 December 2009.

The various competing crime families with interests on the strip also had no cohesive development plan. They could hardly be in the same room without an explosion of violence. The Hunts, Bowers and Matthews wanted luxury flats with a casino. Allen and Sabine dreamt of a mini world trade centre. None of it met national and local planning policy objectives.

The LDA's Compulsory Purchase Order meant the only fight left was over how much the government agency was willing to pay private landowners for their plots. The Matthews family would have to wait for the results of Allen's appeal to the Law Lords before they could get their hands on any of the LDA money. Allen's main ground of appeal was the 'possible bias' by one of the judges. The Law Lords were wholly unimpressed with the argument and in July 2008 ruled that ownership of the land at 1-7 Brunel Street was to remain with the Matthews family.[7]

After four violent and expensive years, the legal battle for the Silvertown strip was finally over. Shortly thereafter, the LDA paid the Matthews family an undisclosed sum

---

[7]Allen's lawyers argued that Lord Justice Ward had an 'unusual interest' in Chic Matthews and the land dispute over 1-7 Brunel Street. Ward was the lead appeal court judge that overturned Matthews' drug factory conviction in 1996 because of police corruption. A decade later Ward heard Matthews' appeal against the decision rejecting his adverse possession claim. The appeal was originally reserved to Lord Neuberger in February 2007. But at the last minute, Ward let both sides know that he was replacing Neuberger and asked if there were any objections. On the police's advice, Allen was not present at the appeal court but he told his barrister to object in the strongest terms fearing that his role as an informant in the drug factory case would count against him. Jane Giret QC supported the concern and tried her best, but Ward refused to recuse himself, saying he didn't recall the details of the drug factory case. Ward and two other judges found in Matthews favour and returned the land to him. Allen then appealed to the Law Lords claiming Ward shouldn't have heard the case and lost.

for the squatted land on 1-7 Brunel Street and Allen paid
their legal fees.[8]

The Bowers brothers also hoped for a good payday from
the LDA without having to rob. They owned several plots
on the strip through the company Abbeycastle Properties
Limited. The main plot was the Peacock Pub, for which
the LDA offered only £1.85 million, pointing out that
the global recession had burst the property bubble. In any
event, whatever sum the Bowers got from the LDA would
be immediately seized under the Proceeds of Crime Act
as part of the brothers' sentence for the Gatwick Airport
robbery.

There was a general feeling among those who privately
owned land on the Silvertown strip, and had held on to
it as an investment, that the LDA was muscling them
with offers that failed to reflect the 'Olympic effect' on
Canning Town. Actor Billy Murray was firmly in this
camp. He grew up there in the fifties and sixties. His
sister owned a number of pubs in the area when young
Murray was training as an amateur fighter and thinking
of a career in acting. He knew the Kray twins through
boxing and from painting their club during his stint as a
decorator. One day they lent him the money to pay the
first term of drama school and three decades later Murray
was a household name from his television roles as a bent
detective in *The Bill* and a crime boss in *EastEnders*.

The Silvertown strip always looked like a good sleeping
investment and in 1998 he bought a derelict building

[8]Terry Sabine was not compensated by the LDA. Allen had two other plots on
the Silvertown strip and through his trustees in bankruptcy began negotiations
with the LDA for a good price. They couldn't agree and the matter went to the
Land Tribunal for independent assessment.

on the southern tip of the strip where Peto Street and Victoria Dock Road meet, which became the local nightspot, Twilight. Murray was familiar with many of the local families but didn't see them as gangsters. He'd campaigned for the Bowers after their conviction for the Gatwick robbery signing a petition that criticised the police for suggesting the brothers behind the Peacock Gym had 'terrorised' the local community.

'The Hunts were a big family like the Bowers. I just know them as businessmen. They have a reputation as people who go out and earn their money. People have got a lot of respect for them. I don't know them. Socially, I've met about four times David Hunt at charity functions that he's arranged where they get a so-called celebrity like myself sitting on a table,' Murray explained. He remembered attending boxing and charity functions, including one at Hunt's Woolston Manor Golf Club, where the Long Fella was on the next table and 'an absolute gentleman.'

The Newham crime squad had intelligence from local sources that the Adams crime family had expressed an interest in buying Twilight from Murray. He was holding out for the right consortium of developers but the actor declined to comment on whether the north London crime family had approached him. In the end, it was the LDA that eventually made Murray an offer he didn't like but couldn't refuse.[9]

As 2008 came to a close, the anti-corruption squad sent its file on Mac, Guntrip and Clark to an independent

[9] Telephone interviews with Billy Murray 14 May 2010 and 15 May 2018.

barrister to see if there were any grounds for bringing
disciplinary charges.

The trio had spent many sleepless nights wondering
what really lay behind the decision to only abandon
the two trials of Chicky Matthews junior and Danny
McGuiness. Incompetence? A cover-up? Perhaps an
informant was being protected. The more they thought,
the more one thought became unshakeable. Did Davey
Hunt have someone in the DPS who, as Guntrip put it,
'could influence the decision without fear of being too
closely questioned?'

The idea wasn't altogether far-fetched. After all, the
DPS was sitting on the secret 2002 Tiberius report, which
concluded that Hunt had penetrated Scotland Yard's
detective branch at a senior level. Furthermore, the anti-
corruption squad was made up of detectives on rotation
from other branches. It was not a posting for life.

Three months later, in early April 2009, the external
barrister advised the DPS that there was no prospect
of successfully disciplining the three officers. After 529
days under investigation the trio processed the news in
different ways. Mac was depressed, Guntrip stoic and
Clark furious.

The youngest of the three by age and service sent a
blistering email to the DPS. It railed about the cost of
Operation Kayu during a recession and the 'disgraceful'
treatment of three once loyal officers. Clark was still on a
career break and trying to patch things up with his wife
but feared for his family's physical and financial safety.
The wage was the only reason he'd consider returning to
the force that had betrayed him. On a detective's salary he
could earn enough to take the edge off the austerity that
was coming. 'Me and my family will never forget how we

have been treated and hope those involved never forget either,' he wrote. Did anyone at Scotland Yard have 'the bottle' to question what had gone on, he asked the DPS.

Surprisingly, some did and in September 2009 an officer from outside the DPS was brought in to conduct one-on-one interviews with Operation Kayu officers across the ranks. Ashfaq Siddique wasn't one of them. Ironically, the debriefing took place at the same police sports club where, four and a half years earlier, Pelé Mahmood blew the whistle on corruption in Newham council. It concluded that there was an atmosphere of 'mistrust and disharmony' inside the DPS and Operation Kayu. Senior DPS management and the Gold Group had exerted 'too much influence' on operational decisions and the 'interventions were perceived to be political and not based on the developing investigation.'

More junior anti-corruption detectives were effectively kept in the dark about what had been done and those lines of enquiry that should have been looked into were 'under-resourced and abandoned too soon'. The lower ranks felt they were not being listened to and those in charge 'put their own spin on the material which was not supported elsewhere ... The briefings were overhyped and opinionated rather than having any proper basis. This overhyping manifested itself to some as close to bullying them into carrying out enquiries and actions without properly sourced material. There was confusion over leadership and decision making.'

The most stinging feedback, however, concerned the decision to abandon the Matthews trial and its knock on effect for the prosecution of McGuinness. 'Whilst the decision to stop the [Matthews] trial was made by the CPS and Prosecution Counsel there was a perception

that briefings given to them were overhyped and excitable
and should have been more measured. Had they been
more measured it was felt the trial could have progressed.
There was an issue in relation to the minute keeping at
the meeting to discuss the trial and this led some to be
concerned about the content of those discussions.'[10]

[10]1 December 2009 Operation Kayu Debrief Report by Clive Walker SDC1 and
signed off by DCI Simon Rose DPS.

The Met's decision to abandon the Aladdin's den trial of Chicky Matthews
junior in October 2007 had ramifications for the force's investigation of the
£14m Hatton Garden Security Deposit robbery which took place over the Easter
weekend in 2015. The jewellery found at London City Metals (LCM) by Mac's
team in March 2006 was traced to the sophisticated 2004 robbery of Giggy's,
a jeweller in Hatton Garden. Stolen items from the August 2010 robbery of
Chatila, a jeweller in Old Bond Street, was also found at LCM when the police
raided it in August 2015. Detectives were in fact looking for the proceeds of the
Hatton Garden robbery and had reason to suspect that Matthews was acting as
a fence.

Car number plate recognition technology revealed that Terry Perkins, one
of the Hatton Garden robbers, had visited LCM on three Saturdays between
February and March 2015 in the weeks leading up to the robbery. The police
later bugged Perkins's car in the weeks directly after the heist. He was secretly
recorded plotting with Danny Jones to offer someone they called 'Frank' from
LCM a 'parcel' of stolen items. It appeared from one bugged conversation that
'Frank' had fenced for them before.

'I'll take it to Frank not all at once and I hope we get a decent fix … Any shit
I'll give to Frank, but I want to give him a bit of cream as well, do you know
what I mean? … Whatever he says about that let's hope its about a million
pounds worth,' Perkins tells Jones. Perkins is also recorded saying he was willing
to melt whatever Frank did not want, in particular coins and an Indian gold
bracelet he described as 'my pension'.

On 19 May 2015, Perkins and Jones were arrested for the Hatton Garden heist,
along with Brian Reader, John Collins, Carl Wood, Hugh Doyle and much later,
Michael Seed. The first four men pleaded guilty after seeing the surveillance
evidence against them. Jones also pleaded guilty to the Chatila robbery. Perkins
was due to stand trial for that alongside Matthews, but died in prison aged sixty-
nine in February 2018.

Very little in Scotland Yard that is supposed to be kept
secret remains so and eventually leaks out to other officers
in some digested form. Mac knew about the lower rank
criticisms of Siddique and others but hadn't appreciated
the 'political' dimension to what had happened to him
and his crime squad. For now, he was more annoyed
that the DPS was still intent on punishing him by
insisting that he should go through something called the
'adverse inference procedure'. Little is known about the
procedure, and Scotland Yard want it this way. It began
as a secret blacklist – the Service Confidence Policy – of
officers the Yard did not want in the police but lacked
the necessary evidence to discipline, sack or prosecute
criminally. Officers found by a judge to have lied during
trial can also be referred to the adverse inference unit and
put on the blacklist.

However, the whole system is wide open to abuse and
has been used vindictively to damage whistle-blowers
and officers who cross the DPS or senior management.
Intelligence about an officer is fed into the system

Detectives suspected other Hatton Garden robbers were also involved in the
Giggy's and Chatila heists and had fenced their swag through Matthews. A man
called Frank who worked at LCM was eliminated from enquiries but Matthews
was charged with handling diamonds, a ruby and sapphire-encrusted bracelet
and emerald earrings stolen during the Chatila robbery. Matthews claimed he
was storing them (in the ceiling at LCM) for his family friend James Tibbs
junior. However, after the jury found him guilty in January 2019, he accepted
buying them from Tibbs, who was never charged.

Matthews, fifty-five, sold LCM before his trail for a 'high price', making him
a 'wealthy man', his barrister told Judge Korner, who jailed him for four and a
half years, banned him from being a company director for ten years and branded
Matthews 'a professional handler' of stolen gems.

In March 2019, Michael Seed, 58, was found guilty of involvement in the
Hatton Garden robbery and jailed for 10 years.

and designed to linger, effectively ending their career. Alternatively, officers the force wants to get rid of without the embarrassment of any disciplinary or criminal action are simply allowed to resign.

In Mac's case, the DPS sent a poisonous three-page document to the adverse inference unit that contained the same demonstrably false intelligence behind the now internally-discredited Operation Kayu. For example, it claimed his mishandling of informants had led to the collapse of the Matthews trial and that he had some indirect responsibility for the shooting of Newham council contractor Charlie Butler.

There were new claims too, that he had 'talked up' his mental health issues to avoid being interviewed and eventually appeared as 'Banana Man'. The report ended with a devastating critique from which there was no way back for Mac. 'It is the overall assessment that DCI McKelvey is a corrupter of other officers. This is in the sense that his disregard for the rules, systems and procedures and the fact that he appears to be stuck in a time warp in the 70s Gene Hunt style of policing, an individual that he genuinely appears to model himself on.'

Gene Hunt was the fictional television detective of a recent BBC hit-drama, *Life on Mars*, who evoked nostalgic laughter among viewers largely because of his politically incorrect views in the office. But Gene Hunt was also an effective detective who, by getting the job done, spoke to the public's need to believe the police, not violent criminals, still controlled the streets.

If looked at objectively, a senior police source explained, what Mac needed was better supervision and management training – that he was now too senior to be tearing around 'on the plot' with his detectives. Instead, the DPS made sure that his career was over. Mac knew it too and all that was left was to leave.

The force psychiatrist, however, refused to support his retirement on medical grounds. Mac appealed, and a hearing on 11 March 2010 found that he *was* suffering from 'chronic post-traumatic stress disorder with severe depression and personality change.' He retired in May after twenty-eight years' service and a few weeks shy of his forty-eighth birthday.

The leaving do was a bittersweet affair. Mac was the only one who wore fancy dress. He came as Gene Hunt. But the low theatre of his leaving do wasn't Mac's final middle finger to Scotland Yard. Now on the outside with good friends on the inside, he was determined to become a guerrilla cop, much like Jimmy Holmes became a guerrilla gangster.

The next two years leading up to the Olympic opening ceremony were going to be a very important time for the image of Scotland Yard and Davey Hunt for different reasons – security for the police and legitimacy for the crime boss. The Long Fella was diversifying into the worlds of premiership football and prime time television. The whiff of gangster was by now faint enough not to repel the right people, and yet evocative enough to guarantee their respect.

14

Hammer Time

Mike Law hadn't felt right about crossing the floor to join the Tories in Newham council and when he got there discovered they were little better than his own party. The New Labour administration of Sir Robin Wales had, he felt, covered up whistle-blower allegations of corruption, but the Tories were too in love with the mayor to do anything about it.

Law saw no option but to step down at the 2006 local elections, but he was unable to leave politics altogether. He had always liked the idea of being a journalist but was now pushing fifty. A job came up managing a betting shop. It paid the bills while he reinvented himself as a respected blogger on shenanigans in the Olympic borough. Law's blog was called Newham Nettles as a nod to the Aaron Hill poem about those with the mettle to grasp difficult problems.

A former fellow councillor, Sarah Ruiz, said of Law, 'many people thought he was a nutter. But he isn't. He's very thorough, anal in fact.' She too resigned as a Labour councillor after thirteen years over Sir Robin's style of leadership. 'Robin never does anything straight. The

instruction would go out, you make this happen, and
he doesn't actually care how it happens. He is a dictator.
He never forgives anybody he sees as going against him.
You've got to live in Newham to understand how corrupt
it all is at times,' she said.

Law's blog was an immediate success and he had
many disgruntled sources coming to him on a range
of subjects – from the huge fees paid to consultants to
rancour over the company awarded the casino license at
the soon to be opened Westfield Stratford City shopping
centre. Law would do his own digging then write up
the results, enjoying the discomfort that each tap of the
keyboard was causing the mayor and his communications
department.

'When [the] council announced [in 2010] that it would
be supporting West Ham United in its bid to secure the
Olympic Stadium as its new home venue, I took some
interest, especially as it was reported that the council
would secure a loan of £40 million to finance the football
club's bid,' Law explained. 'It was a bizarre partnership
between a deprived local authority and a failing football
club.'

Sir Robin had struck a deal with the Treasury to
borrow £40 million if West Ham won the bid. The vote
in favour of the deal went through the council easily
enough but some councillors privately griped that they
had not been given enough detail and reporters weren't
told what would happen if West Ham defaulted on the
loan repayments. The government and the office of the
mayor of London had set up the Olympic Park Legacy
Company (OPLC) in 2009 to ensure that after the
Games the stadium and athletes' village did not become
ghostly white elephants in the middle of a recession.

The OPLC's immediate task was to handle the bidding process among football clubs interested in relocating to the new stadium on a long lease.

Tottenham Hotspurs had been looking to move to a bigger ground in north London but was persuaded by the mayor's office and the new Tory-led coalition government of David Cameron to bid for the 80,000-seater £486 million Olympic stadium. Tottenham made it clear to the politicians that they would rebuild it without a running track so supporters could be nearer the pitch and offered £30 million to upgrade Crystal Palace in south London as an alternative international athletics venue.

Bidding closed in September 2010. Two months later the OPLC announced its shortlist. The battle for the Olympic stadium was between West Ham and its partner, Newham council, and premier league rivals Tottenham in association with the sports and entertainment group AEG, who ran the O2 arena, formerly the Millennium Dome.

On 11 February 2011, the OPLC voted unanimously – thirteen to zero – for the West Ham bid, which did not involve demolishing the stadium or removing the athletics tracks. The government and London's mayor, Boris Johnson, approved the decision in March.

Law had two good sources inside Newham council who only contacted him using withheld numbers and told him to never call on their work phones. Soon after West Ham was named the preferred bidder, one of the sources mentioned that two former senior Newham council executives had been seen visiting the town hall during the OPLC's deliberations. It was interesting – not for the fact the couple were in a relationship, but because one now worked for West Ham and the other for the OPLC.

Ian Tompkins was Newham council's former head of communications and a close ally of Sir Robin Wales. Some said he was the mayor's chief propagandist and enforcer. The 53-year-old left the council in 2008 for West Ham United, which already had a close relationship with the council and lavished gifts on the mayor. The council took a £15,000 box at the club.[1]

Tompkins was put in charge of masterminding West Ham's joint bid for the Olympic stadium. His lover was 33-year-old Dionne Knight, a law graduate and the former head of procurement at Newham council, where they met. The couple were already in a relationship when she went to work for the OPLC in May 2010 as its £80,000-a year director of corporate services.

Law eventually had enough to make a request under the Freedom of Information Act for details of the couple's visits to the council between September 2010 and March 2011. He particularly wanted to know if they'd met with Sir Robin, who also sat on the OPLC board but had no vote on who would get the stadium. The council refused Law's request on the grounds it was too costly to answer.[2] The blogger's actions had not gone unnoticed by a private investigator based in Manchester. Howard Hill used the fake name 'Graham Benson' to contact Law looking for any leads on Tompkins and Knight that could be chased down on behalf of his client.

[1]Newham council's new chief executive Joe Duckworth cut the communications budget after a review.
[2]The council eventually responded in June 2011. The reply said: 'We can confirm that Ian Tompkins visited the London Borough of Newham's offices on regular occasions during the stadium bidding process as part of the agreed partnership [with] West Ham United on the stadium project. Ms Knight did not to our knowledge visit the LBN offices on any official OPLC business.'

Tottenham had hired Hill two days before the OPLC bid decision to do a discreet but deep dive around those involved in the process because the club suspected foul play by West Ham and the OPLC.

Daniel Levy, the chairman of Tottenham, thought his bid had been leaked to his rival between the preliminary and final stages. That suspicion only hardened after the unanimous OPLC decision and when Tottenham was allowed to see a redacted version of the executive report on both bids. It was 'very biased' against the club, said Selwyn Tash, Tottenham's lawyer. 'The report was so strongly worded in favour of West Ham/Newham that any committee member would be very hard pushed not to vote for it ... The documents disclosed have been so heavily redacted it begs the questions what don't [the OPLC] want us to see? I think the feeling we have had is that we've been used to leverage a higher offer or a better offer from West Ham Newham because we lost so badly. We thought we had an incredibly strong bid. We were told we failed on two of the five main criteria and we felt we didn't at all, that they had made a decision and worked back to try and justify it.'[3]

Over the next few weeks, legal letters dropped through the mailboxes of the OLPC, Boris Johnson, Newham council and West Ham, threatening court action if answers were not forthcoming about the decision-making process. Meanwhile, according to a Tottenham insider, a report by Hill on the new owners of West Ham was causing Levy to think hard about whom he was taking on.

David Sullivan and David Gold had become multi-millionaires through separate and joint adventures in

[3]Interview with Selwyn Tash 1 July 2011.

the sex business and then as owners of Birmingham City
football club. At forty-nine, Levy was no pushover on the
pitch, but the report is said to have warned him to be
especially careful about mixing it with Sullivan.

At seventy, David Sullivan can look back on a remarkable
career that took on the Establishment and won. In one
interview he went as a far as calling himself a 'freedom
fighter' for tumescent men's right to party singlehandedly
with porn.

In the seventies, the economics graduate stayed away
from Soho, where Bernie Silver was cock of the walk.
Sullivan preferred to make his base in Essex, from where
the young porn baron cornered the market in mail-order
dirty magazines. When punters bounced cheques he
name-dropped the Krays to ensure speedy payment –
until one of the twins complained from prison, that is. As
Sullivan tells it, he and Reggie Kray became pen pals and
were bonded by parents who used to drink together in the
old East End.[4]

In addition to porn through the letterbox, the young
entrepreneur also spotted the coming explosion in blue
movies and separately founded the UK sex shop chain
'Private' to sell them, all of which pushed the boundaries
of the out-dated Obscene Publications Act and brought
Sullivan lots of money and notoriety as the British equivalent
of American porn baron and self-styled libertarian, Larry
Flynt. All that cash had to go somewhere, and Sullivan
invested in Soho real estate, which first brought him into

[4]West Ham blog Claret & Hugh 4 June 2015. David Sullivan and former West
Ham chairman, Terry Brown, later funded the £3 million budget for the 2015
straight-to-DVD feature *The Rise of the Krays*.

contact in the late eighties with Davey Hunt, a man he
would many years later loan £1 million.

Hunt and Jimmy Holmes leased Sullivan's premises
on the corner of Brewer Street and Wardour Street,
which they ran as a lucrative clip joint taking £10,000 a
week. Holmes recalls paying around £300,000 per year
in rent to Sullivan's man who he met every Monday at
the Ambassadors snooker club to hand over the cash.
Sullivan's involvement with 'massage parlours' had earned
him a short spell in prison for living off immoral earnings.
He took the conviction for 'poncing' in his stride – seeing
it as the price of being a freedom fighter.

'Whatever the future held for Sullivan,' observed
journalist Martin Tomkinson at the time, 'by the beginning
of the eighties he could look back on an almost unbelievably
successful decade. Single-handed he has revolutionised
the sex industry by taking porn to the general public ...
Moreover, at thirty-three, by working six days a week, he
was in the enviable position of being able to contemplate
selling out and retiring.'[5]

Only he didn't. Instead, Sullivan teamed up with David
Gold, a true East End rags-to-riches entrepreneur, and
bought ailing Birmingham City football club in 1993.

Gold, the older of the two, had made his fortune
through the Anne Summers chain of upmarket sex shops
and parties, where sales teams cleverly marketed sex toys
at women in the comfort of their living room – a bit like
Avon ladies, but with dildos. In January 2010, Sullivan
and Gold bought a controlling stake in West Ham United,
having sold Birmingham City the previous year for a profit.

---

[5] Martin Tomkinson, *Pornbrokers: Rise of the Soho Sex Barons* (Virgin 1982).

Gold described the purchase of the famous Boleyn ground as a 'boyhood dream' and Sullivan said that, had they not been Hammers fans, the deal made no financial sense as the club was in a 'serious mess' and facing relegation. Karren Brady, their young managing director at Birmingham City, came over as vice chair. She had first worked with Sullivan at *The Daily Sport*, his overtly soft-porn meets celebrity tittle-tattle tabloid whose sales eventually went flaccid. By the time she joined West Ham, Brady was a TV celebrity as Alan Sugar's sidekick judge in *The Apprentice*.

The trio of Sullivan, Gold and Brady were now firmly in the sights of Levy, who had replaced Sugar as chairman of Tottenham in 2001. When Tottenham got no satisfactory answers to its legal letters, in April 2011 the club launched judicial reviews in the high court, which put a major spanner in the OLPC's legacy plans. The handover to West Ham had to be suspended because Levy was questioning the integrity of the process, particularly whether Newham council had acted correctly in getting access to a £40 million loan of public money.

The following month, Tottenham upped the ante by seeking to judicially review the decision of the OPLC, the mayor of London and the minister of sport in making West Ham the preferred bidder. A Tottenham insider said the club had picked up rumours that Lord Coe, the chairman of the London Organising Committee of the Olympic and Paralympic Games, was instrumental in West Ham winning the bid. The Tory peer had 'an emotional attachment to the stadium and a political attachment to it remaining,' the insider said, and Tottenham was hearing that he had threatened to resign from LOCOG if it was knocked down.

While high court judges decided on the merits of Tottenham's legal claims, the club's private investigator was obtaining some potentially damaging information on its rival.

Howard Hill does not look like a private investigator of the Continental Op kind found in the pages of a Dashiell Hammett novel. For starters, he has no hard-boiled law enforcement background and is more likely to have a row with a sommelier than a punchy informant in a dive bar. The jowly investigator in his mid-fifties is part of the newer breed of corporate gumshoe, the accountants whose playgrounds are the boardroom battles when clients find themselves on the wrong end of a criminal or civil prosecution.

Hill was a partner at PKF, a forensic accountancy firm, where he ran the business intelligence team carrying out due diligence inquiries for clients, a fancy name for all manner of investigative techniques, some that straddle the line of legality and plausible deniability. The unwritten agreement between private investigators and their corporate clients in this new world is the same as it ever was: don't get caught, and if you do, you're on your own.

Hill was already on the case when he learned of Mike Law's freedom of information request. The private investigator had turned to the dark arts to gain access to bank statements and phone records of a key West Ham executive. Such private information can be obtained unlawfully by having someone on the inside of a bank or phone company. More typically, it's blagged over the phone. A skilled blagger is a good mimic and has an array of sound effects at hand, such as recordings of a departure lounge flight announcer, to stress the urgency and authenticity of

the request for the bank statements or phone records of the
person he or she is pretending to be. Once in possession of
Ian Tompkins' phone records, Hill noticed that the West
Ham executive was frequently calling one number, which
was traced to Dionne Knight. In May, she was put under
surveillance at her £350,000 Surrey home where she lived
with her teenage daughter.

Meanwhile, Tottenham's investigator obtained copies
of her and Tompkins' bank statements. At 4.52 p.m. on
16 May, NatWest Bank faxed over Knight's statements
from 23 December 2010 to 28 April 2011, the crucial
period before and after the OPLC's bid decision. Among
the humdrum withdrawals of everyday life, two types of
deposit into her bank account caught Hill's eye. The first
was Knight's monthly salary of just under £5,000 from
the OLPC. The other was a series of deposits from 'West
Ham United'.

Over the four-month period, West Ham had deposited
£9915.31 into her bank account – £1,900 in the month
before the stadium decision and £8,000 afterwards. Hill
also discovered another payment of £4,800 from West
Ham in June. There were also regular deposits, described
as 'loan repayments' totalling £2,248, from Tompkins'
Halifax bank account.

On the face of it, during the crucial bidding period
West Ham had an OPLC director on the payroll.
The club had paid almost £15,000 to Knight, who
happened to be in a relationship with the mastermind
of its bid for the Olympic stadium and both of them
had previously worked at Newham council, West Ham's
bid partner. At first blush, it was a sensational discovery
and one that had the potential to re-open the bid for
Tottenham, especially as West Ham had just been

relegated to the Championship, which cast further doubts on its finances.

Hill informed Tottenham about the payments to Knight. The club's lawyers, Olswang, then wrote to the OPLC. The letter did not refer to any payments by West Ham into Knight's bank account but asked if she had access to confidential information about the bid process.

The OPLC already knew about the relationship with Tompkins because Knight had declared it upon joining in May 2010. The couple had been seeing each other for two years by then, after Tompkins separated from his wife. But when Knight was shown the letter from Tottenham's lawyers she said nothing to the OPLC about the money she was receiving from West Ham or what it was for. The OPLC's lawyers therefore wrote back simply saying Knight had no part in the process of selecting the final bidder. Tottenham was not satisfied with the response. The club never thought she had any influence over the decision to give the stadium to West Ham. They wanted to know whether she'd had access to confidential information about the bid and believed that Knight had attended OPLC committee meetings in an advisory capacity with her boss, Jonathan Dutton, who was on the board and did have a vote in the bid decision.

Tottenham's private investigator had also turned his attention to the OPLC and was looking at its board members. Hill obtained the mobile phone records of Andrew Altman, the OPLC chief executive. The American developer had worked in the Philadelphia mayor's office before being recruited in August 2009 for the £195,000 job on a five-year contract. The private investigator was hoping to bottom out his client's suspicion that the OPLC had been holding secret talks with West Ham. To that end, Hill also obtained the phone records of Karren

Brady, who was leading West Ham into the battle for the Olympic stadium. The phone billings for the period December 2010 to February 2011 showed that in the four weeks before the bid decision there had been calls and texts between Altman and Brady. She had also phoned Keith Edelman, the former Arsenal Football Club director, who was chairman of the OPLC's audit committee at the time. Both Altman and Edelman were among the thirteen board members who voted for West Ham.

The question for Tottenham was what could it do with all this potentially explosive intelligence? The club decided to pass it to a newspaper.

At a swanky London hotel in June, Hill explained to reporters from *The Sunday Times* that his client was 'bouncing off the wall' to make public West Ham's payments to Knight. He lent forward and slid a photocopy of the bank accounts and phone records across the table. Days later, the private investigator made it clear that he was reporting directly to Daniel Levy and Selwyn Tash. But the Tottenham chairman didn't want to be seen to be involved. 'They are very anxious to keep Daniel at arm's length from the information I gave you,' Hill told one of the reporters. 'They are paranoid about not wanting to be associated with it.'

On 30 June, a *Sunday Times* reporter knocked on Dionne Knight's front door. Her silver Porsche was parked in the driveway. Moments earlier, Ian Tompkins had arrived with a takeaway. Knight came to the door with a hacking cough and was asked about the West Ham payments into her bank account. 'There's a perfectly good explanation for that, an innocent explanation,' she said, inviting the reporter inside.

Knight stressed she had told the OPLC about her relationship with Tompkins when she was first offered the job. 'Ian and I had an agreement that we wouldn't talk about [the bid],' she said. Tompkins nodded. 'And I declared it to West Ham at the time as well,' he added. They both pointed out that there were 'huge Chinese walls' in place. Knight stopped going to West Ham matches. She still attended the odd club function but not in an official capacity. Tompkins recalled that Brady wanted to take him and a few others for a thank you dinner with their partners but the OPLC advised Knight against it.

However, when asked if she had told her employer about the payments from West Ham into her NatWest account, Knight became defensive. 'I haven't declared and there's no reason for me to declare payments that have gone in and out of my account … What comes in and out my account is not their business … There is nothing that obliges me to inform my employer what goes in and out of my account and who it's from.'

'You are not being bribed in any way?'

'No! I'm not being blackmailed. I'm not being induced. I've not been bribed. I've not even got access to information that's worth … He would know more about the process,' she said, pointing at Tompkins. 'If your implied question is, have you given information to West Ham in exchange for financial sums, categorically not, categorically swear on the Koran, the Holy Bible. I can understand the public perception but the process has been so controlled and I've been so far removed from the process. Even if I did have information, categorically not.'

Knight finally admitted that the payments were for an undeclared consultancy that started in December,

therefore during the bidding process, and continued after
West Ham had won; but she wouldn't say what she did
for the club without its permission.

The couple were painting a muddled picture. Knight
thought it important to declare the relationship to the
OPLC but not that she was moonlighting for West Ham
during the bidding process. Only a few weeks earlier,
at the end of May, she'd failed to come clean about the
consultancy when shown the letter from Tottenham's
lawyers.

'Do you think you should have [told the OPLC]?'

'No, I don't.'

Pressed for the last time to describe the consultancy
work, Knight replied obliquely, 'It's just a one-off piece
of work they've asked me to help because of my technical
expertise in the area ... I'm comfortable telling you it's
technical assurance.'

The next day, the reporter called Daniel Levy for a
comment. Tottenham's chairman was told that the bank
statements obtained by his private investigator had been
put to Knight who admitted having an undeclared paid
consultancy with West Ham.

'Wow!' He said. 'I would rather not comment if I'm
honest, because I don't want the government to feel
we're anywhere near this ... What I'd rather you do is,
can I ask you to speak to our lawyer who's involved with
the whole process on our behalf . . . a gentleman called
Selwyn Tash.'

'Is he dealing with Howard, as Howard mentioned his
name to me as well?'

'Right. Let me give you his number ... We are in litigation
with the government and at the same time although I don't

think this whole process was fair, I certainly don't want to be seen to be the one that was responsible for bringing all this out into the open. So as far as I'm concerned I'm nowhere near this.'

According to the Tottenham insider, Tash was part of a trusted circle around Levy that others in the club called 'the family'. On the phone, Tash confirmed that he reported to Levy but told the reporter that the club was making no comment. Later in the day, the OPLC suspended Knight on full pay pending an independent investigation. 'The auditors Moore Stephens have been appointed to carry out this investigation into our [internal stadium] procedures. We are also investigating the nature of the consultancy work that Dionne Knight undertook without our knowledge or permission. We remain confident that the integrity of our processes has not been compromised,' the statement said.

West Ham followed with a statement revealing for the first time that Knight was doing a procurement contract relating to the Olympic stadium project but unconnected to the bidding process, which the club also insisted had not been compromised.

Over at *The Sunday Times*, the reporters wondered why West Ham would contract Knight in December to carry out procurement work for a stadium bid it hadn't yet won. 'If West Ham was so confident of winning the process in December then it was a done deal,' Tash suggested over the phone.

Just before midnight, Karren Brady provided a statement. It started off explaining that West Ham and Newham council had formed a jointly owned company, the Legacy Stadium Partnership (LSP), to handle its bid, which was aware of 'the long-standing relationship' between Tompkins and Knight. Then this:

> The LSP had to undertake a project in relation to the procurement of a construction partner after the Olympic Games. This work was put out to tender. Ms Brady and Mr [Kim] Bromley-Derry [chief executive of Newham council] were informed by Ian Tompkins that Dionne Knight had permission from the OPLC to undertake this work as a paid procurement project on behalf of the LSP and that there was no conflict of interest with her role at the OPLC.

It wasn't looking good for Tompkins. But there was more:

> Ms Knight was paid for and undertook this project, which involved a substantial amount of work. The work was undertaken on a completely transparent basis and there was no reason for the LSP to believe that she was prohibited from doing so. Ms Knight was neither directly or indirectly part of the bid process nor part of the decision making process within the OPLC. This has been confirmed by the OPLC. Neither Ms Brady nor Mr Bromley-Derry have ever had any dealings with Ms Knight in relation to the bid process and confirm that no aspect of the bid process has ever been discussed between them and her. The LSP has not paid any member of the OPLC for any information in relation to the bid process. The LSP has not received any unauthorised information from the OPLC or any other source in relation to its bid.

West Ham declined to provide *The Sunday Times* with a copy of Knight's procurement contract or information

about the tendering process, crucially, when it was first
advertised, who ran it, and which companies were in the
running. Nor would the club explain why it had taken
Tompkins' word and not checked with the OPLC before
awarding one of its directors with the paid contract. All it
said was Knight won the 'very substantial' work because
she was 'significantly' cheaper.

West Ham suspended Tompkins, who it described as
'the member of staff responsible for appointing [Knight]'
and launched an internal inquiry into 'why [she] agreed
to undertake [the] work without the permission of her
employer.'

That evening, Tompkins was called for a comment. He
hadn't seen West Ham's statement effectively saying that
he had misled Brady and Newham council.

'Is that right?' the reporter asked.

'I'm not commenting on it.'

'It looks like they are hanging you out to dry.'

'I can't say anything.'

The next day, further clarity on what Knight was doing
for West Ham came from her own lawyer. She was a
'procurement specialist' paid £20,400 for preparing a
procurement document for the design of the stadium, he
told the *Sunday Times*. The contract was part of the bid
process and ran from December 2010 to June 2011. Knight
now accepted it was 'inappropriate' to take the contract
and not tell the OPLC, but her work for West Ham 'had
nothing to do with the process' and she was 'the equivalent
to a widget counter filling in a form,' the lawyer added.

It was Tompkins, he said, who had informed Knight
that she'd won the contract but Knight had never
claimed that the OPLC were okay with it. As for the

regular deposits of £557 that Tompkins paid into her
NatWest account, they had nothing to do with West
Ham or the contract. They were repayment of a loan
she had taken out for Tompkins because he had 'bad
credit'. Their relationship was now over, the lawyer
revealed.

In a final call to Tash for his take on these latest
developments, Tottenham's lawyer told the newspaper: 'It
seems to me that people are getting their head together to
concoct a story whereby the Newham West Ham side and
also the OPLC side come out of this, you know, high and
dry with no blemishes, no stigma attached. And the two
people involved, Tompkins and Knight will lose their jobs
and possibly face some sort of prosecution.'

But, Tottenham was also in danger of being hauled
through the courts because lawyers for West Ham were
now taking legal action for the unlawful access to Brady's
phone records. Tash paused when asked to comment
on the club's use of Howard Hill and PKF to conduct
corporate espionage on West Ham and the OPLC.

'We are going to make it clear that the information was
obtained for Tottenham,' the reporter added.

'You are going to make that clear?'

'Yes we are going to make that clear otherwise it leaves
the impression that we obtained it and in the current
climate we can't have that.'

The climate referred to was the phone hacking scandal
engulfing the media, in particular outlets owned by
Rupert Murdoch's News International, which was about
to close sister paper the *News of the World*. The tabloid's
former editor had recently resigned as chief spin-doctor
for David Cameron's government and the prime minister
was days away from announcing a judicial inquiry into

the media. Meanwhile, Scotland Yard had already formed a special squad to investigate journalists, their sources and the use of private investigators to obtain personal details.[6]

Tash was disappointed at the news. 'It seems that now everyone's going to point the finger at Tottenham ... for producing information that everybody suspected was there anyway ... I understand your point of view. I had thought, possibly naively, that you would say the information had been handed into you not that it was either commissioned by the club or anybody, you know, that it was received anonymously,' he said.

'We gave no undertakings ... We are going to say that Tottenham commissioned the investigation. That's the truth.'

After a long pause, Tash said the club was offering no comment.

Following publication in early July, Brady and the OPLC spoke to the police. In a further statement to *The Sunday Times*, the *Apprentice* star said all her dealings with the OPLC chief executive and other board members during the bidding process were 'wholly legitimate, in the normal course of business [and] the integrity of the bidding

---

[6] *The Sunday Times* was part of News International. In a disgraceful episode, external lawyers working with News International executives handed over reporters' emails to the police without due regard for source protection issues. The police's own senior management had close ties to News International and the investigation of journalists should have been handled by another force. Reporters and their sources – the lifeblood of any media organisation – were thrown under the bus to protect the Murdochs, their media empire in the UK and US and its favoured executives.

process for the Olympic Stadium was not in any way compromised.'⁷

The OPLC agreed. Contacts between its board members and Brady or Levy were 'quite usual' and part of the bidding process to ensure the best possible bids and taxpayer value, it said, adding that 'no confidential information from one bidder was ever shared with another bidder'.⁸ Six weeks later, the OPLC's auditors came to the same conclusion in a report that found Knight had no access to confidential information, had not passed on any relating to the bidding process and therefore the integrity of the process was intact and West Ham would remain the preferred bidder.

The government and mayor of London's office agreed the bid did not need to be reopened. West Ham's own review similarly found it did nothing wrong in hiring Knight. However, days later the stadium's future was once again up in the air when Tottenham won its judicial review of the £40 million loan by Newham council to West Ham. Mr Justice Collins said no commercial bank would have made the loan and without it the football club could not have jointly bid for the stadium. Tottenham claimed

⁷'Olympic boss paid secret cash' and 'Lovers suspended in stadium scandal' *The Sunday Times* Insight team; Michael Gillard, Jonathan Calvert, Claire Newell (3 July 2011). 'West Ham calls in police over Olympic spies' Insight team (Michael Gillard, Jonathan Calvert, Claire Newell) 10 July 2011.

⁸Altman and Edelman had spoken to both Brady and Levy, an OPLC spokeswoman said, but the quango would not provide the protocols for how conversations were recorded and minuted. A source close to Brady told *The Sunday Times* that her calls to the two OPLC board members were innocuous. One was asking what could she say about the West Ham bid in her column for *The Sun* and another was the OPLC asking about an article claiming the club was refinancing.

the state aid had given their rival an unfair competitive advantage.

The judge also commented on *The Sunday Times'* revelations about West Ham's payments to Knight. Putting aside the OPLC's findings, he said: 'It looks bad, to say the least,' and suggested that Tottenham should raise it at the next hearing in October. There was much to play for in the intervening months with all sides having big cards. The police investigation into the corporate espionage was gathering pace and Brady was also pursuing Howard Hill and PKF through the civil courts.

On the other side, Tottenham could use its recent court victory as leverage against Boris Johnson and the government to withdraw from the Olympic stadium race in return for public sector funding to rebuild a new stadium at its White Hart Lane home in Harringay.

The area of Tottenham had recently gone up in flames when a riot started there and spread across London following the police shooting in July 2011 of Mark Duggan, a mixed-race man. Public money towards a new football stadium could always be sold as regeneration. In the way of these things, deals were done and pleas entered. West Ham and Newham council re-bid and got the Olympic stadium on a 99-year lease and controversial terms that left its fans and the taxpayer unhappy.

Howard Hill resigned from PKF just before he was arrested with two others he had hired for the *blagging* operation. They eventually pleaded guilty to unlawfully obtaining phone records and bank statements. Hill was fined £100,000.[9] It emerged that four OPLC directors

---

[9]Richard Forrest and Lee Stewart were fined £10,000 and £13,250 respectively.

were targeted along with Brady, Sullivan, Gold and Sir
Robin Wales. Levy agreed to settle with Brady and West
Ham to end further hostilities, at least off the pitch,
without an admission of liability. 'It was proper dough,'
said a Tottenham insider. 'Football deals with all its dirty
business in private.'

15

TOWIE

Woolston Manor Golf and Country Club was back on the map. The venue in Abridge was fast becoming an upmarket fixture in the Essex social calendar. Davey Hunt had successfully erased the image of its violent past as the Epping Forest Country Club by remodelling it to appeal to families and the wedding crowd over drug dealers and pill-popping ravers.

Since 2005, money poured in from the restored golf course and grounds. Then, following a mysterious fire three years later, the listed manor was rebuilt from the ashes as Mooro's, a glitzy eatery and bar named after Sir Bobby Moore, the much-loved captain of West Ham United and England's 1966 World Cup squad. Alongside the country club cash cow, the Hunts were also buying up pubs and bars in Essex. The empire expansion was going smoothly until officers from the Serious Organised Crime Agency (SOCA) and Inland Revenue raided Woolston Manor early one morning before the golfers arrived. The joint operation on 29 June 2010 was looking for paperwork to support long-standing suspicions that Hunt was laundering money through these cash businesses and evading tax.

Almost one hundred law enforcement officers carried out the co-ordinated raids across Essex including his accountants, the office of his property solicitor, Chris Williams and the Morleys, Hunt's family home in Great Hallingbury. Although there were no arrests and only documents were seized, Hunt offered to come in for interview and explain his 'substantial cash expenditure'. Hughmans, his criminal solicitors, also told the police that the cash came from 'realistic and commercial' rent payments, which Hunt had declared to his accountants but didn't always bank.

The SOCA operation also targeted the scrap metal merchant who had sold the Morleys to Hunt in 1993 in an usual house swap and cash deal. Alan Sewell was now a successful Essex car dealer whose larger than life personality had struck a chord with his neighbour Rod Stewart. The international superstar referred to Sewell as Big 'Honest' Al and would tell anyone that he'd helped him get over the break-up of his marriage to model Rachel Hunter. Stewart gave Sewell a loving write-up in his autobiography, and *The Graham Norton Show* showed footage of Big Al cuddling the crying singer after his beloved Celtic beat Barcelona. More than that, Sewell was the long-term manager of Stewart's celebrity football team, the Vagabonds. Over a quarter of the team were Essex police officers who ran out on the singer's well-kept pitch during the weekend sporting the green and white hoops of Celtic. 'Al picked the team,' said one player, 'and had a knack of ingratiating himself with police officers'. He was a guest at the annual dinner of the Essex CID and was also friendly with the east London branch of Scotland Yard's Flying Squad, the source said. It was this football connection and closeness to serving police officers that

separately sparked a major corruption probe inside
SOCA. At the centre of it was a female SOCA officer who
was part of the team that had raided Hunt's country club.
Sheila Roberts and her long-term partner Glyn Evans, a
former senior Essex superintendent, were close friends of
the Sewells, and through them became friendly with Rod
Stewart and his new wife Penny Lancaster. The couples
dined together and Roberts claimed she once saw the
singer pay Sewell £160,000 in cash for a Ferrari. Evans
had bought a Porsche off Sewell and since 1994 played for
the Vagabonds. He also once travelled on Stewart's private
jet to watch Celtic.

SOCA, however, had no interest in Stewart. His best
friend, Big Al, was another story. The UK's leading crime
agency suspected Sewell of corruptly using his friendship
with Roberts and Evans to undermine a mortgage fraud
and tax investigation he was facing. Evans had retired
but Roberts worked in the same SOCA office that was
investigating Sewell. That operation in turn flowed from
the raid on Hunt's mansion and was part of a wider
mortgage fraud inquiry involving Essex brokers.

Sewell contacted Evans for advice. He, Roberts and
another SOCA officer visited Sewell's home twice unaware
they were under surveillance and being listened to. In
Sewell's kitchen, Roberts said she recognised the names
of the SOCA investigators looking into his business. One
of them was her best friend who sat next to her in the
Hainault office. Roberts advised Sewell to lawyer up and
described SOCA as 'shit' and unable to 'investigate their
way out of a paper bag'.

When she was arrested, Roberts told the anti-corruption
investigators interviewing her that Sewell had many
friends in Essex police, Scotland Yard and SOCA that he

knew through football and charity functions. Sewell, she said, was concerned that SOCA's interest in him was all to do with Hunt. She said the raid on Woolston Manor and the Morleys was the talk of Great Hallingbury village – the flyposting by Jimmy Holmes in 1996 by now a distant memory. Ultimately, the Teflon gangster and 63-year-old Sewell had no need to worry. The operations into them were an embarrassment but never led to any charges. Nor did the corruption probe.[1]

[1]On 13 March 2013, SOCA's anti-corruption squad carried out early morning arrests of Alan Sewell, Sheila Roberts, Glyn Evans and Brian Adair.

Roberts, 48, and Evans, 52 were partners for twenty-eight years. They met when she was a special constable and he was an ambitious detective in Essex police. The couple had been friends with Sewell and his wife, Debs, since 1994, a year after Hunt bought the Morleys.

They regularly dined together and socialised with Rod Stewart. Roberts made no secret of her friendship with the singer through 'Big Al'.

As well as the Vagabonds, Evans played football for White Roding, another Essex-based team run by a close friend of Sewell. Around 2008, Davey Hunt's oldest son, David junior, then 20-years-old, was also on the team. 'He turned up to matches in a Range Rover with slicked back hair. Everyone knew whose son he was. He played about five games,' said one team member.

Evans and Roberts split acrimoniously in 2011 and at the time of their arrest two years later they were still dividing assets including a big house in Essex with stables and a gym.

Roberts began a relationship with Brian Adair, a former police officer who joined SOCA and was posted to Central America as a drugs liaison officer. They met working on an international drug operation (Coronary) and were living together at the time of their arrest on suspicion of misconduct in a public office.

Roberts was very talkative during her interview. On legal advice, Adair said nothing and frustrated the interview process by insisting on writing down every question he was asked before refusing to answer it.

During her interview, Roberts said she was 'very unhappy' at SOCA after being suddenly taken off Operation Coronary. She also said a bullying complaint had not been dealt with which made her feel isolated and undervalued. She was also seeing a psychiatrist after the death of her father.

Meanwhile, Woolston Manor Golf and Country Club continued to grow as a money-spinner for Hunt. In fact, the venue's reputation was about to go national with the launch of a reality television pilot on ITV about a group of vajazzled twenty-somethings who, if stupid was an Olympic sport, would have been worthy contenders for Team GB at the forthcoming Games.

However, Roberts denied acting corruptly or under duress from Evans. Adair also denied acting corruptly. During his interview he was asked about his relationship with David Hunt. Adair gave no comment but later claimed that he'd never heard of the gangster until the meetings with Sewell.

Adair and Roberts were suspended and later charged with Evans for offences under the Data Protection Act when police documents were found during searches of their homes. On 16 May 2014, a judge dismissed the charges for lack of evidence and the Crown Prosecution Service dropped the corruption case against all four.

Roberts and Adair remained suspended pending an internal investigation for gross misconduct. A senior source at the National Crime Officers Association said they were being 'hounded out' of the job for whistleblowing.

Friends of Roberts say she fell out of favour for helping uncover a scandal involving three SOCA officers who conspired to fabricate evidence to get one of them off a speeding ticket in 2007. During her interview Roberts admitted she should have told her line manager about Sewell but didn't because she was being bullied and thought her colleagues might be setting her up. She said she was not liked because she was making waves on an internal project into ethnic women's promotion within SOCA's firearms division. A source close to Roberts said the firearms division was 'the last bastion' of white, male officers chiefly from Scotland Yard.

Friends of Adair say his card was marked when he passed on allegations that a SOCA officer stationed overseas was abusing his child and making fraudulent expenses claims. Friends of Evans, Adair and Roberts say the trio believe the operation against them was revenge because of past whistleblowing.

Adair retired after completing his thirty years service and Roberts resigned on ill-health grounds. Adair wanted to bring a civil claim against SOCA, which became the National Crime Agency in October 2013, and needed Sewell's help, but he declined to get involved.

The Only Way is Essex flounced onto British television screens in October 2010 to soon secure an average audience of 1.25 million viewers and a BAFTA.

The scripted not scripted show followed Mark Wright, a good-looking 23-year-old who had just split with his childhood sweetheart and was playing the field. Only Wright didn't have the field to himself as Kirk Norcross, another good-looking Essex lad, also had designs on the local talent's talent for fake tans, fake body parts and absurd chat. *TOWIE*'s new stars were inevitable tabloid fodder as Wright and Norcross, two wannabe club promoters, duelled it out in a battle of pecks and skinny kecks across various venues, among them the Sugar Hut, run by his dad Mick Norcross, and the Hunt family's Woolston Manor entertainment complex.

The Wright family were the anchor of the show, which featured his car dealer dad, also called Mark, mum Carol, her mum, nanny Pat, sister Jessica, an aspiring singer, and young brother Josh, a talented footballer. The Wright boys came from good footballing stock, although Dad, Mark senior, was outshone by his younger brother, Jason Wright, who played for West Ham in the eighties and was branded a 'love rat' by the tabloids for apparently cheating on Page 3 sensation, Maria Whittaker.

Evans had a new partner, a solicitor, when his home was raided in March 2013. She successfully sued for false imprisonment in November 2017.

The author investigated the matter for *The Sunday Times* and spoke to all the parties concerned. Sewell told the author that he had not met Hunt since 1993 and denied the SOCA investigation into his business was linked to the crime boss.

Two days before the story was published on 25 May 2014, the National Crime Agency issued the author with a formal Osman warning of a threat to his life. The NCA warning said: '[Hunt's] organised crime group is actively looking to try and find and cause you serious harm.'

The Hammers had also scouted Mark junior but he too was outshone by his younger brother, Josh, who after a spell at Redbridge United and international caps for England under-19s ended up in the midfield for League One Gillingham FC.

To give the show an edge, Mark Wright senior was portrayed as having something of the Essex underworld about him. 'He's a man's man. He's the *TOWIE* Godfather. Mess with him and you'd face a world of pain,' fans were told on the dedicated ITV website. However tongue-in-cheek the write-up was supposed to be, seeing Mark Wright senior as a television celebrity brought a smile to the faces of some retired organised crime and anti-corruption detectives who had worked east London and Essex. The police had significant intelligence about Mark and his three brothers Eddie, George and Jason, and their relationship with the Hunts. In September 1992, for example, the regional crime squad received word that Eddie and Jason had enlisted Davey Hunt to go to Spain to confront a Dutch cartel that had seized their assets over an unpaid £1 million drug debt.

The most interesting material was contained in the secret Tiberius report into police corruption written in 2002, eight years before *TOWIE* was first aired. The report described Mark Wright as 'an upper echelon criminal' with contacts in UK and Europe who was suspected of getting close to police officers in order to corrupt them. Operation Blackjack, the report said, was 'no better example' of this.

Wright had an intriguing role in the story of Paul Cavanagh, who Hunt almost killed over a £10,000 Land Rover. Wright was the friend who left messages on Cavanagh's phone warning him not to go to Palmer's

Motors the morning that Hunt slashed his throat in
November 1997. After the assault, bugs and phone taps
inside the car showroom suggested Hunt was using
Wright to see if Cavanagh was going to grass.

Wright was a former business partner of Stevie Hunt
in a Romford car showroom during the nineties. The pair
had sponsored West Ham's then top striker, Trevor Morley,
with a car. Jason Wright was closer to Davey Hunt but
they all went to the Boleyn ground when the Hammers
played at home, which is how Cavanagh got to know Mark
Wright. A senior police source said Operation Blackjack
had amassed 'a lot of intelligence' about the Hunts chasing
Mark and Eddie Wright for repayment of substantial debts.

After the attack on him, Cavanagh alleges that he,
Mark and Eddie Wright made common cause to engage
in a dodgy scheme to raise some quick cash and get the
Hunts off their backs. The trio fell out, leaving Cavanagh
suspecting he had been had over by the Wright brothers.
What Cavanagh didn't know was that, as described in
the Tiberius report, Mark and Eddie Wright were police
informants registered to detective sergeant Ray Ahearne,
who ran the source unit for Operation Blackjack. Neither
Wright brother was aware that the other was also an
informant.[2]

The world of informant handling is a wilderness of
mirrors and there are a number of reasons why people

---

[2]According to the 2002 Tiberius report, Mark Wright was registered under the
pseudonym 'Michelle Banner' on 19 February 1998. Wright denies he was an
informant. It is possible he was unaware he had been registered as one, although
this was common practice at the time. The Tiberius report said Eddie Wright
was registered as 'Michelle Poole'. Two senior sources on Operation Blackjack
confirm this.

talk to the police: revenge, taking out the opposition, and for protection are high on the list. However, handlers have to be most wary of informants whose real motive is to find out what the police know about them and their associates – the so-called double agent. Was Mark Wright hoping to get rid of his debt by helping put Hunt behind bars? Was he playing both sides? Or was it something else that Ahearne had yet to discover?

'[Mark] Wright was specifically tasked with giving intelligence on Hunt,' a police insider explained. However, the Tiberius report says that the anti-corruption squad questioned whether Wright was in fact a double agent who while giving information about Hunt's organisation was also passing information back about the police. For example, he was secretly recorded at Palmer's Motors talking about a police officer he claimed to have in his pocket and alerted one of Hunt's associates that 'his man' had revealed that the Long Fella's finances were being monitored.

Wright never named Ahearne as his source. Nevertheless, the detective was secretly investigated during Operation Blackjack. The anti-corruption squad found no evidence to bring any criminal or disciplinary charges for corruptly working with Mark Wright or the Hunts. However, the anti-corruption squad did suspect Wright as a potential corrupter of police officers.[3] The detective retired unaware that he had been suspected of any misconduct, which he denies. Wright declined to answer a long list of specific questions but denied he was ever a police informant or a

---

[3]One of Ahearne's former colleagues said they never saw any corrupt activity in the source unit and believed the detective had correctly handled tricky informants such as Wright.

double agent for the Hunts. The TV celebrity described the brothers as former 'business associates' against whom there was 'no evidence' of any criminality.

'I have known Stephen Hunt for thirty years and David Hunt for twenty-five years. I probably speak to Stephen once or twice a month on the phone as friends,' he said. Wright claimed not to have seen Davey Hunt in years. He described the Long Fella as 'laid back' and 'a very reserved man'.[4]

Hunt did not watch *TOWIE* but Woolston Manor became a fixture in the show and the go-to venue when its stars wanted to throw a birthday bash, engagement party or charity function.[5] In the summer of 2012, with just weeks before the Olympic Games started, Mark Wright senior and junior could also be found enjoying a round of golf on Hunt's course.

[4] The quote was given when approached by *The Sun on Sunday*. 'Brentwoodfellas Exclusive: *Only Way Is Essex Shock*' by Michael Gillard, Ryan Parry and Daniel Sanderson, 9 March 2014.

[5] Gemma Collins had a birthday party at Woolston Manor in 2012, Sam Faiers and Joey Essex hosted their engagement party there in 2013, Amy Childs and Denise Van Outen, the voice of *TOWIE*, launched charity events there in 2016 and 2017 respectively.

16

Games

The Olympic torch landed in Cornwall on 18 May 2012 to begin its seventy-day journey across the UK, spreading a message of respect and friendship. Just in case the message didn't get through, a special detail of Scotland Yard officers was on hand to protect the flame from anyone angry at austerity, corporate greed, Olympic corruption and the so-called war on terror.

On its arrival at Newham, a grinning Sir Robin Wales was there to welcome the torch. 'This flame represents harmony and goodwill and these are demonstrated in our borough, where people get along fantastically and enjoy doing things together,' he asserted. This was not how *Trainspotting* director, Danny Boyle, was experiencing preparations for the opening ceremony, now only six days away. His left-leaning vision of Britishness through the ages had annoyed the Tory-led coalition government, in particular the culture secretary Jeremy Hunt, who tried to slash the section on the embattled National Health Service until the artistic director threatened to resign. The Tory backed off. Harmony was restored.

In the opening ceremony on 27 July, Boyle took 900 million viewers on a 'journey along the Thames' from its source to the centre of London. The eyes of the world fleetingly passed Hunt's waste recycling plant in Dagenham where the Long Fella's joint venture with Brendon Kerr, the Tory-loving demolition tycoon, was in the process of unravelling. The reasons for the divorce were not made any clearer on speaking to Keltbray's finance director, John Keehan, and its managing director, John Price. They simply kept repeating that Keltbray had 'no dealings' with Davey Hunt, which would be true but for the demolition group long-leasing his waste disposal site, paying rent to his offshore and UK companies and keeping his name on the joint venture and his best friend as a director-shareholder. Eventually, the two Keltbray executives settled on blaming 'the recession' for the separation.[1]

'Nothing then to do with the fact that SOCA made a public statement that they regarded [Hunt] as a leading organised crime figure?'

'Well, the only thing is that we don't know him. He is nothing you know as far as we are concerned. We lease a site off EMM and another company. They were nothing to do with David Hunt. We don't know him. We haven't met him. We know nothing about him. Other than, you know, there's been some article in the paper. But we know nothing about the guy. We don't have any association with him,' Keehan continued to insist.

The Sunday Times had published an article in May 2010, during Keltbray's joint venture with Hunt, naming him as a leading organised crime figure. SOCA confirmed this in a public statement in October 2011, which was the same month that the demolition company started

[1]Phone interview with John Price and John Keehan 3 February 2012.

to back away from Hunt.[2] The thrust of the newspaper article concerned the battle for the Silvertown strip and how Scotland Yard had thrown the Newham crime squad under the bus for trying to protect the borough from organised crime.[3] The Long Fella's reaction to the story was swift. No horse's head but a legal letter announcing the unthinkable, the never-before-done by a leading British underworld figure. Davey Hunt was going to sue for libel.

Many rich and powerful figures use the UK's perverse libel courts like legal deodorant, but this was a first. It was a remarkable statement on how far Hunt believed he had snuffed out the whiff of gangster and the profession of violence. It was also a massive gamble and one that suggested something else was at stake. For now, the historic libel trial would have to take a back seat to the world's greatest sporting event where, over two weeks in July and August, 10,000 Olympians had their own day of reckoning.

[2]Keltbray moved out of the Dagenham site and sold the business back to its original owners in 2013. Keltbray Hunt was renamed Keltbray Environmental Limited (KEL). Kerr retains a 51 per cent controlling interest. Phil Mitchell, Teddy Barham and Lawrence Lillie are equal shareholders of the remaining shares. Keltbray's statement said: 'The waste recycling business was not profitable and in 2013 KEL sold the business back to LL and PM although the leases with EMM Ltd and Hunts (UK) Properties Ltd remained with KEL. In 2015 the lease was surrendered and a compensation payment made for the unexpired term of the lease. LL, PM and EB resigned as directors of KEL following sale of the waste business at Dagenham. KEL has other business operations but it has a negative net worth and LL, PM and EB remain shareholders because of this but have no other connection with the KEL or Keltbray Group. Mr Kerr has not met Mr Hunt on any social occasions, and only met him in 2015 to negotiate the surrender of the leases.'

[3]'Taxpayers fund land purchase from crime lords' by Michael Gillard, (*The Sunday Times*, 23 May 2010).

The London 2012 Games were considered a success with sixty-five medals for Team GB including gold in rowing, cycling, athletics, sailing, canoeing, tennis, horse riding, taekwondo and boxing at the ExCel centre in Hunt's old stomping ground.

The Long Fella almost had the last word when his waste management plant caught fire, threatening the closing ceremony on 12 August. Millions watched Hunt's Waste go up in flames and a perfectly formed toxic balloon slowly drifting towards the Olympic Stadium. But few could see the corrosive effect the Long Fella had on the host city, nor the greed and institutional corruption that had allowed him to prosper. The London Fire Brigade managed to get on top of the emergency and put out Hunt's fire by 5.30 p.m. Meanwhile, over at Scotland Yard, the senior management were still trying to cover up their failure to do just that.

Former detective chief superintendent Albert Patrick has done about all an officer interested in chasing real villains could want out of a police career at Scotland Yard. He's served on and led murder, robbery and drug squads targeting most of London's major crime families and run informants, bugging operations and police rugby teams. Yet after thirty years and mandatory retirement, the large Scotsman still couldn't give it up and returned to solve cold cases and other problems.

One such 'problem' was an application from the recently retired David McKelvey for an injury award. Mac wanted compensation for damage to his mental health caused by Operation Kayu. Patrick led a team of three experienced detectives to investigate if the claim had any merit. To do the job properly he negotiated access to the officers

GAMES 313

and intelligence behind Kayu. The anti-corruption squad
agreed that he would be able to see their files but not take
any away.

Four months later, Patrick concluded in a fifty-page
report that an injury award was warranted. Not only
that – he starkly exposed the anti-corruption squad as
incompetent and raised the question whether something
else more malign was at work. Operation Kayu, he said,
was 'a fatally flawed investigation'. The Matthews and
McGuinness trials should never have been abandoned
because anti-corruption officers had 'misled' prosecution
barristers and the Crown Prosecution Service with that
eight-page memo. Mac, Guntrip and Clark had not
mishandled any informants, nor invented intelligence
about a possible threat to life and all other remaining
disclosure issues could have been overcome simply by
talking to them.

'The Anti-Corruption Command acted far too quickly
in their submission of the [eight-page memo] without
checking their suspicions first ... [It] contained inaccurate
and misleading information that would have influenced
the decision by Counsel and the CPS to abandon the trial
of Matthews and others.'

The report went on: 'The Review Team are concerned
that having investigated Mr McKelvey on a number
of occasions and apparently cleared him of any wrong
doing, a different section of the [anti-corruption squad]
later used and continue to use the original allegation
as a "cause for concern" or continued evidence of his
supposed corruption.'[4] Information exonerating Mac had

[4]A Thematic Review of the application for an injury award by David McKelvey.
January 2011.

been omitted from official minutes or not mentioned. Checking calls were not done before highly prejudicial statements were committed to paper as fact or irresistible inference.

In an interview following his retirement, Patrick once again pulled no punches. The decision-making, particularly by Ash Siddique, was 'disgraceful' and involved 'bigging up' the facts, he said.[5] It was not Patrick's remit to examine how, in his view, Siddique and others 'totally misled' the prosecution. 'I would have loved to have done it,' he said. 'But I never got to the bottom of why the report went to the CPS, who authorised that everything was accurate.'

In a further indictment of modern policing, he wondered how it was that a detective willing to go the extra mile in the fight against organised crime was in today's world considered corrupt. 'He's doing his fucking job', Patrick said of Mac. Similarly, the Newham crime squad was 'quietly getting on with what they are paid to do – investigating crime on their patch. And they were quietly nipping away at the edges and of course they were getting closer to the bigger fish,' Patrick explained.

During the review he saw documents showing 'a hint of untoward things happening in [Newham] council', but again it was not his remit to investigate this aspect of the saga. However, Patrick had a lot to say about the decision to abandon the prosecutions:

Just out of the blue they pulled the plug without consultation. If they had just asked the right questions, there were answers to everything counsel had worries

[5]Interview with Albert Patrick 17 and 19 February 2012 and 19 June 2018.

about. It's just so wrong. Was that corruption? Incompetence? Honestly, I will sit on the fence on that one. It could easily be either. It definitely was incompetent officers dealing with that investigation.

Patrick confirmed that only the Matthews and McGuinness trials were abandoned. Could Hunt have had someone on the inside of the anti-corruption squad, as the Newham crime squad suspected?

Hunt has never been nicked properly for years and years and years. He's been nicked but never been convicted. He's never served a sentence for ages. Now, knowing the likes of Hunt, the Adamses, the criminal gangs of London, then the only way they can survive is to have police in their pocket, whether its police, local authorities etc. It's the only way to operate … I can't understand why someone hasn't said, let's go and get him properly. It just hasn't happened.

Patrick stressed that his report was based on the unanimous conclusion of his team, but received no feedback from senior officers.

Scotland Yard's continued defence of the indefensible was also frustrating a senior police intelligence officer who was close to the internal machinations around Mac's damages claim. There were several reasons why coming clean wasn't an option, the source maintained. In essence, Scotland Yard couldn't admit its serious failings.

Firstly, Hunt was 'assisted throughout his rise by corrupt officers' but nothing had been done about them and this corruption had, in the source's view, played a part in the downfall of the Newham crime squad. Secondly, the Gold group had failed to question what they were being told by Operation Kayu about the threat to kill three police officers.

It was a good point, that when put to Rod Jarman, the retired commander who led the first Gold group, elicited this valuable insight. 'It was a very unusual case,' Jarman recalled. 'It's the only time where I've had a Gold group where I've had superintendents from almost every command in the [Yard] turn up because they were worried about what was going to be discussed and revealed in a meeting.'[6]

Thirdly, the frustrated police source queried why no one at Scotland Yard was interested in knowing how a 'factually wrong' eight-page memo was ever passed to the prosecution.

Siddique is retired and now runs a mosque in Barking, east London, which is a key part of the government's controversial Prevent strategy to stop the radicalisation of young British Muslims, without tackling the hypocrisy at the heart of Western foreign policy towards the Middle East.

Operation Kayu still leaves a bad taste in Siddique's mouth but he refuses to accept the personal criticism by his own junior officers or the Patrick review. Remarkably, he feels Mac beat the rap and did it with the help of other corrupt Scotland Yard officers: 'In my experience those with the best contacts get the best response. If you are corrupt and have the best contacts then you get the

---

[6]Jarman made this comment to the author on 8 June 2018 but declined to engage further.

best response ... corruption had the better reach,' he wrote in an email, but refused to expand further on such a loaded comment.[7]

Siddique said he feared for the safety of his family but never made clear where the supposed threat was coming from and declined to answer any further questions without Scotland Yard's permission. The police press office refused to assist nor would it put forward the still serving officers who Siddique had recommended for interview, namely, superintendent Paul Trevors and commander Peter Spindler of the anti-corruption squad.

Separately, Scotland Yard refuses to discuss the decision-making behind Operation Kayu that led to the abandonment of two major organised crime trials and the cover up of corruption in the Olympic borough and the biggest police force in the UK. So it was back to the frustrated police intelligence source to summarise what had gone on. As a veteran of the wilderness of mirrors, the source counselled against looking for one big joined-up conspiracy in Scotland Yard and Newham council. There were 'several small conspiracies' all running at the same time.

No one in *The Sunday Times* legal team really believed that Davey Hunt would take the newspaper all the way to court. Libel trials were now very rare because lawyers are so expensive. But Hunt had a lot more to lose besides

---

[7]Email exchange with Ash Siddique in June 2018. There is no love lost between him and McKelvey, who is privately investigating the murder of the boyfriend of Siddique's niece. In his 2012 civil claim against Scotland Yard, McKelvey accused Siddique of acting corruptly during Operation Kayu. He repeated the claim during his evidence for *The Sunday Times* in the libel trial brought by David Hunt in 2013.

money – a judge's finding that he was a major organised
crime figure could have a serious effect on his ability to
financially function in the straight world – at least, that
was the theory. Yet, as 2013 began, the Long Fella showed
every sign of going the distance having hired Hugh
Tomlinson QC to defend a reputation he didn't have and
deny one he most certainly did.

The Sunday Times was running two defences for
the article. Firstly, that it was true that Hunt was an
organised crime figure, and secondly, that the journalism
underpinning the story was responsible and in the
public interest. However, before the trial could start,
the newspaper had to fight the law. Scotland Yard and
SOCA were trying to prevent *The Sunday Times* from
using the leaked police documents that the reporter had
relied on to write the story. Such material would have
to be disclosed to Hunt as part of any defence to his
claim. The documents inevitably contained sensitive
police intelligence and, mindful of who he was, the
reporter thought it responsible to enlist the help of the
police and SOCA to make any additional redactions
before they were handed over to Hunt. The offer was
met with the Yard's usual arrogance of power. Both law
enforcement bodies joined forces to sue *The Sunday
Times* and the reporter for breach of confidence. The
Yard also launched a leak inquiry to identify his sources.

'It's disgraceful,' said Gavin Millar QC, the newspaper's formidable barrister, 'and an infringement on
a journalist's right to rely on documents in defence of
his own reporting.' The police, he said, were in effect
assisting a crime boss to bring 'a corrupt claim.' The
two law enforcement bodies wanted a private hearing

with a judge without the newspaper present. Millar
saw them off, but the judge nevertheless agreed to
prevent *The Sunday Times* from relying on some of the
most explosive leaked documents, which weakened its
defence.

Scotland Yard also wanted to heavily redact other
documents that weren't obviously sensitive. When
Millar cross-examined Roger Critchell, the head of the
Covert Policing Standards Unit who wielded the thick
black pen, it was apparent that the vast majority of
his proposed redactions were without foundation and
Scotland Yard was being obstructive or protecting itself
from embarrassment. For example, the senior officer had
redacted a comment on a SOCA report saying the Hunts
were 'too big' for Scotland Yard. As an aside, Critchell
was one of the intelligence officers who had turned down
Mac's request for help in 2006.

On the positive side, although *The Sunday Times* was
now fighting with one hand behind its back, at least the
two main law enforcement agencies in the UK had to give
the court a public assessment of David Hunt. Legitimate
businessman, as he was claiming, or successful crime
lord? Scotland Yard and SOCA told the judge they
regarded the claimant as 'the head of an organised crime
group'.[8] Such a statement was enough to question the
merits of continuing the libel claim, but Hunt wasn't for
backing down and neither was *The Sunday Times*.

Pia Sarma, the newspaper's recently appointed legal
manager, hadn't had an easy ride since joining News
International at the height of the hacking scandal and

[8]Stephen Evans of SOCA 18 July 2011.

its preparations for Lord Leveson's judicial inquiry into media standards.[9] Sarma was a striking presence in the pale, male libel world and a tenacious defender of press freedom in the face of hypocrisy and greed by the Hacked Off lobby, a group of mainly celebrities who claimed to be about holding the tabloid press to account for unethical practises. It didn't go unnoticed in some circles that Hunt's barrister chaired Hacked Off. Sarma also knew a corrupt claim when she saw one and persuaded her bosses not to yield to it, despite the financial risk of losing in the high court, where the reputation of journalism was already at rock bottom.

March 2013 was a crucial month away from the start of the libel trial. *The Sunday Times* had turned the tables on Scotland Yard with subpoenas against retired and serving officers and court orders to disclose police documents it knew would undermine Hunt's claim.

A source inside the Yard said a lot of time was spent by the Gold group discussing how not to help the newspaper. Eventually, however, because the judge had ordered it, the disclosure came, albeit in drips and drabs, and certainly boosted the defence that Hunt *was* an organised crime boss.

The time had come to exchange witness statements and prepare for trial. The Long Fella used his to explain how

---

[9]Sarma replaced Alastair Brett, who made the initial decision to fight Hunt's claim in 2010. Brett's thirty-three years of service to press freedom counted for nothing when that year he was sacrificed on the altar of corporate blame-shifting during the hacking scandal. His crime was to help reporter Patrick Foster who, along with *The Times* news desk, thought it a good idea to out an insightful police whistle-blower. In 2014, Foster accepted a police caution for an offence under the Computer Misuse Act. He went to work in public relations for Lexington.

he had become 'successful' while 'unfairly' targeted by the police. In all other respects the lengthy witness statement was a total denial of any wrongdoing. No murder, no drugs, no pimping, no witness intimidation, no threats, no fraud, no money laundering.

'I am the youngest of thirteen children from loving, caring Christian parents ... Like many east London families at the time, we experienced hardship, but we had love, dignity, respect and a strong work ethic, all instilled in us by our parents. The area I grew up in was tough. The friends I made and the people I mixed with were diverse. Some ended up getting in trouble with the police. I myself got involved in some petty crime as a youth. As a young man, when I was fifteen to twenty-one years old, I was a very accomplished boxer. I was a former amateur light heavyweight boxer and was undefeated. I gained a reputation in some circles as a very capable fighter. Due to my reputation as a fighter, I was employed by the landlords of a number of pubs to provide security. More often than not, my presence alone was sufficient to prevent problems, as people were aware that I was an undefeated boxing champion. Unlike many people in the security business, I have never taken drugs and I have never touched a drop of alcohol. Over the years, because of the respect in which I was held, I became someone who local people would turn to resolve disputes. Unfortunately, because I was well known, people tried to use my name to support their claims [and] to threaten others. This is not something that I can control.

'I moved away from the [Canning Town] area many years ago. Today the once tight-knit community has disappeared. There is a lot of drug abuse. People do not respect each other. I know very few people in the area now. However, I have heard from people I still know in the area that my name is still being used. I think it must be in this way that my reputation grew and appears to have developed (in the minds of some police officers) into an unfounded belief that I was behind various serious crimes.

'During the late 1980s and 1990s I was working hard building up my scrap and waste business and starting a young family. My wife and I have been happily married for 35 years. Our eldest is now 27 and our youngest is 13. I still work very long hours. I get up at 4 a.m. every day. I look after my pigeons. I go to work, where I put in many hours. I go to the gym and I come home to my family.

'I have very substantial commercial property interests, built as a result of hard work over many years. I own a number of companies. Hunt's (UK) Properties Limited owns a portfolio of commercial properties including Woolston Manor Golf Club and No 9 Jetty at Hunt's Wharf, which together produce an annual rental income of £457,000. EMM Limited is the owner of the waste yard, which produces an annual rental income of £561,600. I pay UK income tax on this income. The waste business I built up from scratch was so well known and reputable that Keltbray entered into a joint venture, the company was called Keltbray Hunt Limited.'[10]

The Sunday Times article in May 2010 had come as a 'massive shock' and made Hunt feel 'sick to the pit of his stomach' that anyone would think he had anything to do with murder, drugs, fraud and violence. 'I am an innocent man of previously unblemished repute fighting to clear my name,' he insisted and bemoaned that his anonymity on Google was now lost.

[10]David Hunt's witness statement 15 March 2013.

The statement had to address a number of thorny issues from his past, such as the fall out with his former business partner and self-confessed pimp, drug dealer, enforcer and money launderer. Hunt said he was introduced to Jimmy Holmes as someone with 'the Midas touch' when it came to renovating properties but the dandy gangster ran off in 1995 with £100,000 that was earmarked for doing up 2 Green's Court in Soho.[11] On Hunt's account, he had no idea the property was a brothel. But just before he made his witness statement, it was apparently sold for £715,000.[12]

[11]David Hunt's witness statement said he rented 2 Green's Court to Gary Oxley, once Jimmy Holmes' man in Soho, but denied that Oxley was part of his crime group.

At the time of the libel trial, Oxley was serving 21 years for shooting Joey Olliffe on 4 March 2009. He was the son of Ronnie Olliffe, the south London gangster and former business partner in the Barking Road massage parlour with Davey Hunt and Jimmy Holmes.

The transcript of the sentencing at the Old Bailey on 12 October 2009 revealed that Oxley owed a drug debt of £6,500 to Paul Bingham, who was in prison and had asked enforcers Joey Olliffe and Perry Hunt to collect his money. They threatened Oxley's parents and fiancé. He reported it to the police but then took matters into his own hands. Oxley arranged to meet the pair at a cafe in Mottingham. They were waiting with coffee and a chocolate bun when Oxley arrived. He shot Olliffe twice in the head at point blank range. Perry Hunt managed to escape. Oxley called 999 and sat on the floor of the empty cafe next to Olliffe's slumped body with the unloaded gun displayed in front of him. Oxley pleaded guilty but would not give evidence against Perry Hunt because his barrister said the killing of Olliffe had in his client's mind restored 'a certain equilibrium of pain' to the situation. It is not clear if Perry Hunt has any relation to David Hunt's side of the family. In a letter to the judge, Oxley said he had been 'tipped over the edge'. He said a relative had sexually abused him as a child. He later forced the man to pay him money leading to a prison sentence for blackmail in 2001.

Jimmy Holmes never forgave Oxley for switching sides and said he regularly sends him postcards in prison.

[12]Livecourt Properties Limited based in Bromley bought 2 Green's Court, which remained a brothel.

Hunt described Holmes as mentally unwell and said he became 'fixated' with him, eventually writing *Judas Pig*, which contained some of the imaginary 'sadistic fantasies' they were supposed to have done together. The book was part of a 'campaign of vilification' waged against him and Chris Williams, his commercial solicitor. More recently, he accused Holmes of threatening to shoot his criminal lawyers Peter Hughman and Matthew Jenkins.[13]

The Long Fella's statement also dealt with the attack in 1997 on the man he sent to find Holmes. Once again, Hunt denied slashing Paul Cavanagh's throat and claimed the victim withdrew the allegation because it was false and made under police pressure. To support this, Hunt asked Cavanagh to provide a new statement for the libel trial.

The reporter visited Cavanagh and found a broken man who needed an oxygen tank nearby at all times in case of sudden respiratory failure. His crippled hand from a car accident rested on his lap making channel hopping from news to the racing results and back again more of a challenge than he would like at sixty. The light from the

---

[13]Davey Hunt had a misplaced concern that *The Sunday Times* would rely on Jimmy Holmes as a witness in the libel case even after both sides had received a remarkable email from the avant-garde gangster on 25 October 2011 making all sorts of claims. Holmes had first made contact with the author soon after the May 2010 article was published. Then, wrongly fearing that he was going to be subpoenaed as a witness against Hunt, he reverted to his renegade ways and wrote a comical but mendacious email claiming *The Sunday Times* had paid him £50,000 in cash for a witness statement but welched on providing him with the other £50,000 so he was withdrawing co-operation. Through the October email, Holmes wanted Hunt to know that he had talked to the author about the murder of Nicky Gerrard and the double murder of Maxine Arnold and Terry Gooderham. He signed off the email claiming he had been 'in a long-term homosexual relationship' with Hunt and that *Judas Pig* was 'a work of fiction'. This was not a view shared by Scotland Yard.

window where he sat illuminated the long, deep scar on his face that ran from his left ear down to and across his throat then up to the tip of his chin; a disfigured reminder every morning of the attack. At night he still had malignant dreams of men with swords that woke him with the horrors.

Cavanagh told the reporter that he was frightened of saying no to Hunt so he produced an undated, hand-written note addressed 'to whom it may concern' exonerating the Long Fella but in a way that would never stand up in court. Tellingly, Hunt's lawyers didn't ask for a proper statement and Cavanagh was never called as a witness.

The land dispute was always going to be tricky territory for the Long Fella, especially after the newspaper disclosed to him a copy of the CCTV from the court fight. Nevertheless, Hunt maintained that Chic Matthews was an old family friend who had asked him to get involved because he was being 'intimidated' by Billy Allen's thugs. Hunt felt sorry for old man Matthews and on the first day turned up alone at court. He spoke with Danny Woollard, Allen's chief minder, and told him that the land was worth nothing like the £110 million his boss was claiming. The next day, Matthews asked Hunt and his brother Stevie to come to court because he feared trouble. Hunt turned up with three friends. But an unknown group of Allen's creditors also arrived and it was these large gentlemen who were involved in the 'commotion' with Woollard.

In fact, but not surprisingly, Woollard now supported Hunt's claim of innocence, but it was a version of events that strained credulity. The immediate difficulty was Woollard had already gone into great detail about the court fight in his 2009 book, *Wild Cats*, which he now said was made up to increase sales. The veteran gangster also claimed that he'd never grassed on Hunt to the

Newham crime squad because he had 'an aversion to the police'. But this was exposed as another lie when the newspaper disclosed to Hunt an official police transcript of Woollard's taped interview at his home in 2006 when Mac broke the antique chair in a fit of giggles over the pet Alsatian.[14]

Part of Hunt's strategy in fighting the libel case was to make the most of the corruption probe into the Newham crime squad, even though the three detectives were by now off the hook and the anti-corruption squad were dangling from it instead.

Woollard was now claiming that Mac was corruptly working with Allen and had pressured him to give the taped interview at his home. However much it irked them to do it, once the official transcript of Woollard was disclosed to Hunt, Scotland Yard had a duty to consider his safety. A police unit looking after the security of police witnesses that the newspaper had subpoenaed for the libel trial contacted Woollard to offer him protection given the Long Fella now knew he had grassed.

'I never said nothing,' Woollard insisted to detective superintendent Frankie Flood, who ran the unit.

'Well, you did,' Flood insisted back. 'And you better be careful about committing perjury in the witness box.'

'To be honest, since the fracas at court I don't remember fuck all about fuck all,' Woollard replied.[15]

---

[14]According to a source, during one of his debriefs, Woollard claimed that a man called Blackwell had taken a contract out on Hunt and Terry Adams tipped off the Long Fella and the contract was called off.

[15]In the run up to the trial, Billy Allen secretly recorded Danny Woollard suggesting they could get a payday from playing both sides. Allen thought the anti-corruption squad would arrest his former minder for attempting to pervert the court of justice but they refused to take the tape recordings.

Davey Hunt was at his reverential best when Mr Justice
Simon entered the courtroom. He shot to his feet and
bowed his head until the judge sat down. Hunt was
wearing a blue suit and white shirt. His grey hair was
just long enough to part at the side and he carried an
embossed glasses case on his way to the witness box, a
creaking dark wooden pulpit to the left of the judge with
a commanding view of the packed courtroom.

Discreetly he crossed himself then swore on the Bible
to tell the truth, the whole truth and nothing but the
truth. His barrister had already accepted that Hunt
hadn't been honest in the past over his tax affairs. 'But
what we say is he is not a conventional businessman.
He is a rough diamond. He is a man from Canning
Town. He has not gone through higher education and
the professions, or anything of that kind. But he is not a
criminal mastermind.'[16]

Hunt continued the religious theme and told the
judge through a dry mouth that the article had 'crucified'
him. He looked nervous. The Long Fella was about to
go into unchartered territory. Many a time he had sat
in front of a detective and growled no comment or
worse, but that wouldn't play in Court 13. Mr Justice
Simon was not only studying Hunt's answers, but
also his demeanour under pressure to see if the mask
of legitimacy slipped when Millar started what would
turn out to be a marathon cross-examination. The Long
Fella, who had just turned fifty-two, asked to take his
jacket off as he was directed to the bundle of documents
arranged in front of him.

[16]Hunt denied evading justice by corrupting police or having any relationship
with the intelligence services.

'Could I point out that I don't read very well and I
would like a bit of assistance if possible?'

Millar agreed and at 10.47 a.m. gently lobbed the
first question about his early run-ins with the police in
Canning Town. Hunt denied he was a racist or a Sniper,
or that he was business partners with Jimmy Holmes in
any drugs and prostitution rackets. He'd never threatened
anyone, even when working the doors of rough local pubs.

'It was a close community. Most of the people knew
most of the people and you could approach them in
a manner without using muscle. It could be done in a
diplomatic way.'

'Right, so you acted as a diplomat?' asked Millar.

'Of course Sir, yes.'

The newspaper's barrister continued to score points as
he took Hunt through the sustained police operations
against him, his family and criminal friends. All Hunt
could do was deny any involvement in violent crime.
Every so often, when he took a sip of water, there followed
a pronounced biting movement that made him appear
like a human shark.

After lunch, Millar went to work on the witness's
weakest defence: his finances. Legitimate businessmen
fill in tax returns and don't lie in mortgage applications
about the source and size of their income. Nor do they
hide assets in offshore companies set up by a money
launderer. The judge gave Hunt a timely reminder that
he didn't have to answer anything that could incriminate
him. Instead, the besieged witness fell back on the staple
response of the scoundrel. 'I can't recall,' he said countless
times when asked how he could afford a mansion, a waste
management plant, a car showroom and a Soho brothel
while being a tax ghost.

Hunt apologised for his tax evasion and, in mitigation, pointed out that he recently paid 'in the region of £1 million in tax on a property business that bought in £30,000 per week.

'I'm just a naive businessman who's good at his job but not in the paperwork.'

During the difficult afternoon session, Hunt had become visibly riled by the presence of four large gentleman sitting in the court staring at him in the witness box. All overcoats and earpieces, they looked like nightclub bouncers of the kind the Long Fella had seen off all his life. The muscle quartet was sold as 'niche threat management specialists' by Will Geddes, founder of International Corporate Protection. The security department for News International, owners of *The Sunday Times*, had contracted ICP to protect non-police witnesses coming in and out of court, some of whom wanted to give evidence from behind a screen.

The reporter behind the article wanted nothing to do with the ICP goons. Their presence sent totally the wrong message to a man like Hunt. So rather that tell them where he was staying, the reporter chose a nearby police station as the pickup point for the next morning.

Louis Charalambous, the external solicitor running the case, called the reporter at 9.30 a.m.

'Have you left yet?' he asked.

'Just about to.'

'Don't. The security firm's walked off the job.'

It turned out that Geddes was flaky, one of those posh types in the growing corporate security world whose website boasted of derring-do. Word had got back to Charalambous that Geddes had initially claimed to News

International that two of his men were warned overnight
of 'repercussions' to their families if they turned up at
court. However, when the police spoke to Geddes that
morning he said he had pulled out for corporate reasons.
None of the ICP men would make statements to the
police, which meant there was a lack evidence to arrest
Hunt for being behind the intimidation.

The newspaper's executives rang around for a replacement
security firm, but word seemed to have got out. Eventually,
a discreet group from outside London stepped in.

Meanwhile, Hunt was back in the witness box and
getting a hard time about the money moving around his
businesses. The Long Fella felt it was 'unfair' that he was
being asked about what his companies were doing twenty
years ago. Then, something snapped in him and he broke
into a long speech about hard work and broken dreams. It
turned out that Hunt had one day hoped to hand over his
multi-million pound waste business to his children. But
the police and, more recently, *The Sunday Times* reporter,
had ruined that 'dream'.

A 'fantastic relationship' with Barclays bank, who was
going to loan him up to £20 million to grow the business,
suddenly went cold in 2000, which he put down to police
interference. Luckily, a price war broke out in the metals
trade making his Dagenham plant more valuable. A
British and a Dutch firm were bidding for Hunt's business
and this gave him 'another shot at the title for my kids,' he
told the mesmerized courtroom. Everything was back on
track until 2010 when *The Sunday Times* article appeared
and crucified him, his dream and his children's future.

The day ended with a surreal reminder of what happens
to those who crossed the Long Fella. Millar took Hunt
slowly though the chilling attack on Paul Cavanagh then

asked about a bugged conversation at the car showroom where a plan was discussed to send Mark Wright with a tape recorder to visit Cavanagh and see if he was grassing to the police. Hunt was reminded that Wright was now the patriarch of the star family in *TOWIE*, which was in its third series.

'I don't watch it to be quite honest,' he replied. 'But I know his boy is in the programme.'

'Is this very important,' Mr Justice Simon inquired, 'because if so I have not made a note of it.'

'It is important to my daughters, my Lord, but to nobody else,' Millar assured the judge.

That afternoon, detective superintendent Frankie Flood and his number two, David Johnson, briefed the Gold group at Scotland Yard about the day's developments. A decision was taken to give Hunt a formal warning using the reverse Osman procedure – when the police approach the source of the threat and warn them against carrying it out. The Yard felt that Hunt's broken dreams speech was a direct threat to the reporter, who he also blamed for 'hounding' his business partner, Keltbray.

The next day, Flood and Johnson approached the Long Fella at court. The detectives warned him that were anything to happen to any of the newspaper's witnesses the police response would be robust. Hunt nodded.[17]

---

[17] The incident with Will Geddes's security firm ICP and the reverse Osman warning were kept from the judge to avoid any prejudice to David Hunt. Mr Justice Simon was a replacement judge after Hunt's legal team had objected to the original libel trial judge, Michael Tugendhat, in part because he had found for the author in a previous libel trial (Flood v Times Newspapers). Tugendhat's replacement had recently allowed SOCA to seize the house of Manchester businessman Arran Coghlan, who had previously been cleared of three murders and a major drugs conspiracy. Simon ruled the property was bought with criminal proceeds.

Mr Justice Simon gave his judgment at the beginning of July 2013. It was a complete victory for *The Sunday Times*. David Hunt *was* 'the head of an organised crime network, implicated in extreme violence and fraud' and had also engaged in money laundering and witness intimidation to avoid prosecution.

Journalism had managed to do what policing couldn't in thirty years. That failure was in significant measure down to the many levels of corruption in Scotland Yard that had gone unaddressed and which assisted an undoubtedly world class gangster to evade justice.

The judge found that Hunt had assaulted journalist Peter Wilson when he door-stepped him in 1992 about the gruesome and still unsolved double murder of Maxine Arnold and Terry Gooderham. Wilson's 'compelling' evidence was preferred over Hunt's 'courteous and mild-mannered' demeanour while telling a pack of lies. The Long Fella was capable of 'sudden violence when his interests were directly threatened' and he was not frightened to 'take on a journalist regardless of the consequences,' Mr Justice Simon ruled.

Paul Cavanagh was moved to hear that the judge believed Hunt had slashed his throat in 1997 and then tried to cover it up. It gave him the courage to finally reveal what had really gone on, even though it did not reflect too kindly on him.[18]

Mr Justice Simon also found that Billy Allen was intimidated by Hunt, who had lied about what happened at court in 2006 to disguise the fact that he 'orchestrated

---

[18]'Revealed: Gang Boss's Bloody £25,000 bribe' and 'I feared a beating – but the Long Fella asked for a knife' by Michael Gillard & Tim Rayment, (*The Sunday Times*, 14 June 2015).

a brazen and violent attempt to pervert the course of justice'. The judge found that the Long Fella wanted Allen to drop his land claim because he stood to gain financially if Matthews won.

Throughout the trial Hunt had claimed he relied on the professional advice of Chris Williams, his property solicitor of the last eighteen years. But the judge rejected Williams as a truthful witness and found that the lawyer 'knew or suspected' Hunt was involved in 'a money laundering exercise'. Jersey-based Galleons Reach Limited, for example, was set up for an illicit purpose to launder criminal proceeds and hide Hunt's ownership of a brothel. Meanwhile, his waste business was run as a legitimate cash-based front to put off the taxman.

Although Mr Justice Simon did not find that the newspaper had justified Hunt's involvement in murder and drug trafficking, he said the reporter's journalism was responsible and in the public interest and therefore a complete defence to the claim.

Money, they say, has no smell. And soon after the libel trial, Lloyds TSB bank, one of the three official sponsors of the London Olympics, stepped in to loan the Long Fella some £4 million after Barclays Bank felt it had to pull out.

During the trial, Hunt had spoken of his 'great' eight-year relationship with Barclays and even boasted that one bank manager wanted to jump ship and work for his property company. That all changed when the bank learned of *The Sunday Times* investigation into their client. Barclays gave Hunt a year to find another lender and in June 2013 called in £4.2 million in loans to his property company. Lloyds immediately stepped in with three loans to Hunt's (UK) Properties Limited, whose prize asset was Woolston Manor Golf and Country Club. Two of the loans in May and June 2013 were secured against the land used for the waste disposal business.

The third loan on 2 July was agreed one day after Hunt was branded an organised crime boss involved with money laundering and two days before the damning libel judgment was published. This third loan was secured against a £1 million life insurance policy that Hunt had recently taken out with Legal & General.

At the time of making these loans, Lloyds Banking Group was 25 per cent owned by the taxpayer after a government bailout following the 2008 global financial crisis, which in turn was caused by greed, irresponsible lending and poor regulation. Lloyds defended its decision to be banker to a British godfather claiming it had followed 'clear account opening and lending processes, including customer identification, credit and anti-money laundering checks in line with internal policies, legal and regulatory obligations.' But John Mann, a Labour MP on the Treasury select committee, was not impressed and demanded that the supposedly tough new regulator launch an inquiry.

'There are honest and solvent businesses in my constituency that Lloyds have refused to lend money to who will be shocked to see how lax their systems have been on this,' he told *The Sunday Times*.[19]

However, the Financial Conduct Authority and the Treasury were happy leaving it to the 'banksters' to sort out – a sure sign that self-regulation was back.

[19]'Crime Lord Lent £4m by Lloyds Bank' by Michael Gillard & Carl Fellstrom, (*The Sunday Times*, 11 May 2014).

Hunt found another lender who was equally unperturbed by his designation as a crime boss. Losing the libel claim had cost almost £2 million in legal fees, £805,000 of which Hunt owed to *The Sunday Times*.

On 3 October 2013, GC CO NO 102, a finance company, loaned the Long Fella £1 million, which ten days later he used to pay the newspaper's costs. The finance company belonged to David Sullivan. Hunt had approached the co-owner of West Ham for help and, the story goes, from one Hammers fan to another, Sullivan agreed. The loan was secured against Woolston Manor, Mooro's bar-restaurant and some land that Hunt owned in Broxbourne, Hertfordshire.

West Ham had just secured a controversial 99-year lease from the government to start playing at the Olympic stadium in 2016. Both Sullivan and Hunt were keen to stress that the £1 million loan was a personal matter made on commercial terms and neither the football club nor any of its directors had done any business with the Long Fella or his companies. Hunt's spokesman said he'd known Sullivan for 'many years' through a shared interest in West Ham.

No mention was made of their other shared interest in the sex business.[20]

Joanna McKelvey had stood by her husband throughout his mental breakdown and other problems in their marriage, but after five years fighting Scotland Yard she wanted closure. Mac swore it would come as soon as Scotland Yard wised up and settled the civil claim

[20]When Sullivan wound up GC NO CO 102 in January 2014, the liquidator said Hunt repaid the £1 million loan.

for damages that he, Guntrip and Clark had served on Scotland Yard shortly before the libel trial. The trio had given valiant evidence for the newspaper and were delighted by the judge's devastating finding that Operation Kayu was 'misdirected' and 'undoubtedly assisted' Hunt avoid prosecution for his involvement in the violence and intimidation around the Olympic land dispute.

On her way to the local Tesco one day, Joanna felt someone was tailing her in an expensive car. The good-looking young man followed her around the shopping aisles and was right behind Mac's wife at the checkout counter, clearly wanting his presence noticed. When Mac found out he reported it to the police protection team who pulled the supermarket CCTV and identified the driver from his personalised number plate as 26-year-old David Hunt junior. The eldest son had been a co-director of various Hunt companies and ran Mooro's bar-restaurant at Woolston Manor, where he was photographed with *TOWIE*'s Mark Wright junior and TV presenter Holly Willoughby.

Officers immediately turned up at The Morleys but got no response so a reverse Osman warning, the second, was served on Hunt senior through his solicitor. While the police response to the perceived threat had been rapid, Scotland Yard was determined not to concede an inch on Mac's civil claim, and threw even more taxpayers' money at defending it for another two years.

Finally, on 30 November 2015, deputy assistant commissioner Fiona Taylor, who took over responsibility for the Gold Group, apologised to Mac, Guntrip and Clark and their families 'for the injury and damage caused to them as a result of the investigation'. Mac was paid almost £150,000 in damages. The two others shared just under £100,000. Guntrip decided to stay on in the police. Clark made it clear he was never coming back.

Mark Lake, their tenacious solicitor, had a legendary thirst acquired from a long history of acting for police officers. The unconventional veteran of exposing the antics of Scotland Yard's anti-corruption squad thought on this occasion that the so-called Untouchables had outdone themselves. 'This was a colossal injustice. Three committed detectives tried to bring to justice people they believed to be premier league villains or their associates. Once they realised they were dealing with a complex web of serious organised crime, local authority corruption in and around the Olympic zone, and police corruption, including within [the] anti-corruption squad, they sought assistance from units with far better resources than a borough crime squad.

'Their quest was futile. [Scotland Yard] was uninterested citing a variety of bewildering reasons such as a lack of resources. They courageously persevered but were stymied when out of the blue a corruption operation was launched into them. The burning question is why did the anti-corruption squad behave in this perverse and reckless way?

'One answer is that corrupt officers deliberately derailed attempts to imprison members of Hunt's organised crime network. The most charitable answer is that the anti-corruption squad relied on ancient and demonstrably false intelligence about McKelvey and set out to prove it. Clark and Guntrip were collateral damage but the [Yard] did not care. The operation was a ghastly failure but this came as no surprise to anyone with any knowledge of the methodology of the anti-corruption squad. It is inevitable that no one ever faced the music for the shambles that they deliberately created.'

Mac now runs a private investigation firm and delights in showing up the Untouchables. He still gets up in the middle of the night and sends ranting emails to various senior officers when a policing scandal makes the news. The betrayal and hurt from a career cut short have not gone away.

'We tried everything to resolve this matter internally and even wrote to the prime minister, the home secretary, the mayor, MPs and senior police officers to raise our concerns about the endemic corruption we uncovered in the police linked to organised crime. We were ignored. We believe a secret cell of corrupt police sleepers exist to assist organised crime.

'For eight years we've had to endure rumours that there's no smoke without fire. The question that the commissioner and politicians should be asking is who started the fire and why? Until that question is asked corruption will exist in the police and Newham council and organised crime will flourish.'

Epilogue

Truth Commission

It was the summer of 2013 and Sir Robin Wales could afford to pour himself a congratulatory double scotch for overseeing a lasting 'legacy' in Newham.

The mayor had hosted a successful Olympic Games with boxing gold in Canning Town for soon-to-be world heavyweight champ, Anthony Joshua. While over in Stratford, the dirty fight for the Olympic stadium had gone to West Ham United, his partners and the home side. With this, and twenty-three years at the helm of Newham council, Sir Robin had every reason to believe his political future was assured as long as he wanted one which, at fifty-eight, he still did. There was, after all, no significant opposition from the other mainstream parties. To all intents and purposes, he was the untouchable mayor of a one-party state.

In a corner of his backyard, however, a secret coup was taking shape that in five years' time would depose Sir Robin and lead to calls for a 'Truth Commission' into his legacy, and the links between organised crime, police, big business and the council.

In June 2013, Rokhsana Fiaz and four other left-wing Labour activists met in Newham to discuss overthrowing

their despised Blairite leader.[1] The Fiaz five were doing
the reverse of a famous power-sharing pact almost twenty
years earlier that Tony Blair, Sir Robin's mentor, had
struck with Gordon Brown at an Islington restaurant
to take control away from the left and reposition New
Labour on the centre right.

Fiaz and the other plotters represented a growing
membership of the Newham Labour party who, by 2013,
were tired of what they saw as Sir Robin's anti-democratic
style of leadership. 'What Robin did over the years was
decimate, in its totality, the ability of open scrutiny of
the decision making of the mayor,' Fiaz explained to me.
'[He] had used the prominence and dominance of Labour
locally to sustain his hegemony and it's led to a really
corrosive effect in local politics.' Another concern, she
said, was alleged cronyism and the misuse of public funds
in development projects, among them the controversial
deal that saw the council borrow £40 million to support
West Ham's bid for the Olympic stadium.

In the past, such resentment had led independent-
minded Labour councillors such as Mike Law to cross
the floor or leave the party altogether. However, 42-year-
old Fiaz and her supporters were not for walking away
or waiting for Wales to step down or die. The plan was
to work secretly inside the local party to build 'a pincer
movement' and make her the Labour candidate for

---

[1]Four of the original five were: Rokhsana Fiaz (current mayor of Newham);
Charlene McLean (deputy mayor and cabinet member for youth safety), John
Gray (cabinet member for housing services) and Terry Paul. A source close
to Fiaz said Paul, a councillor for Stratford, dropped out soon after the first
meeting in June 2013. Although, on her election in May 2018 she appointed
him cabinet member for finance.

mayor, knowing whoever won that battle would end up controlling Newham.

Fiaz accepted the challenge. 'I said, okay, if we are going to do this we are going to absolutely fucking do this. I'm not interested in losing. We're going to win.'

The secret monthly meetings grew in numbers especially among the West Ham branches of the Newham Labour party, where Sir Robin was less popular. He controlled the East Ham side of the borough, but for the plot to succeed Fiaz needed to win over all twenty local branches in Newham. The plotters weren't ready to mount any serious challenge in 2014, when Sir Robin won his successive third term as mayor building on a record of no rise in council tax and progressive policies in housing, education and local employment.

Fiaz was elected a councillor for Custom House that year and publicly paid lip service to the mayor while secretly building a democratic socialist alternative to his administration. The split mirrored a wider division in the UK Labour party and growing discontent with Blairism and his brand of unfettered capitalism, especially after the disastrous interventions in the Middle East and the global financial crisis.

Jeremy Corbyn becoming leader of the Labour party in 2015 boosted the Newham plotters' confidence, as did the election of Sadiq Khan, a friend of Fiaz, who became Labour mayor of London one year later.

By 2017, Sir Robin became aware that Fiaz, whose father called her his 'little lion', was going to mount a challenge as Labour candidate in the May 2018 mayoral election. Similarly, it was clear to Fiaz that her opponent was going to fight hard to hold on to power. Under the rules, Sir Robin was automatically re-selected as Labour's mayoral candidate. This was the trigger for the plotters to come fully out of the shadows. Fiaz and her supporters wanted an open selection of candidates and threatened legal action if Sir Robin didn't concede.

He did so eventually, and so began what the Fiaz camp called a 'dirty' campaign. Conversely, Sir Robin's supporters believed the party in Newham had been 'infiltrated' by Momentum, a left-wing grassroots organisation that grew up after Corbyn's election as Labour leader, and by Muslim extremists.

Being called a left-wing extremist didn't bother Fiaz as much as whispers that she was a Muslim one too. The Wales camp certainly felt that 'Islamists' had infiltrated the party and that election fraud involving bogus voters from the Bangladeshi and Pakistani communities was taking place.

Fiaz lived in the north of the borough with her Muslim parents, who'd come over from Pakistan and ran a successful clothing factory in the East End before retiring. Their daughter considered herself a practising Muslim, albeit one who drank and smoked. Her own career, after gaining a law degree and a stint as a journalist, was largely spent in policy research on race and counter-terrorism strategies for British Muslims and building bridges with the Jewish community. Her mentor was Richard Stone, the Jewish doctor who sat on the Home Office-appointed panel that investigated Scotland Yard's mishandling of the 1993 murder of Black teenager Stephen Lawrence, and concluded that the force was 'institutionally racist'.

The focus of Fiaz's mayoral campaign was to 'Clean up Newham'. It clearly resonated within the party and with voters, who decided to end Sir Robin Wales's reign as the longest-serving British mayor. In March 2018, Fiaz won the Labour candidacy by 861 votes to 503. Two months later, she was elected mayor of Newham with a 73 per cent share of the vote.

Her acceptance speech called for an end to the sniping and promised to build on Sir Robin's legacy, but behind the scenes she was plotting once more, this time to purge her party and her predecessor's legacy with what she was privately calling a 'Truth and Reconciliation Commission.'

Council insiders, it was said, had been coming forward with 'horror stories' about the 'culture and practices' they'd had to endure under Sir Robin. Fiaz did her own 'deep dive' which she said left her with the impression of a council 'so removed from people, [that it had] lost its sense of compassion and empathy.' The council she was inheriting had 'zilch emotional intelligence' and 'institutional indifference' toward its voters, she felt. The idea behind a truth commission, therefore, was to allow 'traumatised' council officers to tell their story while also showing the people of Newham that there was a new breed of politician and politics coming.

'I'm very different from the previous dude,' she said.[2]

One of Fiaz's closest advisers brought the new mayor up to speed on the story behind this book, starting with Pelé Mahmood's dramatic allegations that the council's enforcement division was corrupt and racist which had led to the Kelly report in September 2005. Amanda Kelly's conclusions about a rotten state of affairs 'tantamount to corruption' had resulted in back door exits for those in charge.

[2]Author's interview with Rokhsana Fiaz 22 August 2018.

Fiaz was also told about what had happened to Mac and the Newham crime squad when they tried to prosecute corrupt contractor Danny McGuinness, who'd been allowed to continue working for the council despite the Kelly report.

To recap, when Mac's team arrested McGuinness in February 2006 with over one hundred stolen vehicles he made it clear his defence would allege corruption in the council and its revolving door with the local police. 'This'll never get to court, you'll see,' he'd said as the handcuffs clicked around his wrists and he was led off the Silvertown strip. He was right. The trial was abandoned in late 2007.

Years later, in December 2015, I had approached McGuinness to try and understand why he had felt so certain during his arrest that a masonic brotherhood of crooks, crooked cops and council officers would come to his rescue. The retired contractor was in a chatty mood on the phone. He recalled the events as if they were yesterday and made some explosive claims about corruption in divisions of Newham council, which, if true, supported Kelly's findings.[3]

McGuinness was angry after his trial collapsed and insisted on a meeting with Sir Robin Wales, he said. The arrangement was made through Councillor Kevin Jenkins, a close ally of the mayor and a friend of McGuinness, who confirmed this.[4]

[3]Phone interview with Danny McGuinness 16 and 22 December 2015.
[4]In an interview with the author on 6 October 2018, Kevin Jenkins confirmed that he had put Danny McGuinness in touch with mayor Wales. Jenkins believed that McGuinness shouldn't have been prosecuted. The councilor was involved with the charity Community Links at 105 Barking Road and sub-let office space to DM Security before the 2006 arrest of McGuinness. Jenkins didn't attend the meeting between Wales and McGuinness but recalled that the council's finance director Bob Heaton was tasked to investigate. Jenkins said he was unaware about the council's payment to McGuinness.

Council records also confirm that the meeting with Sir Robin took place on 26 February 2008. McGuinness said he told the mayor that he should never have been prosecuted because of an understanding with the council that he could personally profit from removing and selling abandoned cars as long as, so he alleged, he kicked back money and the vehicles didn't reappear in the UK.

'We could send it to Ghana, anywhere outside the UK ... we never had a written contract ... and that's what made it awkward,' he claimed over the phone to me.

McGuinness went further and said that the council ultimately authorised a substantial payment effectively for his silence and for the inconvenience caused by the recently abandoned prosecution. The payment, he alleged, was to help rescue his company, DM Security, which had gone into liquidation.

'To be truthful, I went into liquidation and [the council] got me the money so we could get ourselves out of liquidation.'

'That's good of [the council],' I replied.

'Well the thing is, it wasn't good of him it was in [the council's] own interest?'

'In what way?'

'Because at the end of the day we could prove beyond doubt that enough people knew what we had the right to do and what we never had the rights to do. I could have brought them to court myself and ... they would have had a lot of egg on their face. As I say [the council] gave us something like nearly half a million pounds for the receivers to sort it all out. So at the end of the day if we wasn't within our rights believe me they wouldn't have parted with no money.'

'Was it coming up to the Olympics and they didn't want egg on their face?'

'Possibly. At the end of the day I knew about [people] on the take, all getting brown envelopes, whatever. But other people didn't know that. Know what I mean?'

'Did you witness that type of corruption?'

'Yeah. The bottom line of it was they knew that if they pushed and upset me so much I would have got out me own packet, know what I mean? Obviously I think [it] had a lot of bearing on the outcome of the case to be quite truthful ... They were all within their own masonic parts although they denied all the masonic side, but what can you say.'

McGuinness, a prominent freemason, promised to meet up after he was done appearing as a local Santa Claus and handing out another type of gift, but he became ill in the New Year and died in February 2016. However, inquiries I made with the liquidator of DM Security confirmed that Newham Council *had* paid money to the beleaguered company. Such a payment, coming so soon after Scotland Yard had caused the crooked contractor's trial to be abandoned, had the hallmarks of a conspiracy to shut down a major corruption scandal in the Olympic borough.[5]

[5]Companies House records show that DM Security (London) Limited (04367530) was incorporated in February 2002 and registered at 105 Barking Road. James Duckworth was appointed liquidator on 8 October 2007 in the run up to the trial of McGuinness. DM Security had filed no accounts for 2005 and 2006. The company was dissolved on 26 June 2014. Mr Duckworth declined to provide his notes on the approach from McGuinness or the 'deed of settlement' with Newham council but confirmed that one had taken place. He said that well into the process of sorting out the insolvent company's affairs, McGuinness had called out of the blue claiming that Newham council was a significant debtor.

Sir Robin Wales agreed to discuss these and other issues over several meetings, the first at a cafe in Westfield, the largest shopping centre in Europe built during his time at the helm of Newham council. 'We did some interesting things,' he said, clearly proud of his record as mayor.[6]

Beefing up the enforcement division to deal with the major problem of abandoned cars in Newham was one of his political pet projects, Sir Robin agreed, but he denied being involved in any attempt to cover up corruption.

'My line is if there is any suggestion of any wrongdoing – investigate. The only thing you can be done for as a politician is if you hide things. Never hide anything. I don't care, because I haven't done anything wrong … If people do things wrong, prosecute every time, if you can. It's always a question is it worth the effort? Have you got the evidence? You get rid of people … I told the chief executive at the time [Dave Burbage] if you think you can prove it, make the judgement, go ahead and do it … So we got rid of him. It was John Page and [others]. I believe [they] left with no golden handshake. [They] just left.'[7]

Sir Robin couldn't explain why McGuinness was allowed to remain the council's principle contractor after the Kelly report and until the Newham crime squad arrested him months later in February 2006.

Until that point, the liquidator had no record of money owed to the company. Newham council's legal department acknowledged the debt and paid a sum of money but the liquidator refused to say how much.
[6]Author's interview with Sir Robin Wales 5 and 11 October 2018.
[7]John Page died in 2017.

To recap some more, soon after the arrest, the top cop at Newham 'bollocked' Mac and Guntrip because he felt the operation had embarrassed him in front of the council. In May 2007, with the trial of McGuinness just months away, Nigel Mould, an enforcement official at the council, emailed Guntrip expressing concerns for the political ramifications if the prosecution went ahead.

Sir Robin said word that McGuinness was threatening to reveal a culture of brown envelopes in the council's enforcement division had not reached him in the run up to the trial. 'My view is if you get a brown envelope, we'd want to know, we'd prosecute. I knew nothing about it. If I had done I would have asked for an inquiry,' he told me.

However, Sir Robin recalled that in his meeting with McGuinness after the trial was abandoned the contractor made some 'allegations' and wanted money. Sir Robin was hazy on the detail – he found McGuinness hard to understand because of his thick cockney accent – but recalled asking finance director, Bob Heaton, to investigate. I asked Sir Robin if he was aware of the arrangement McGuinness claimed he had with the council to sell seized cars?

'Let me say, it's a fucking lie. He's a fucking liar,' he replied in a thick Glaswegian accent. Sir Robin also denied personally authorising any hush money payment to the contractor, but didn't deny that one could have been made.

'I'm not saying other people may not have done it. I can't say what other people did or didn't do around corruption. I can tell you that I didn't … What you are describing is a whole bunch of people working together in a conspiracy which I can't tell you I know anything about ... As far as I'm concerned I've asked [executive officers] to investigate. I let them get on with it.'[8]

My findings were passed to the new mayor for comment. Word came back that Fiaz had asked the council's most senior lawyer to investigate the payment to McGuinness as part of the preparation for her Truth Commission.

The possible links between organised crime in Newham and local politicians is another area the new mayor said she intended to explore in the Truth Commission. It

[8]During his February 2008 meeting with Robin Wales, Danny McGuinness also made allegations against Nick Dennett, the council employee he blamed for his arrest in February 2006. McGuinness had threatened to kill Dennett, who the council equipped with a bulletproof vest. McGuinness told Wales that Dennett was corruptly working with a local Gypsy family, the Ferriers, some of whom used to be in the Snipers. Bob Heaton investigated the allegation, which was uncorroborated. It may be coincidental that a secret trawl of Dennett's work computer found he had accessed legal porn and he resigned in April 2008 rather than face a disciplinary hearing where he expected to be sacked. Dennett sued the council for constructive dismissal and discrimination as a whistle-blower to the Kelly inquiry. Pelé Mahmood supported his claim with a statement. Dennett sought disclosure from the council of seven former employees who had sued for various discriminatory conduct and received settlements with confidentiality agreements. He also wanted the disciplinary records of senior employees against whom discrimination had been alleged and details of contact between the council and Scotland Yard over corruption allegations involving serving officers and retired ones working for the council. The council unsuccessfully tried to resist disclosure of the secret appendix of the Kelly report but handed it over one week before the opening ceremony of the Olympic Games on 27 July 2012. However, on 16 October, the employment tribunal dismissed Dennett's claim but accepted he had made protected disclosures to the Kelly inquiry and criticised Newham council for not acting more clearly and robustly when dealing with his clearly deteriorating mental state.

Dennett impolitely declined to discuss any matters with the author. He is now a trustee of the Peacock Gym. 'Fuck off and leave me alone', he said.

was a concern already flagged up sixteen years earlier by Scotland Yard's 2002 Operation Tiberius Strategic Intelligence report which identified Peacock gym owners, the Bowers brothers, as criminals who'd set out to make political and police friends through the guise of charity work for underprivileged local youth.

A man who for a long time was a government informant inside the Bowers crime syndicate spoke extensively to me about their activities and an allegedly corrupt relationship with an influential local Labour politician.

The source, whom we shall call Kurtz, claimed that Danny McGuinness was the first to mention the existence of compromising sex tapes of the politician cavorting with prostitutes and taking cocaine in early nineties Newham.[9]

'[The politician] was caught in a two-way mirror with toms [prostitutes] … The honey trap was in a block of flats behind the Railway Tavern in Plaistow,' said Kurtz, who learned of these details in 2000.

Tony Bowers also referred to the sex tapes when issues arose about the Peacock gym, said Kurtz. He talked about 'getting out the file' and it was Kurtz's impression that

[9]Danny McGuinness was legally represented by Janice Brown, the sister of Lyn Brown, a former councillor in the Wales administration and MP for West Ham. Janice Brown told the author that the Bowers, who were family friends since childhood, had referred McGuinness to her law firm and that corruption in the council was going to be a large part of his defence.

According to Kurtz, Martin and Tony Bowers are freemasons, along with McGuinness, former police officers and council officers in the enforcement division. Sir Robin Wales, who denied being a freemason, said he believed the problem of masonic influence had been largely tackled when he joined Newham Council in the early 1980s. The freemasons were said to control Housing and Enforcement, while the Catholic Knights of Colombus controlled Education in the council.

other crime families – the Hunts and the Adams – also knew about the existence of the sex tapes.

A senior adviser to Fiaz confirmed that they had picked up the same allegation from inside the local Labour party, and former councillor, Mike Law, said he too had heard it from a criminal source. None of them, however, had seen the sex tapes, although Kurtz was adamant they existed. The now retired politician at the centre of the honey trap allegation denied being beholden to or blackmailed by any gangsters.

'Really? Fuck me mate! I've never been with a prostitute and I've never taken cocaine. It's bollocks. It's a great story and maybe it will push my street cred. I'm just a very, very boring straight-laced person,' he said.

Separately, the Bowers had openly lobbied Jim Fitzpatrick, their local Canning Town MP, when they needed help furthering their business plans. The still sitting MP had no issue disclosing to me his correspondence file, which showed that in August 2001, while serving as a Treasury whip in the Blair government, Fitzpatrick met Tony and Martin Bowers unaware they were secretly plotting the £1 million Gatwick heist and lorry hijacks across the UK.

The Bowers brothers had their eye on a council unit under the Silvertown flyover and, more importantly, wanted to build a rooftop casino on the strip, part of a vision shared with the Hunts and Matthews. Fitzpatrick wrote to the brothers that he had 'put out feelers regarding the Silvertown Way site' with Newham council and enclosed a copy of the recommendations of the Gambling Review Body set up by then home secretary, Jack Straw.

According to Kurtz, the two Bowers brothers had once met Fitzpatrick on the House of Commons terrace to listen to their casino plans. The MP said it was possible he had done so but certainly recalled seeing the 'larger than life' brothers at the Peacock gym.

In summer 2002, Fitzpatrick and the Bowers lobbied senior Newham council figures after the gym's private landlord had significantly increased the rent. The council was the freeholder of the land on the Silvertown strip and in November agreed to buy the head lease off the landlord and rent the gym back to the Bowers at a peppercorn.

'I was quite supportive of the gym in principle given the role it played helping local young people stay out of trouble,' said Fitzpatrick, adding dryly, 'not sure how the subsequent convictions for armed robbery helped with that ambition though.'

In March 2003, the Bowers were caught red-handed during the Gatwick Airport robbery, which they claimed was motivated by a desire to save the gym. Sir Robin Wales recalled an amusing incident, just before the arrests. 'Finally, I was persuaded to go down [to the Peacock gym] ... I came out and I got a call from [the borough commander] saying what the fuck have you been doing?' The gym was being 'staked out' as part of a major investigation, the senior officer confided in him.

'We knew [the Bowers] were at it but at the same time they were doing stuff for the kids as well,' Sir Robin explained.

After prison, Martin and Tony Bowers continued to schmooze Newham's rising political stars. Rokhsana Fiaz, for example, used to train at the Peacock gym and in 2009 was introduced by her trainer to the two brothers.

'In a typical east London manner, they sat me down,' Fiaz recalled. 'They'd found out I was going to be awarded an OBE and without me knowing or my approval they took out a quarter page advert [in the local press] that said, THE PEACOCK GYM CONGRATULATES ROKHSANA FIAZ OBE. PROUD AS A PEACOCK.'

Nine years later, Fiaz heard that Tony Bowers was 'unhappy' on learning she had won the 2018 mayoral election. A senior member of her team told me that the new mayor was nevertheless determined to probe the 'development interests' of organised crime in Newham as part of the Truth Commission.

The furore over the £40 million loan that Newham council made to secure the bid for the Olympic stadium forced Sir Robin Wales to order an independent review of the decision-making and oversight process. The review reported seven months later in July 2018 after he had been kicked out of office. Its conclusions, specifically that the council had partnered with West Ham United to bid for the stadium despite external advice that a £3 million annual return on the £40 million loan was never possible, was seized on by Rokhsana Fiaz.

She announced 'a much broader review into the culture and practices within the council that have developed over the last two decades.' Sadiq Khan welcomed the move. Since his election as mayor of London in 2016, Khan had been at loggerheads with West Ham over the leasing arrangement for the stadium that he'd inherited from his Tory predecessor, Boris Johnson.

The football club's owners, David Sullivan and David Gold, had secured a 'deal of the century' when they agreed to pay just £2.5 million per year to play at the stadium on a 99-year lease. Khan's team felt that Sir Robin's council couldn't be trusted to keep private their discussions about plans to recoup additional costs from West Ham and were leaking information to the football club.

A senior source in the Fiaz camp said Khan had likened the old Newham council to '1960s Chicago', a reference to the one-party machine politics of patronage and corruption in the US city where the mafia also held huge sway. Khan promised Fiaz whatever help she needed cleaning up Newham and expressed particular concern about the revolving door between the council and West Ham United.

Fiaz was also concerned about the revolving door with the local police. Nick Bracken, the deputy chief executive, was the former borough commander for Newham when Mac and his team were thrown under the bus. He went on to run Sir Robin's enforcement department in 2011 and rose to be chief operating officer. Bracken jumped before he was pushed. Daniel Fenwick, the legal director of the council, however, was kept on because the new mayor had complete trust in him. So much so, in the two months before she took up office in May 2018 Fiaz asked Fenwick to take secret measures to mitigate the effect of any attempt to destroy evidence that could be relevant to her Truth Commission.

According to the same well-placed source, Fenwick ensured that 'tags' were put on the work computers of selected executives and council officers between March and May to prevent the permanent deletion of emails and documentary evidence. When Fiaz and her team took over they discovered there had been, 'an attempt to shred loads and loads of things.' According to the source, additionally, 'some ten thousand emails were deleted.'

At the time of writing, Fiaz and her team were going through these 10,000 emails retrieved from the backup server to determine the terms of reference for her Truth Commission. Part of it, she said, will investigate 'the nexus of a criminal network,' in Canning Town and its 'links' to the council, police and West Ham United.

The football club had problems with its own supporters over the move to the Olympic stadium. At one point in early 2018, Andy Swallow, the thuggish co-founder of West Ham's hooligan element, the Inter City Firm, fronted a demonstration of fans to demand the sacking of Sullivan and Tory-appointed life peer Baroness Karren Brady from the board.

Swallow's ICF was involved in the rave scene back in the 1980s and 1990s along with the Bowers and the Hunts, all diehard West Ham fans. He now has interests in a pub and is the chief executive of Grays Athletic Football Club in Essex, where he moved because the East End had become 'too cosmopolitan', to put it in the new language of those representing old far-right politics. Swallow happily identifies with the Football Lad's Alliance, an umbrella group of fans apparently concerned with the terrorist threat posed by Britain's Muslim community.

The word on the terraces was that Davey Hunt was unhappy that his name was being associated with Swallow and his protest against the West Ham board. The Long Fella, after all, was friendly with Sullivan, who had loaned him £1 million to pay our legal costs after the libel battle.

According to a source close to these events, Hunt was present at a meeting between Sullivan and Swallow after which the protest march planned for March 2018 was called off. Swallow thought other fan groups would follow suit and end the protest, but Mark Walker, the elected head of the West Ham United Independent Supporters' Association, took up the baton. That's when the trouble started.

Walker was a Labour activist who had campaigned for Sadiq Khan and at the time was seeking election as a councillor. He received threats from other West Ham fans because of these left-wing associations. Separately, Swallow, whose reputation for violence needed no introduction, denied threatening Walker over the phone if he didn't call off the march. 'This is bigger than you know,' the thug is said to have told a very frightened 36-year-old Walker, who, while his wife and young sons slept, stayed by his front door all night, the police on speed dial, waiting for it to be kicked in.

Privately, Rokhsana Fiaz is also concerned for her safety if she goes ahead with a Truth Commission into the last two decades of political, masonic, commercial and criminal alliances in Newham. It was this hidden wiring that Mac and his team of detectives stumbled across when they tried to take out Davey Hunt and his associates, and in turn were ruthlessly taken out by their own bosses at Scotland Yard. Fiaz should be applauded for having the idea of a Truth Commission, which maybe a more experienced politician would have avoided for its wild card nature that could lead to unpredictable and dangerous places.

Sir Robin, who is right to be proud of the difference his administration made to ordinary people's lives in this depressed London borough, initially felt disinclined to appear before any inquiry. But then the idea of one last stage to defend his record started to appeal as our lunch progressed. 'Bring it on,' he said. 'I don't fucking care.'

Scotland Yard is unlikely to appear having done its own secret settlement and damage limitation exercise with the three detectives it so badly damaged. Mac is now a high-profile critic of the police and may well take the chance to rap about his ordeal at a Truth Commission. His despair with the way police forces have lost control of the streets led him to offer a private 'local bobby' service to some of the more affluent parts of London, and to privately investigate violent crimes linked to the organised crime groups he spent his detective career chasing.

Davey Hunt is thriving as a businessman.[10] The publicity-shy Long Fella is unlikely to tell his story to a Truth Commission and there is little sign of any activity around him by Scotland Yard's specialist units or the National Crime Agency that might put him before a criminal court.

Over at Newham, there is resistance among old guard members of the Labour party to a far-reaching inquiry. Fiaz will have to show political courage and guile if she is to honour her pledge to clean up Newham and win over her cabinet. One cabinet member familiar with the Hunts and Bowers took the new mayor aside to whisper concern for her safety if she launched a Truth Commission. Push too hard, he warned, and you could be 'taken out'.

Sometimes, the only choice is the hardest one.

---

[10]Hunt's Holdings Ltd is the parent company through which David Hunt owns Hunt's (UK) Properties Limited, which declared in its accounts for the year ending June 2017 a shareholder fund of £15.75m and assets of £23.72m. Hunt's Holdings Limited declared a shareholder fund of £2.64m for the same accounting period.

Index